S0-FBR-552

# LITERARY ESSAYS

BY
GEORGE EDWARD WOODBERRY

NEW YORK
HARCOURT, BRACE AND HOWE
1920

COPYRIGHT, 1900, 1905, 1907, BY
GEORGE EDWARD WOODBERRY

COPYRIGHT, 1920, BY
HARCOURT, BRACE AND HOWE, INC.

# CONTENTS

Crabbe, 3
Landor, 17
On the Promise of Keats, 35
Byron's Centenary, 49
On Browning's Death, 59
Matthew Arnold, 73
Coleridge, 91
Shelley's Work, 107
Cervantes, 129
Scott, 157
Milton, 183
Virgil, 209
Montaigne, 237
Shakespeare, 263
Swinburne, 289

*The author makes grateful acknowledgment to Messrs. Harper & Brothers for their permission to use the text of the authorized American edition of Mr. Swinburne's poems published by them.*

# LITERARY ESSAYS

# CRABBE

WE have done with Crabbe. His tales have failed to interest us. Burke and his friends, as we all know, held a different opinion from ours; and their praise is not likely to have been ill founded. The cultivated taste of Holland House, thirty years later, is also against our decision. Through two generations of markedly different literary temper Crabbe pleased the men best worth pleasing. Indeed, we owe him to Burke's approval; for when Lord North, Lord Shelburne, and Lord Thurlow had neglected his entreaties for recognition and aid, and had left him to write, pawn, and go hungry, Burke saved him from the debtor's prison, took him into his friendship, welcomed him to his home, and gave him to literature.

Yet the verses which won this recognition from Burke, and gained for Crabbe, besides, praise from Johnson and talk with Fox and idle mornings in Reynolds's studio, were only his fledgeling flights. It was not until after more than twenty years of silence, spent in the obscurity of a country clergyman's life, that he showed the richness and abundance of his vein. Then Burke and his friends had given place to those younger men, in whose lives a new age was dawning; but as warm a welcome awaited Crabbe among them as he had ever met with in Burke's club. With them he passed his old age, pleased with Byron's praise, and with the friendliness of Moore and Rogers, and with Scott's kindly regard and correspondence. They liked to see him, with his beautiful white hair, his formal, old-fashioned garb and old-school manners, the last of that long line of poets through whom the Queen Anne taste had tyrannized for a century in English verse, sitting familiarly among themselves, who were preparing the way for the next generation to ignore the traditions which Burke and Johnson had fixed in his poetic faith. Especially did Sir Walter honor him; like Fox, he chose Crabbe's poems to be read to him just before he died.

Without reckoning the approval of others, what was the strong attraction in Crabbe's work for Scott and Fox? Their judgment was not so worthless that it can be disregarded with the complacent assurance with which the decisions of Gifford and Jeffrey are set aside; on the contrary, Scott had such health and Fox such refinement that their judgment ought to raise a doubt whether our generation is not making a mistake and missing pleasure through its neglect of Crabbe.

Crabbe is a story-teller. He describes the life he saw, — common, homely life, sometimes wretched, not infrequently criminal; the life of the country poor, with occasional light and shadow from the life of the gentlefolk above them. He had been born into it, in a village on the Suffolk coast, amid stern and cheerless natural scenes: landward, the bramble-overgrown heath encompassing crowded and mean houses; eastward, —

"Stakes and sea-weed withering on the mud."

Here he had passed his boyhood, in the midst of human life equally barren and stricken with the ugliness of poverty, among surly and sordid fishers given to hard labor and rough brawl, —

"A joyless, wild, amphibious race,
With sullen woe displayed in every face," —

and the sight had been a burden to him. The desire to throw off this twofold oppression of mean nature and humanity must have counted for much in determining him on that long-remembered December day, when, as the bleak twilight came down, darkening the marshy pool on the heath where he stood, he took his resolve to go up to London and seek poetical fame; and glad at heart he must have been, that morning of early spring, when he left all this ugliness behind him, ignorant of the struggle and distress he was to meet where he was going.

In that early poem which Johnson praised Crabbe described this village life with the vigor of a youth who had escaped out of its dreary imprisonment, and without a touch of that tenderness for early associations which softened Goldsmith's retrospect of the scenes of his early days. Crabbe told of exhausting labor leading on to prematurely useless and neglected age; of storms sweeping away the shelter of the poor; of smugglers, poachers, wreckers, tavern debauchery, and, worst of all, the poorhouse — a terrible picture, perhaps the best known of all his drawing — with its deserted inmates cut off from all human care except that of the heedless physician and the heartless parson; a miserable tale, but too much of it only what his own eyes had seen. We do not know the contents of those piles of manuscripts which he wrote during his twenty years of silence, and — not much to the world's loss, some think — made bonfires of to amuse his children; but his first poem after that long interval was the same story, the experience of those whose names appeared in the year's parish register of births, marriages, and deaths, and was a sorrowful survey of seduction, desertion, crime, discontent, and folly. In his later tales he dealt less in unrelieved gloom and bitter misery, and at times made a trial at humor. There are glimpses of pleasant English life and character, but these are only glimpses; the ground of his painting is shadow — the shadow that rested on the life of the English poor in his generation.

Where else would one turn for an adequate description of that life, or gain so direct an insight into the social sources and conditions of the Methodist revival, or into the motives and convictions of reformers like Mary Wollstonecraft? Where would one obtain so keen a sense of the vast change which has taken place in the conditions of humble human life within this century? Mr. Leslie Stephen, in that essay which is so good-humored but so unsuccessful an attempt to appreciate Crabbe, mentions the few illustrations in modern literature of the life Crabbe described; it is seen in Charlotte Brontë's Yorkshiremen, and George Eliot's millers, and in a few other characters, "but," he says, "to get a realistic picture of country life as Crabbe saw it, we must go back to Squire Western, or to some of the roughly-hewn masses of flesh who sat to Hogarth." The setting of Crabbe's tales has this special historic interest. The schools, houses, books, habits, occupations, and all the external characteristics of the tales belong to the time: the press-gang comes to carry off the lover just before his wedding-day, and leaves the bride to nurse an unfathered child, to receive the courtship of a canting and carnal preacher, and to find a refuge from him, and from the father who favors him, in suicide; orphan boys are bound over to brutal taskmasters; pictures of the sects (from the pen of a respectable clergyman of the Established Church, it is true) recall the beginnings of Methodism with a vividness only to be equaled by the books and pamphlets of the early converts' own writing. This historic value of the tales, however, great as it is to the student of manners, is secondary to their poetic value, which lies in the sentiment, feeling, and pathos with which the experience of life embodied in them, the workings of simple human nature, in however debased surroundings, is set forth. It is an experience which results usually from the interplay of low and selfish motives, and of ignoble or weak passions; it is, too often, the course of brutal appetite, thoughtless or heartless folly, avarice, sensuality, and vice, relieved too seldom by amiable character, sympathy, charity, self-sacrifice, or even by the charm of natural beauty. Yet if all the seventy tales be taken into account, they contain nearly all varieties of character and circumstance among the country poor; and, though the darker side may seem to be more frequently insisted upon, it is because the nature of his subject made it necessary, because he let his light, as Moore said, —

> "Through life's low, dark interior fall,
> Opening the whole, severely bright,"

rather than because he had any lack of cheerfulness of temper.

Crabbe does not, in a true sense, give expression to the life of the poor; he merely narrates it. Here and there, throughout the poems, are episodes written out of his own life; but usually he is concerned with the experience of other men, which he had observed, rather than with what his own heart had felt. A description of life is of course far inferior to an utterance of it, such as was given to us by Burns, who dealt with the life of the poor so much more powerfully than Crabbe; and a realistic description has less poetic value than an imaginative one, such as was given to us by Wordsworth at his best. Crabbe's description is perhaps the most nakedly realistic of any in English poetry; but it is an uncommonly good one. Realism has a narrow compass, and Crabbe's powers were confined strictly within it; but he had the best virtues of a realist. His physical vision — his sight of what presents itself to the eye — was almost perfect; he saw every object, and saw it as it was. Perhaps the minuteness with which he saw was not altogether an advantage, for he does not seem to have taken in the landscape as a whole, but only as a mosaic of separate objects. He never gives general effects of beauty or grandeur; indeed, he seldom saw the beauty of a single object; he did little more than catalogue the things before him, and employ in writing poetry the same faculty in the same way as in pursuing favorite studies of botany and entomology. Yet, with these limitations, what realist in painting could exceed in truthfulness and carefulness of detail this picture of a fall morning? —

"It was a fair and mild autumnal sky,
And earth's ripe treasures met th' admiring eye;
The wet and heavy grass where feet had strayed,
Not yet erect, the wanderer's way betrayed;
Showers of the night had swelled the deep'ning rill,
The morning breeze had urged the quick'ning mill;
Long yellow leaves, from osiers strewed around,
Choked the small stream and hushed the feeble sound."

Or this sketch of light in a decayed warehouse turned into a tenement for the poor? —

"That window view! oiled paper and old glass
Stain the strong rays, which, though impeded, pass,
And give a dusty warmth to that huge room,
The conquered sunshine's melancholy gloom;

> When all those western rays, without so bright,
> Within become a ghastly glimmering light,
> As pale and faint upon the floor they fall,
> Or feebly gleam on the opposing wall."

Nor is this carefulness of detail a trick, such as is sometimes employed, to give the appearance of reality to unreal human life. Crabbe's mental vision, his sight into the workings of the passions and the feelings, although not so perfect as his physical vision, was yet at its best very keen and clear; the sentiments, moods, reflections, and actions of his characters are seldom contrary to nature. It would be difficult to show a finer delineation of its kind than his description of the meeting of two long-parted brothers. As Richard approaches his brother's hall, he reflects, —

> " 'How shall I now my unknown way explore, —
> He proud and rich, I very proud and poor?
> Perhaps my friend a dubious speech mistook,
> And George may meet me with a stranger's look.
> How stands the case? My brother's friend and mine
> Met at an inn, and set them down to dine;
> When, having settled all their own affairs,
> And kindly canvassed such as were not theirs,
> Just as my friend was going to retire,
> "Stay! you will see the brother of our squire,"
> Said his companion; "be his friend, and tell
> The captain that his brother loves him well,
> And when he has no better thing in view
> Will be rejoiced to see him. Now, adieu!"

> " 'Well, here I am; and, brother, take you heed,
> I am not come to flatter you and feed.
> You shall no soother, fawner, hearer, find;
> I will not brush your coat, nor smooth your mind;
> I will not hear your tales the whole day long,
> Nor swear you're right, if I believe you wrong;

> I will not earn my dinner when I dine
> By taking all your sentiments for mine;
> Nor watch the guiding motions of your eye
> Before I venture question or reply.
> Yet, son of that dear mother could I meet —
> But lo! the mansion, — 'tis a fine old seat!'
>
> "The brothers met, with both too much at heart
> To be observant of each other's part.
> 'Brother, I'm glad!' was all that George could say,
> Then stretched his hand, and turned his head away;
> Richard, meantime, made some attempt to speak,
> Strong in his purpose, in his trial weak.
> At length, affection, like a risen tide,
> Stood still, and then seemed slowly to subside;
> Each on the other's looks had power to dwell,
> And brother brother greeted passing well."

These qualities of fine, true physical and mental vision are the essential qualities for valuable realistic work; if there be room for regret in Crabbe's share of them, it is because their range is contracted. The limitations of his physical vision have been mentioned; in respect to his mental vision Crabbe saw only a few and comparatively simple operations of human nature, — the workings of country-bred minds, not finely or complexly organized, but slow-motioned, and perplexed, if perplexed at all, not from the difficulty of the problem, but from their own dullness. Yet within these limits his characters are often pathetic, sometimes tragic, or even terrible, in their energy of evil passion or remorse.

One other quality, without which clear mental and physical vision would be ineffective, is essential to realism like Crabbe's, — transparency, the quality by virtue of which life is seen through the text plainly and without distortion; and this is the quality which Crabbe possessed in most perfection. He not only saw the object as it was; he presented it as it was. He neither added nor took away; he did not unconsciously darken or heighten color, soften or harden line. Whatever was before his mind — the conversation of a gossip, the brutality of a ruffian, the cant of a convert — he reproduced truthfully; whatever was the character of his story, mean or tragic, trivial or pathetic, he did not modify it. There was no veil of fancy, no glamour of amiable deception or dimness of charitable tears, to obscure his view: if he found nudity and dirt, they reappeared in his work nudity and dirt still; if he found courage and patience, he dealt the same even-handed justice. His distinction is that he told a true story.

It was, perhaps, because he was thus able to present accurately and faithfully the human life which he saw so clearly that he won such admiration from Scott; for Scott had the welcome of genius for any new glimpse of humanity, and he knew how rare, and consequently how valuable, is the gift of simple and direct narration of what one sees. Fox had great sensibility and tenderness of heart; and Crabbe presented the lot of the poor so vividly, so lucidly, so immediately, that he stirred in Fox the same feelings with which a better poet would have so charged his verses that natures not so finely endowed as Fox would have been compelled to feel them too. Scott and Fox knew what a valuable acquisition this realistic sketch of humble life in their generation was, so faithful, minute, and trustworthy; they felt that their experience was enlarged, that real humanity had been brought home to them, and in the sway of those emotions, which Crabbe did not infuse into his work, but which his work quickens in sympathetic hearts, they could forgive him his tedious-ness, his frequent commonplace, his not unusual absurdity of phrase, his low level of flight with its occasional feebleness of wing.

In their minds, too, his style must have had more influence than we are apt to think, — the style of the great school which died with him, the form and versification which they had been taught to believe almost essential to the best poetry, and from a traditional respect for which they could hardly free their minds as easily as ourselves. Crabbe used the old heroic rhymed couplet, that simplest form of English verse music, which could rise, nevertheless, to the almost lyric loftiness of the last lines of the Dunciad; so supple and flexible; made for easy simile and compact metaphor; lending itself so perfectly to the sudden flash of wit or turn of humor; the natural shell of an epigram; compelling the poet to practice all the virtues of brevity; checking the wandering fancy, and repressing the secondary thought; requiring in a masterly use of it the employment of more mental powers than any other metrical form; despised and neglected now because the literature which is embodied in it is despised and neglected, yet the best metrical form which intelligence, as distinct from poetical feeling, can employ. Crabbe did not handle it in any masterful way; he was careless, and sometimes slipshod; but when he chose he could employ it well, and should have credit for it. To take one more example from his poems, how excellently he uses it in this passage! —

> "Where is that virtue which the generous boy
> Felt, and resolved that nothing should destroy;
> He who with noble indignation glowed
> When vice had triumph; who his tear bestowed
> On injured merit? He who would possess
> Power, but to aid the children of distress!

Who has such joy in generous actions shown,
And so sincere they might be called his own;
Knight, hero, patriot, martyr! on whose tongue
And potent arm a nation's welfare hung, —
Where now this virtue's fervor, spirit, zeal?
Who felt so warmly, has he ceased to feel?
Or are these feelings varied?  Has the knight,
Virtue's own champion, now refused to fight?
Is the deliverer turned th' oppressor now?
Has the reformer dropt the dangerous vow?
Or has the patriot's bosom lost its heat,
And forced him, shivering, to a snug retreat?
Is such the grievous lapse of human pride!
Is such the victory of the worth untried!"

Scott felt an attraction in such poetic form which we have perhaps ceased to feel; and Fox, had he lived to read it, would equally have acknowledged its power.

But Wordsworth said Crabbe was unpoetical; he condemned him for "his unpoetical mode of considering agreed with Wordsworth, and disagreed with Scott and human nature and society;" and, after all, the world has Fox. Wordsworth told Scott an anecdote in illustration of his meaning. Sir George Beaumont, sitting with himself and Crabbe one day, blew out the candle which he had used in sealing a letter. Sir George and Wordsworth, with proper taste, sat watching the smoke rise from the wick in beautiful curves; but Crabbe seeing — or rather smelling — the object, and not seeing the beauty of it, put on the extinguisher. Therefore, said Wordsworth, Crabbe is unpoetical, — as fine a bit of æsthetic priggishness as is often met with. Scott's opinion was not much affected by the anecdote, and Wordsworth was on the wrong track. It is true, however, that Crabbe was unpoetical in Wordsworth's sense. Crabbe had no imaginative vision, — no such vision as is shown in that stormy landscape of Shelley's, in the opening of "The Revolt of Islam," which lacks the truth of actuality, but possesses the higher imaginative truth, like Turner's painting, or that shown in that other storm in "Pippa Passes." Crabbe saw sword-grass and saltwort and fen, but he had no secret of the imagination by which he could mingle them into harmonius beauty; there is loveliness in a salt marsh, but Crabbe could not present it, nor even see it for himself. As in landscape so in life. Goldsmith was untrue to the actual Auburn, but he was faithful to a far more precious truth, the truth of remembered childhood, and he revealed with the utmost beauty the effect of the subtlest working of the spirit of man on practical fact; it is his fidelity to this psychological and spiritual truth which makes Auburn the "loveliest village of the plain." Crabbe exhibited nothing of this imaginative transformation of the familiar and the commonplace, perhaps saw nothing of it; he described the fishing village of Aldborough as any one with good powers of perception, who took the trouble, might see it. Through these defects of his powers he loses in poetic value; his poetry is, as he called it, poetry without an atmosphere; it is a reflection, almost mirror-like, of plain fact.

Men go to poetry too often with a preconceived notion of what the poet ought to give, instead of with open minds for whatever he has to give. Too much is not to be expected from Crabbe. He was only a simple country clergyman, half educated, with no burning ideals, no reveries, no passionate dreams; his mind did not rise out of the capabilities and virtues of respectability. His life was as little poetical, in Wordsworth's sense, as his poetry. Yet his gift was not an empty one. Moore, Scott, and Byron were story-tellers who were poetical, in Wordsworth's sense; but is Crabbe's true description of humble life less valuable than Scott's romantic tradition, or Moore's melting, sensuous Oriental dream, or Byron's sentimental, falsely-heroic adventure? Has it not another value, because there is more of the human heart in it; because it contains actual suffering and joy of fellowmen; because it is humanity, and calls for hospitality in our sympathies and charities? Unpoetical? Yes; but it is something to have real life brought home to our tears and laughter, although it be presented barely, and the poet has trusted to the rightness and tenderness of our hearts for those feelings the absence of which in his verse led Wordsworth to call these tales unpoetical. But it is only when Crabbe is at his best that his verse has this extraordinary power.

# LANDOR

MANY of the most sensitive and discriminating critics of this century have, in the suffrage for fame, listed themselves for Landor. He seemed almost to achieve immortality within his lifetime, so continuously was the subtle appreciation of the best yielded to him, from the far-off years when Shelley used, at Oxford, to declaim with enthusiasm passages from "Gebir," to the time, that seems as yesterday, when Swinburne made his pilgrimage to Italy, to offer his tribute of adoration to the old man at the close of his solitary and troubled career; and still each finer spirit,

> "As he passes, turns,
> And bids fair peace be to his sable shroud."

During his long life he saw the springtime, and outlived the harvest, of the great poetic revival, and the labor of the Victorian poets of the aftermath was half accomplished before his death; but from all these powerful contemporary influences he was free. He remained apart; and this single fact, attesting, as it does, extraordinary self-possession and assurance of purpose, suffices to make his character interesting, even were his work of inferior worth. As yet, however, even to the minds of cultivated men, he is hardly more than a great figure. He is known, praised, and remembered for particular scenes, dramatic fragments, occasional lyrics, quatrains. This is the natural fate of a discursive writer. It matters not that Landor was wide ranging; it matters not what spoils of thought, what images of beauty, he brought from those far eastern uplands which it was his boast to haunt: he failed to give unity to his work, to give interest to large portions of it, to command public attention for it as a whole. Indeed, his work as a whole does not command the attention even of the best. What does survive, too, lives only in the favor of a small circle. He forfeited popular fame at the beginning, when he selected themes that presuppose rare qualities in his audience, and adopted an antique style; but such considerations, at least in their naked statement, do not tell the whole story. Other poets have missed immediate applause by dealing with subjects that assumed unusual largeness of soul, range of sympathy, and refinement of taste in their readers: like Shelley, singing of unheeded hopes and fears to which the world was to be wrought; like Wordsworth, narrating the myth of Troy. Other poets, in style, have set forth the object plainly, and left it to work its will on the heart and imagination, unaided by the romantic spell, the awakening glow, the silent but imperative suggestion, the overmastering passion that takes heart and imagination captive; and they have not lost their reward. A remote theme, an impersonal style, are not of themselves able to condemn a poet to long neglect. They may make wide appreciation of him impossible; they may explain the indifference of an imperfectly educated public; but they do not account for the fact that Landor is to be read, even by his admirers, in a book of selections, while the dust is shaken from the eight stout octavos that contain his works only by the professional man of letters.

What first strikes the student of Landor is the lack of any development in his genius. This is one reason why Mr. Leslie Stephen, seizing on the characteristic somewhat rudely, and leaping to an ungracious conclusion, calls him "a glorified and sublime edition of the sixth-form schoolboy." Men whose genius is of this fixed type are rare in English literature, and not of the highest rank. They exhibit no radical change; they are at the beginning what they are at the end; their works do not belong to any particular period of their lives; they seem free from their age, and to live outside of it. Hence, in dealing with them, historical criticism — the criticism whose purpose is to explain rather than to judge — soon finds itself at fault. When the circumstances that determined the original bent of their minds have been set forth, there is nothing more to be said. With Landor, this bent seems to have been given by his classical training. To write Latin verses was the earliest serious employment of his genius, and his efforts were immediately crowned with success. These studies, falling in with natural inclinations and aptitudes, pledged him to a classical manner; they made real for him the myths and history of Greece and Rome; they fed his devotion to the ancient virtues, — love of freedom, aspiration for the calm of wisdom, reverence for the dignity of heroism, delight in beauty for its own sake; they supported him in what was more distinctively his own, — his refinement in material tastes, his burning indignation, his defense of tyrannicide. These characteristics he had in youth; they were neither diminished nor increased in age. In youth, too, he displayed all his literary excellences and defects: the fullness and weight of line; the march of sentences; the obscurity arising from over-condensation of thought and abrupt and elliptical constructions; his command of the grand and impressive as well as the beautiful and charming in imagery; his fondness for heroic situation and for the loveliness of minute objects. This was a high endowment; why, then, do its literary results seem inadequate?

With all his gifts, Landor did not possess unifying power. He observed objects as they passed before him at hap-hazard, took them into his mind, and gave them back, untransformed, in their original disorder. He thought disconnectedly, and expressed his thoughts as they came, detached and separate. This lack of unity did not result simply from his choice of the classical mode of treatment, or from a defect in logical or constructive power, although it was connected with these. The ability to fuse experience, to combine its elements and make them one, to give it back to the world, transformed, and yet essentially true, the real creative faculty, is proportioned very strictly to the self-assertive power of genius, to the energy of the reaction of the mind on nature and life; it springs from a strong personality. To say that Landor's personality was weak would be to stultify one's self; but yet the difference between Landor the man and Landor the author is so great as to make the two almost antithetical; and in his imaginative work, by which he must be judged, it is not too much to say that he denied and forswore his personality, and obliterated himself so far as was possible. He not only eliminated self from his style, and, after the classical manner, defined by Arnold, "relied solely on the weight and force of that which, with entire fidelity, he uttered," but he also eliminated self, so far as one can, from his subject. He did not bind his work together by the laws of his own mind; he did not interpenetrate and permeate it with his own beliefs, as the great masters have always done. His principles were at the best vague, hardly amounting to more than an unapplied enthusiasm for liberty, heroism, and the other great watchwords of social rather than individual life. These illuminate his work, but they do not give it consistency. It is crystalline in structure, beautiful, ordered, perfect in form when taken part by part, but conglomerate as a whole; it is a handful of jewels, many of which are singly of the most transparent and glowing light, but unrelated one to another, — placed in juxtaposition, but not set; and in the crystalline mass is imbedded grosser matter, and mingled with the jewels are stones of dull color and light weight. A lovely object caught his eye, and he set it forth in verse; a fine thought came to him, and he inserted it in his dialogues; but his days were not "bound each to each by natural piety," or by any other of the shaping principles of high genius. He was a spectator of life, not an actor in life. Nature was to him a panorama, wonderful, awful, beautiful, and he described its scenes down to its most minute and evanescent details. History was his theatre, where the personages played great parts; and he recorded their words and gestures, always helping them with the device of the high buskin and something of a histrionic air. He was content to be thus guided from without; to have his intellectual activity determined by the chance of sensation and of reading, rather than by a well-thought-out and enthusiastic purpose of his own soul. And so he became hardly more than a mirror of beauty and an Æolian harp of thought; if the vision came, if the wind breathed, he responded.

This self-effacement, this impersonality, as it is called, in literature, is much praised. It is said to be classical, and there is an impression in some minds that such an abdication of the individual's prerogatives is the distinctive mark of classicism. There is no more misleading and confusing error in criticism. Not impersonality, but universality, is that mark; and this is by no means the same thing, differently stated. In any age, the first, although not the sole, characteristic of classical work is that it deals with universal truth, of interest to all men: and hence the poet is required to keep to himself his idiosyncrasies, hobbies, all that is simply his own; all that is not identical with the common human nature; all that men in large bodies cannot sympathize with, understand, and appreciate. Under these conditions direct self-revelation is exceptional. The poet usually expresses himself by so arranging his plot and developing his characters that they will illustrate the laws of life, as he sees these laws, without any direct statement, — though the Greek chorus is full of didactic sayings; and he may also express himself by such a powerful presentation of the morality intrinsic in beautiful things and noble actions as "to soothe the cares and lift the thoughts of men," without any dogmatic insistence in his own person. In these ways Æschylus obliterated himself from his work just as much as Shakespeare, and no more; Swift just as much as Aristophanes, and no more; but the statement that Shakespeare or Swift obliterated themselves from their works needs only to be made to be laughed at. The faith of Æschylus, the wisdom of Sophocles, are in all their dramas; Anacreon is in all his songs, Horace in all his odes. The lasting significance of their productions to mankind is derived from the clearness, the power, the skill, with which they informed their works with their personality. These men had a philosophy of life, that underlay and unified their work. They rebuilt the world in their imagination, and gave it the laws of their own minds. Their spirits were active, molding, shaping, creating, subduing the whole of nature and life to themselves. It is true that the ancients accomplished their purpose rather by thought, the moderns rather by emotion; but this difference is incidental to the change in civilization. Either instrument is sufficient for its end; but he who would now choose the ancient instead of the modern mode, narrows, postpones, and abbreviates his fame only less than Landor, in his youth, by writing in Latin. Whatever be the mode of its operation, the energy of personality is the very essence of effective genius.

That Landor had no philosophy of life, in the same sense as Shakespeare or Æschylus, is plain to any reader. Those who look on art, including poetry, as removed from ordinary human life, who think that its chief service to men lies in affording delight rather than in that quickening of the spirit of which delight is only the sign and efflorescence, would consider Landor's lack of this philosophy a virtue. It accounts largely for his failure to interest even the best in the larger part of his work, and especially for the discontinuity of his reflections. These reflections are always his own; and this fact may seem to make against the view that he eliminated self from his productions so far as possible. But the presence of personality in literature as a force, ordering a great whole and giving it laws, is a very different thing from its presence as a mere mouthpiece of opinion. The thoughts may be numerous, varied, wise, noble; they may have all the virtues of truth and grace; but if they are disparate and scattered, if they tend nowhither, if they leave the reader where they found him, if they subserve no ulterior purpose and accomplish no end, there is a wide gulf between them and the thoughts of Shakespeare and Æschylus, no less their own than were Landor's his. In the former, personality is a power; in the latter, it is only a voice. In Landor's eight volumes there are more fine thoughts, more wise apothegms, than in any other discursive author's works in English literature; but they do not tell on the mind. They bloom like flowers in their gardens, but they crown no achievement. At the end, no cause is advanced, no goal is won. This incoherence and inefficiency proceed from the absence of any definite scheme of life, any compacted system of thought, any central principles, any strong, pervading, and ordering personality.

In the same way the objectivity of Landor's work, its naturalism as distinguished from imaginativeness, results from the same cause, but with the difference that, while the faults already mentioned are largely due to an imperfect equipment of the mind, his mode of art seems to have been adopted by conscious choice and of set purpose. The opinion of those who look on naturalism as a virtue in art is deserving of respect. We have been admonished for a long while that men should see things as they are, and present them as they are, and that this was the Greek way. The dictum, when applied with the meaning that men should be free from prejudice and impartial in judgment, no one would contest; but when it is proclaimed with the meaning that poets should express ideas nakedly, and should reproduce objects by portraiture, there is excuse for raising some question. No doubt, this was in general the practice of the ancients. The Athenians were primarily intellectual, the Romans unimaginative. But by the operation of various causes — the chief of which are the importance bestowed on the individual and the impulse given to emotion by the Christian religion — mankind has changed somewhat; and therefore the methods of appeal to men, the ways of touching their hearts and enlightening their minds, have been modified. In literature this change is expressed by saying that the romantic manner has, in general, superseded the classical. The romantic manner aims at truth no less than the classical; it sets forth things as they are no less completely and clearly. The difference is rather one of methods than of aims. The classical poet usually perceives the object by his intellect, and makes his appeal to the mind; the romantic poet seizes on the object with his imagination, and makes his appeal to the heart. Not that classical work is without imagination, or romantic work devoid of intellectuality; but that in one the intellect counts for more, in the other imagination. The classical poet, having once presented ideas and objects, leaves them to make their way; the romantic poet not only presents them, but, by awakening the feelings, predisposes the mood of the mind, makes their reception by the mind easier, wins their way for them. In classical work, consequently, success depends mainly on lucidity of understanding, clearness of vision, skill in verbal expression; in romantic work, the poet must not only possess these qualities, but must superadd, as his prime characteristics, rightness, one might better say sanity, of passion. The classical virtues are more common among authors, the romantic far more rare; and hence error in the romantic manner is more frequent, especially in dealing with ideas. But with all its liability to mistake in weak hands, romantic art, by its higher range, its fiercer intensity, especially by its greater certainty, has, in the hands of a master, a clear increase of power over classical art, and under the changed conditions of civilization its resources are not to be lightly neglected. Indeed, one who voluntarily adopts the classical manner as an exclusive mode seems to choose an instrument of less compass and melody, to prefer Greek to modern music. He sings to a secluded and narrow circle, and loses the ear of the world. Certainly Landor made this choice, and by it he must stand.

Let us take an example from the best of Landor's work, and from that region of classical art where it is wholly competent, — the brief description of small objects: —

> "The ever-sacred cup
> Of the pure lily hath between my hands
> Felt safe, unsoiled, nor lost one grain of gold."

How completely, how distinctly, the image is given, — its form, its transparent purity, its fragile and trembling gold! How free from any other than a strictly artistic charm! And yet how different is its method of appeal from Shelley's

> "tender blue-bells, at whose birth
> The sod scarce heaved;"

from Shakespeare's

> "daffodils
> That come before the swallow dares, and take
> The winds of March with beauty."

Or, to select an illustration, also of Landor's best, when the image, no less objective, yields of itself an infinite suggestion: —

> "Borgia, thou once wert almost too august
> And high for adoration; now thou 'rt dust.
> All that remains of thee these plaits unfold,
> Calm hair meandering in pellucid gold."

Again, how perfect is the image, how effective the development of the third line; how the melody of the last blends with its selected epithets to place the object entire and whole before the mind; how free is the quatrain from any self-intrusion of the poet! But here, too, the method of appeal is very different from Shakespeare's, as in the lines on Yorick's skull: "Here hung those lips that I have kissed I know not how oft." The difference in mood between these two only emphasizes the difference in method. Enough has been said, however, in description and exemplification of the two kinds of art. Either is sufficient for its ends, nor would any one desire to dispense with that which has resulted in work so admirable as has been quoted from Landor. The distinctively romantic poets do not consign the classical style to disuse. In the presentation of images, Keats has frequent recourse to it, as in his picture of Autumn lying

> "on a half-reaped furrow sound asleep,
> Drowsed with the fume of poppies, while thy hook
> Spares the next swath and all its twinèd flowers."

So Wordsworth, in expressing ideas, is sometimes more bald than the least imaginative of the classics. But such poets do not employ this style alone; they are characterized by the modern manner; they give us those "sweet views" which in the ancient mode "can never well be seen." Landor droops below his great contemporaries, not by merely adopting the classical method, but by adopting it exclusively. Whether this choice was entirely free, or partly determined by natural incapacity, is doubtful. Violent and tempestuous as his nature was, with all his boyish intensity of indignation, his boyish delicacy of tenderness, he seems to possess temper rather than true passion. In the verses to his poetic love, Ianthe, there are many fine sentiments, graceful turns;

there is courtliness of behavior; but the note of passion is not struck. Ianthe is only another poetic mistress of the cavalier school, and in the memory her name is less, both for dignity and pathos, than Rose Aylmer's. Without passion, of course, a poet is condemned to the classical style. Passion is the element in which the romantic writer fuses beauty and wisdom; it is the means by which personality pervades literary work with most ease, directness, and glow. In the great modern poets it is the substance of their genius. But just as neither by a philosophy of life nor in any other way did Landor fill his subject with himself, so neither by passion nor by any other quality did he breathe his own spirit into his style.

The consequence is that Landor, unclassified in his own age, is now to be ranked among the poets, increasing in number, who appeal rather to the artistic than to the poetic sense. He is to be placed in that group which looks on art as a world removed; which prizes it mainly for the delight it gives; which, caring less for truth, deals chiefly with the beauty that charms the senses; and which therefore weaves poetry like tapestry, and uses the web of speech to bring out a succession of fine pictures. The watchwords of any school, whether in thought or art, seldom awake hostility until their bearing on the details of practice reveals their meaning. Art is, in a sense, a world removed from the actual and present life, and beauty is the sole title that admits any work within its limits. Of this there is no question. But that world, however far from what is peculiar to any one age, has its eternal foundations in universal life; and that beauty has its enduring power because it is the incarnation of universal life. What poem has a better right to admission there than "The Eve of St. Agnes"? and in what poem does the heart of life beat more warmly? "Laodamia" belongs in that world, but it is because it voices abiding human feelings no less than because of its serenity. Nature in itself is savage, sterile, and void; individual life in itself is trifling: each obtains its value through its interest to humanity as a whole, and the office of art is to set forth that value. A lovely object, a noble action, are each of worth to men, but the latter is of the more worth; and, as was long ago pointed out, poetry is by the limitations of language at a considerable disadvantage in treating of formal beauty. But without developing these remarks, of which there is no need, the only point here to be made is that in so far as poetry concerns itself with objects without relation to ideas, it loses influence; in so far as it neglects emotion and thought for the purpose of gaining sensuous effects it loses worth; in both it declines from the higher to the lower levels. Landor, notwithstanding his success in presenting objects of artistic beauty — and his poetry is full of exquisite delineations of them — failed to interest men; nor could his skill in expressing thought, although he was far more intellectual than his successors, save his reputation. Landor mistook a few of the marks of art for all. His work has the serenity, the remoteness, that characterize high art, but it lacks an intimate relation with the general life of men; it sets forth formal beauty, as painting does, but that beauty remains a sensation, and does not pass into thought. This absence of any vital relation between his art and life, between his objects and ideas, denotes his failure. There are so many poets whose works contain as perfect beauty, and in addition truth and passion; so many who instead of mirroring beauty make it the voice of life, — who instead of responding in melodious thought to the wandering winds of reverie strike their lyres in the strophe and antistrophe of continuous song,—that the world is content to let Landor go by. The guests at the famous late dinner-party to which he looked forward will indeed be very few, and they will be men of leisure.

Thus far, in examining the work of Landor as a whole, and endeavoring to understand somewhat the public indifference to it, the answer has been found in its objectivity and its discontinuity, both springing from the effacement of his personality as an active power; or, in other words, in the fact that, by failing to link his images with his thoughts, and his thoughts one with another, so as to make them tell on the mind, and especially by eliminating the romantic element of passion, he failed to bring his work into sympathetic or helpful relations with the general emotional and intellectual life of men.

Why, then, do the most sensitive and discriminating critics, as was said at the beginning, list themselves in Landor's favor? They are, without exception, fellow-workers with him in the craft of literature. They have, by their continued eulogy of him, made it a sign of refinement to be charmed by him, a proof of unusually good taste to praise him. His admirers, by their very divergence in opinion from the crowd, seem to claim uncommon sensibilities; and the coterie is certainly one of the highest order, intellectually: Browning, Lowell, Swinburne, to name no more. They are all literary men. They are loud in their plaudits of his workmanship, but are noticeably guarded in their commendation of his entire contents; the passages for which they express unstinted enthusiasm are few. Landor was, beyond doubt, a master-workman, and skill in workmanship is dear to the craft; others may feel its effects, but none appreciate it with the keen relish of the professional author. The fullness, power, and harmony of Landor's language are clearly evident in his earliest work. He had the gift of literary expression from his youth, and in his mature work it shows as careful and high cultivation as such a gift ever received from its possessor. None could give keener point and smoother polish to a short sentence; none could thread the intricacies of long and involved constructions more unerringly. He had at command all the grammatical resources of lucidity, though he did not always care to employ them. He knew all the devices of prose composition to conceal and to disclose; to bring the commonplace to issue in the unexpected; to lead up, to soften, to hesitate, to declaim; to extort all the supplementary and new suggestions of an old comparison; to frame a new and perfect simile; in short, he was thoroughly trained to his art. Yet his prose is not, by present canons, perfect prose. It is not self-possessed, subdued, and graceful conversation, modulated, making its points without aggressive insistence, yet with certainty, keeping interest alive by a brilliant but natural turn and by the brief and luminous flash of truth through a perfect phrase. His prose is rather the monologue of a seer. In reading his works one feels somewhat as if sitting at the feet of Coleridge. Landor has the presence that abashes companions. His manner of speech is more dignified, more ceremonial, his enunciation is more resonant, his accent more exquisite, than belong to the man of the world. He silences his readers by the mere impossibility of interrupting with a question so noble and smooth-sliding a current of words. The style is a sort of modern Miltonic; it has the suggestion of the pulpit divine in Hooker, the touch of formal artificiality that characterizes the first good

English prose. Landor goes far afield for his vocables; his page is a trifle too polysyllabic, has too much of the surface glitter of Latinity. But in the age that produced the styles of De Quincey, Ruskin, and Carlyle, it would be mere folly to find fault because Landor did not write, we will not say after the French fashion, but after the fashion of Swift, at his highest and on his level, the unrivaled master of simple English prose. Landor, at his best, is not so picturesque as De Quincey, nor so eloquent as Ruskin, nor so intense as Carlyle; but he has more self-possession, more serenity, more artistic charm, a wider compass, a more equal harmony, than any of these.

Landor pleases his fellow-craftsmen, however, not only by this general command of language as a means of expression, but by the perfection of form in his short pieces. Perfection of form is the great feature of classical art; it is an intellectual virtue, at least in literature, and appeals to the mind. The moderns are lacking in it. Landor's command of form was limited, insufficient for the construction of a drama; impressive as Count Julian is, it has not this final excellence. Landor's power in this respect is analogous to Herrick's; it is perfect only within narrow bounds; but it lacks Herrick's spontaneity. His verses are not the "swallow flights of song;" he was not a singer. The lyric on "Rose Aylmer" is entirely exceptional, and much of its charm lies in the beauty of the name, the skilful repetition, and, we must add, in the memory of Lamb's fondness for it. Familiar as it is, it would be unjust not to quote it:—

> "Ah, what avails the sceptred race!
> Ah, what the form divine!
> What every virtue, every grace!
> Rose Aylmer, all were thine.

> Rose Aylmer, whom these wakeful eyes
> May weep, but never see,
> A night of memories and of sighs
> I consecrate to thee."

Ordinarily, however, Landor deals with a beautiful image or one fine sentiment. His objectivity, his discontinuity, help him here; they insure that simplicity and singleness which are necessary for success. The lack of any temptation in his mind to expound and suggest is probably one reason why he rejected the sonnet, certainly the most beautiful poetic mold to give shape to such detached thoughts and feelings. He scorned the sonnet; it was too long for him; he must be even more brief. He would present the object at once, instead of gradually, as the sonnet does; not unveiling the perfect and naked image until the last word has trembled away. His best work of this kind is in the quatrain, which is rather the moralist's than the poet's form, — Martial's, not Horace's.

> "I strove with none, for none was worth my strife.
> Nature I loved, and, next to Nature, Art;
> I warmed both hands before the fire of life,
> It sinks, and I am ready to depart."

This is perfect; but it is perfect speech, not perfect song. When Landor had something to say at more length, when he had a story to tell, he chose the idyl; and his work in this kind is no less perfect in form than are his quatrains. Indeed, on the idyls his poetic fame will mainly rest. They are very remote from modern life, but the best of them are very beautiful, and in the highest rank of poetry that appeals to the artistic sense. Those who are able still to hold fast to the truth of Greek mythology to the imagination will not willingly let them die. To read them is like looking at the youths and maidens of an ancient bas-relief. The cultivated will never tire of them; the people will never care for them. The limitations of their interest are inherent in their subject and the mode of its presentation; but these limitations do not lessen their beauty, although they make very small the number who appreciate it.

Landor's influence over his critics is due chiefly to his power as a stylist, and to the perfection of form in his shorter poems and his idyls; but something is also due to the passages which, apart from those mentioned, they commend so unreservedly; such as the study of incipient insanity in the dialogue between Tiberius and Vipsania, and the scenes from "Antony and Octavius" where the boy Cæsarion is an actor. Not to be conquered by these argues one's self "dull of soul;" and scattered through the volumes are other passages of only less mastery, especially in the Greek dialogues, which cannot here be particularized. For this reason no author is more served than Landor by a book of selections. After all, too, an author should be judged by his best. Nevertheless, when one remembers the extraordinary gifts of Landor, one cannot but regret the defects of nature and judgment that have so seriously interfered with his influence. His work as a whole exhibits a sadder waste of genius than is the case even with Coleridge. There is no reason to suppose that the verdict of the public on his value will be reversed. His failure may well serve as a warning to the artistic school in poetry; it affords one more of the long list of illustrations of that fundamental truth in literature,— the truth that a man's work is of service to mankind in proportion as, by expressing himself in it, by filling it with his own personality, he fills it with human interest.

# ON THE PROMISE OF KEATS

In the domestic, chatty, and nonsense portions of the letters of Keats, and their chaffing, their abandon, their unregarded laughter (and admirable fooling they are, too), there is a spontaneous and irresponsible gaiety, which, being quite natural only to the young heart and mind, charmingly discloses his youthfulness as a prime quality. Of all the famous English poets, he had most of the spirit of April in him. His senses were keen; his temperament was feverish, now jealous and irritable, and straightway humble and indulgent; his imaginary joys and sorrows were spiritual possessions, subjecting him; his humor was scampering, his fancy teeming, his taste erratic, his critical faculty exposed to balking enthusiasms; his opinions of men and affairs were hasty, circumscribed, frequently adopted unreflectingly at second-hand; and, with all these boyish traits, he was extremely self-absorbed. At the center of his individuality, nevertheless, was the elemental spark, the saving power of genius, the temperance, sanity, and self-reverence of a fine nature gradually coming to the knowledge of its faculties and unriddling the secret of its own moral beauty. Hence Lord Houghton, doing more essential justice to Keats than any of his louder eulogists, describes his works as rather the exercises of his poetical education than the charactery of his original and free power; and Matthew Arnold, even when placing him with Shakespeare, excuses him as a 'prentice hand in the wisest art.

Too many of his admirers, seizing upon the external, accidental, and temporal in his biography and the fragmentary and parasitical in his poetry, have really wronged Keats more than did the now infamous reviews; they have rescued him from among the cockneys only to confound him with the neo-pagans. In what did the promise of Keats lie? The first step in the inquiry is the recognition of his immaturity, — the acknowledgment that his memorials must be searched for the germ rather than the fruit.

Sensuous Keats was, as every poet whose inspiration is direct from Heaven must be; unfortunately, the extraordinary beauty and facility of his descriptions of sensation, and his taste for climax and point in his prose have made it easy to quote phrases which seem to show that he was unduly attached to delights of mere sense. To pass by the anecdotes of Haydon, not too scrupulous a truthteller, here is a characteristic paragraph written to his brother George:—

"This morning I am in a sort of temper, indolent, and supremely careless; I long after a stanza or two of Thomson's 'Castle of Indolence'; my passions are all asleep, from my having slumbered till nearly eleven, and weakened the animal fiber all over me to a delightful sensation about three degrees this side of faintness. If I had teeth of pearl and the breath of lilies, I should call it languor; but as I am I must call it laziness. In this state of effeminacy, the fibers of the brain are relaxed in common with the rest of the body, and to such a happy degree that pleasure has no show of enticement and pain no unbearable frown; neither poetry, nor ambition, nor love have any alertness of countenance; as they pass by me, they seem rather like three figures in a Greek vase,

## ON THE PROMISE OF KEATS

two men and a woman, whom no one but myself could distinguish in their disguisement. This is the only happiness, and is a rare instance of advantage in the body overpowering the mind."

With similar zest he enumerates the pleasures of drinking claret or of eating a peach, or he describes his "East Indian" to his brother's wife: "She kept me awake one night, as a tune of Mozart's might do. I speak of the thing as a pastime and an amusement, than which I can feel none deeper than a conversation with an imperial woman, the very 'yes' and 'no' of whose lips is to me a banquet. . . . As a man of the world, I love the rich talk of a Charmian; as an eternal being, I love the thought of you. I should like her to ruin me, and I should like you to save me."

Such quick susceptibility to sensuous impressions of every kind may be plentifully illustrated by opening almost at random in his works. But the characteristics that mark the real sensualist — the content that the lotus-leaf vapors forth, the fierceness of the centaur's pursuit, the struggle of the faun's transformation — are nowhere to be found in the letters or the poems; before his illness, at least, there is no debility, irresolution, or mastery of the instincts over the mind. In fact, without any revolution of his nature, without the slightest effort, by mere growth it would seem, he passed on into the "Chamber of Maiden Thought," as he phrased it, and became absorbed as deeply in his reflections as previously in his impulses. At no time, indeed, was he wholly unthoughtful. The passages that have been given above are parenthetical, and should be read in connection with such as these, of the opposite tenor:—

"I must think that difficulties nerve the spirit of a man;

they make our prime objects a refuge as well as a passion."

"I am becoming accustomed to the privations of the pleasures of sense. In the midst of the world, I live like a hermit. I have forgot how to lay plans for the enjoyment of any pleasure. I feel I can bear anything, — any misery, even imprisonment, — so long as I have neither wife nor child."

"Women must want imagination, and they may thank God for it; and so may we, that a delicate being can feel happy without any sense of crime."

"Scenery is fine, but human nature is finer; the sward is richer for the tread of a real nervous English foot; the eagle's nest is finer for the mountaineer having looked into it."

Many a remark, based like these immediately upon his own experience, shows that Keats had an insight into his own life and an outlook on the world inconsistent with the portrayal of him as merely impassioned with sensuous beauty.

So far, in fact, was Keats from being either lapped in Lydian airs or fed on food of sweetest melancholy that he was sometimes a disagreeably unhappy person, if his brother George's description of him be entirely true, since his moodiness was vented in complaints, irritable jealousies, and like ways. However exceptional such occasions were in the intercourse of the brothers, this exposure, taken together with some of the upbraidings in the letters to Fanny Brawne, is very significant. Keats himself refers to the strain of morbidity in him, and, although from time to time he felt the strong awakening of the philanthropic instinct, frequently expresses his distaste for society, his misanthropy, his indifference to the public, his wish to live withdrawn, free from human relations, engaged in poetizing for his own sake. Toward women especially he had a bitter tongue, before he fell in love with Fanny Brawne.

"When I was a schoolboy, I thought a fair woman a pure goddess; my mind was a soft nest in which some one of them slept, though she knew it not. . . . When I am among women, I have evil thoughts, malice, spleen; I cannot speak or be silent; I am full of suspicions, and therefore listen to nothing; I am in a hurry to be gone. You must be charitable, and put all this perversity to my being disappointed since my boyhood. Yet with such feelings I am happier alone, among crowds of men, by myself, or with a friend or two."

He ascribes this peculiarity to his love for his brothers, "passing the love of women:"

"I have been ill-tempered with them, I have vexed them, — but the thought of them has always stifled the impression that any woman might otherwise have made on me."

He saw but little to choose, in his satirical moods, between men and hawks:—

"The hawk wants a mate; so does the Man. Look at them both; they set about it and procure one in the same manner; they want both a nest, and they set about one in the same manner. The noble animal man, for his amusement, smokes a pipe; the hawk balances about the clouds: that is the only difference of their leisures."

Experience did not teach him more charity, though it made him more discriminating:—

"The more I know of men the more I know how to value entire liberality in any of them. Thank God, there are a great many who will sacrifice their worldly interest for a friend. I wish there were more who would sacrifice their passions. The worst of men are those whose self-interests are their passions; the next, those whose passions are their self-interest. Upon the whole, I dislike mankind. Whatever people on the other side of the question may advance, they cannot deny that they are always surprised at hearing of a good action and never of a bad one."

This temper toward man in the abstract is the general feeling of which his mood toward the public is a special instance. He simply disregarded men who stood in no intimate relation to him, whether he met them in society or wrote verses for them to read. He was not, if his word be literally taken, sensitive to criticism or ambitious of popularity: he neglected the one because he put faith in his own judgment, and he despised the other because it was to be got at a vulgar cost. His depreciation of the life of men, as he saw it, arose partly from a consciousness of power, partly from a sense of the distance between his thoughts and hopes and those of his fellows. The aloofness of genius he had in full measure. That curiously complex emotion, into which so many instincts and perceptions enter that it is scarcely analyzable at all, and is forced to go under the name of pride, was often dominant in his moods when others than his friends were before his attention. In short, Keats was as incompatible with his surroundings as ever any young poet left to the oblivion of his own society; and he was as indignant at stupidity, as tired of insignificance, as thoroughly world-weary, as a solitary enthusiast for the ideal could well be. In his last letter to George he sums the whole matter up more fully than at first but to the same purport:—

" 'Tis best to remain aloof from people, and like their

## ON THE PROMISE OF KEATS

good parts without being eternally troubled with the dull process of their every-day lives. When once a person has smoked the vapidness of the routine of society, he must either have self-interest or the love of some sort of distinction to keep him in good humor with it. All I can say is that, standing at Charing Cross and looking east, west, north, and south, I can see nothing but dullness. I hope while I am young to live retired in the country. When I grow in years and have a right to be idle, I shall enjoy cities more."

In this opinion he did retire to one place or another, — the Isle of Wight, or Winchester, or Teignmouth, and there isolating himself dreamed out his poems. He lived in a sort of ecstasy during no small portion of these solitary hours, when he could call the roaring of the wind his wife, the stars through the window panes his children, and rest contented in the abstract idea of beauty in all things. This absorption in the idea of beauty which determined the formulation of his creed in the oft-quoted lines, —

"Beauty is truth, truth beauty, — that is all
Ye know on earth, and all ye need to know;"

which also led him into that much misunderstood exclamation, "O for a life of sensations rather than of thoughts;" this intoxication, as it were, with the loveliness of earth, was in his belief a true Pythian inspiration, the medium of the divine revelation. The world takes such expressions as extravaganzas, or as mystical philosophy; but to Keats they were as commonplace as the proverbs of the hearth; he meant them as entirely lucid expressions of plain sense. This point in the criticism of Keats has been too little insisted on and brought to notice. He put his faith in the suggestions of the spirit; he relied on the intimations of what is veiled from full sight; he had little patience with minds that cannot be content with half-knowledge, or refuse to credit convictions because they cannot be expressed in detail, with logical support, and felt with the hand of sense all round, if one may employ the phrase; in other words, he believed in the imagination as a truth-finding faculty, not less valid because it presents truth in a wholly different way from the purely logical intellect. This was the deepest and most rooted persuasion of his mind from the time when he first comes under our observation. To bring together a few expressions of it is the only right way of setting forth his creed in this matter. The following extracts are from various parts of his letters, from the earliest to the later ones:—

"At once it struck me what quality went to form a man of achievement, especially in literature, and which Shakespeare possessed so enormously — I mean *negative capability*, that is, when a man is capable of being in uncertainties, mysteries, doubts, without any irritable reaching after fact and reason. Coleridge, for instance, would let go by a fine isolated verisimilitude caught from the penetralium of Mystery, from being incapable of remaining content with half-knowledge. This pursued through volumes would perhaps take us no further than this, that with a great poet the sense of Beauty overcomes every other consideration, or rather obliterates all consideration."

"Many a man can travel to the very bourne of heaven, and yet want confidence to put down his half-seeing."

"I never feel quite certain of any truth but from a clear perception of its beauty, and I find myself very young-minded, even in that perceptive power."

## ON THE PROMISE OF KEATS

"The whole thing must, I think, have appeared to you, who are a consecutive man, as a thing almost of mere words. But I assure you that, when I wrote it, it was a regular stepping of the imagination toward a truth."

"What the imagination seizes as beauty must be truth, whether it existed before or not. . . . The imagination may be compared to Adam's dream — he awoke and found it truth. I am more zealous in this affair because I have never yet been able to perceive how anything can be known for truth by consecutive reasoning, and yet [so]· it must be. . . . However it may be, O for a life of sensations rather than of thoughts! It is a 'vision in the form of youth,' a shadow of reality to come."

*A shadow of reality to come!* What a light that sentence throws on the aspiration for sensations rather than thoughts, for beauty rather than logic, for the sight rather than the inference, for the direct rather than the mediate perception of the divine! So, at least, it is plain, Keats understood himself; and whether one counts his faith a vague self-deception, meaningless except to a mystic, or has found the most precious truth borne in upon his heart only by this selfsame way, the recognition of the poet's philosophy not merely lifts Keats out of and above the sphere of the purely sensuous, but reveals at once the spiritual substance which underlies his poetry, and which gives it vitality for all time. To other men beauty has been a passion, but to him it was a faith; it was the substance of things hoped for, the evidence of things unseen, — *a shadow of the reality to come*. It was not, as with other poets, in the beauty of nature, the beauty of virtue, the beauty of a woman's face, singly that he found his way to the supra-sensible; he says in his most solemn words, "I have loved the principle of beauty *in all things*."

Dying he said it proudly, as one who had kept the faith that was given him; and since he chose that declaration as the summary of his accomplishment, it needs to be borne in mind, with all its large and many-sided meaning, by those who would pluck out the heart of his mystery.

But although to Keats the worship of beauty in all things was the essence of his life, and the delight that sprang from it the essence of his joy, he did not find in these the whole of life. At first he had been satisfied if the melancholy fit fell on him, "sudden from heaven, like a weeping cloud," — eager to let the passion have its way with him, until it wreaked itself upon expression; but he felt this overmastering of his own will an injury, not merely exhausting but wasteful.

"Some think I have lost that poetic ardor and fire 't is said I once had; — the fact is, perhaps I have; but, instead of that, I hope I shall substitute a more thoughtful and quiet power. I am more frequently, now, contented to read and think, but now and then haunted with ambitious thoughts, . . . scarcely content to write the best verses for the fever they leave behind. I want to compose without this fever. I hope I one day shall."

Similarly, he wishes to know more, and is determined to "get learning, get understanding," if only that he may keep his balance in the "high sensations" that draw him into their whirl.

"Although I take poetry to be the chief, there is something else wanting to one who passes his time among books and thoughts on books. . . . I find earlier days are gone by — I find I can have no enjoyment in the world but continual drinking of knowledge. I find there is no worthy pursuit but the idea of doing some good to the world. . . . There is but one way for me. The road lies through application, study, and thought. I will pursue it; and, for that end, purpose retiring for some years."

The years that should have perfected his powers were denied to him; his account was made up. In these broken plans, however; in this constant expansion of his view and faithful laying of his experience to heart; in the wisdom of his interpretation of what came within his scope; in a word, in his teachableness as well as in his steadier enthusiasm, his uncloyed sensibility, his finer spirituality, as the promise of Keats seems brighter, so his worth seems greater. These letters show that more had passed into his character than was ever reproduced in his poems. We come back to Lord Houghton's decision. Fine as the work of Keats is, his genius was, nevertheless,

> "The bloom, whose petals, nipt before they blew,
> Died on the promise of the fruit."

It has been suggested in some quarters that, notwithstanding his early death, he would probably have done no better work, if indeed he even maintained himself at the height he had reached. In support of this it is urged that Wordsworth's best poetry was written in youth, and that Coleridge's powers were employed on really excellent verse only for two years. These letters make it folly to entertain such a belief; they (and the works too) exhibit not only an increase of intellectual, but also of artistic power. No criticism of his poetry is intended here; but, in connection with this point, it may be remarked that his principal defect is in style, as is shown by the necessity he continually felt of studying literary models, which nevertheless affected his productions hardly at all, except in linguistic handling, — in the choice and flow of words, after Spenser, the structure of sentences, after Milton, and later (in "Lamia"), after Dryden, and in a movement and kind of verbal *esprit*, after Ariosto. This restless change from one master to another, as well as some few critical remarks, indicates a power to form a distinctive style of his own. Again, the marked pictorial character of his poetry — the quality it has to impress one like a cartoon or a bas-relief ("the brede of marble men and maidens"), the grace of form and attitude in the figures of his poetic vision — was clearly recognized by him to be in excess in his compositions. Originally, this was due, in a high degree, to the accident of his friendship with Haydon; the portfolios of the masters helped his imagination in definiteness, in refinement, and especially in power of grouping. As the mind became more to him, and the eye less, he was dissatisfied with this trait of his works. He condemned even the most perfect composition of this kind in English: "I wish to diffuse the coloring of St. Agnes' Eve throughout a poem in which character and sentiment would be the figures to such drapery." One who could speak of such a poem as "drapery" was far from the conclusion of his artistic education. Lastly, he was from the beginning ambitious of writing dramas. "Otho" and "King Stephen" are by no means unmistakable prophecies of success, had he continued in this hope. The effort, however, proves an interest in humanity of a different order from that shown in the mythological or lyrical pieces, and makes evident how far the naturalism of his published poetry was from expressing the fullness of his mind. These three things — the incipiency of his style, the acknowledged insufficiency of picturesque art in creating the best poetry, and the ardent desire to deal with human life directly, and on the large scale, in the drama — are enough to convince us that Keats was truly a Chatterton, only less unfortunate, —"born for the future, to the future lost;" one who, though he wears, Adonis-like, the immortal youth that lies in the gift of early death, would have been even dearer to the world, had his name lost in pathos and gained in honor, as it assuredly would have done if his grass-grown grave wore the wheaten garland of England instead of the Roman daisies.

# BYRON'S CENTENARY

THE absence of any widespread interest in the centenary of Lord Byron is a marvelous illustration of the vicissitudes of literary reputation. Only in Greece was public notice taken of it. The brilliancy with which his fame burst forth, the unexampled rapidity with which it spread through Europe, the powerful influence it continued to exert on the youth of the next age, were to the men who witnessed them sure signs of the magnitude of his future renown. The decadence into which it has fallen would have been incredible to them. It was Byron's distinction to have been the first man of letters who enjoyed an international reputation at once; and one can hardly credit the fact that he has shrunk so wonderfully. In the month of his death Sir Walter Scott, in a brief article which attracted wide attention, said that it seemed almost as if the sun in heaven had been extinguished; and when Scott soon followed him, Landor, writing to Crabb Robinson, remarked that the death of these two had "put the fashionable world into deep mourning," and drew gloomy predictions, in the well-known manner of contemporaries, because the great men were leaving no successors.

Something of the shock of Byron's death and of the exaltation of his genius at the moment was due to the manner in which he met his end; he had fallen like one of his own heroes, died in a cause, and appealed to the romantic feeling of the age. Even then, however, to admire him was found to be a different thing from approving him. When the thirty-seven guns had been fired at Missolonghi, and the Turks had responded with "an exultant volley," and the ship had brought home the remains, the Abbey was refused, and he was buried in the common soil of England. Two incidents of the funeral bring him very near to us. Lady Caroline Lamb met the cortège as she was driving, and, on being told, in answer to her question, that it was Byron's, fainted in her carriage; and Mary Shelley, as she saw the procession winding down, reflected on the short-sightedness of human life, asking who could have foretold at Lerici such changes as she had witnessed in two little years.

Hobhouse, with all his efforts, could raise only a thousand pounds for a memorial, but with this he got Thorwaldsen to make a statue which was sent to England in 1834. The Abbey was again refused, and, to the discredit of the nation, this work was allowed to remain stored away in the Customhouse eleven years, because no fit place could be got to put it in. At last, in 1845, Dr. Whewell gave permission to set it up in the Library of Trinity, which it still adorns. Thirty years later came the miserable fiasco of Beaconsfield's Committee, which, far from making Newstead Abbey a national possession and gathering there the relics of Byron, placed in Hamilton Park (other sites being refused) that statue of the poet leaning on the rocks, with his dog Boatswain beside him, which can only be described as popular melodrama in stone, beautiful only for the mass of red marble which the Greek Government gave for its base. It is to be remarked, also, that at this time the Abbey was a third time practically refused, as Dean Stanley, out of respect to the action of his two predecessors, but not appparently for any other reason, precluded application for erecting a tablet there by a letter in which he said he preferred the subject should not be brought before him.

The history of monuments, however, is not necessarily proof of fame. Others of England's greatest do not sleep in the Abbey, and the hero not infrequently waits for his statue a long age. The place of fame is on the lips of men, and Macaulay, when Moore's "Life" came out, could speak of Byron as "the most celebrated man in Europe." The decline of his vogue was nevertheless rapid and unmistakable. We all remember Carlyle's oracle: "Close thy Byron; open thy Goethe." This must have been about 1840. But, unfortunately, as one writer observes, to open Goethe is to return to Byron's greatness. Did not Goethe tell Eckermann that a man of Byron's eminence would not come again, nor such a tragedy as "Cain"? He thought him greater than Milton — "vast and widely varied," whereas the latter was only simple and stately. Perhaps, as we have been told, Goethe was flattered by Byron's imitation.

Whatever was the reason, the critical judgment of Goethe is one to be weighed with regard to Byron, and to himself also, for that matter. What part Goethe's praise may have had in making Byron the hero of "Young Germany" we have no means of determining, but his works were vital in the new age there, and still his hold seems greater on the Germans, if we may judge by the test of translations and biography, than it is elsewhere on the Continent. Heine was more than touched by him, though he was far from being his duplicate, and could see the humorous side of those young Parisians — Musset the foremost — who were melancholy in the full glow of first manhood, and went about in despair dining sumptuously every day. One pities Musset, for Byron was, as much as another man can be, the secret of his fate. Lamartine caught only the sentimentality of Byron, but Musset assimilated his darker spirit, his recklessness, and license, and skepticism, and transmuted his very coarseness into a Parisian vulgarity. Stendhal and Sainte-Beuve paid tribute to him; and, to cut the subject short, Mazzini thanked him in the name of Italy, in Spain Espronceda drew his inspiration from him, and Castelar, in the later time, eulogized him for his liberating influences in the peninsula with Spanish amplitude of phrase. Karl Elze thinks that the Russian poet, Pushkin, was his child; if it were so, Byron might well be proud of what such an influence was the beginning of in Russia. This rapid survey, with its brilliant names, impresses the mind with the range and dominance of this man, although Landor's sneer, when he hoped that "the mercies which have begun with man's forgetfulness may be crowned with God's forgiveness," does not now seem so absurd as formerly.

To look at the matter from this point of view, however, is to confuse Byron with Byronism. There was a European mood, a temperament of the revolutionary time, that fed on Byron, but he was not its creator, and to regard him as more than a single influence of many that molded the young men of the next generation is to give him vastly more than his due. This is the secret of his vogue in Europe, not that he liberated their minds, but that he set the fashion for minds expanding in a new age of intellectual pride and moral irresponsibility, helped to form their attitude, and was a rallying name for the faction. He was licentious, but he was neither democratical nor atheistical; he had no body of opinions properly thought out and correlated with social facts, either in politics or religion; he had no strong convictions even; but, with prejudices of rank and reminiscences of Scottish theology from which he could not free himself, he was an impulsive and therefore uneven revolter from the old régime, and never quite at home in the new camp. He preferred, he said, to be beheaded by the King and not by the mob; and the whole aristocrat spoke in the saying. Shelley wrote of him, "The canker of aristocracy needs to be cut out;" and he hits off Byron's inconsequence in religion where he speaks of him under the name of Maddalo, and contrasts him with himself. Maddalo, he says, took a wicked pleasure in drawing out his taunts against religion; but, he adds, "What Maddalo thinks on these matters is not exactly known." Byron is believed to have talked with Shelley more seriously than with any other man. He did not himself know what he thought; and his state of mind was well expressed by his remark to Lady Byron, "The trouble is, I *do* believe." In substance, therefore, unlike Shelley, who was democratical and atheistical on principle, Byron was far from being the ideal of the various "young" nationalities, France, Germany, Italy, and Spain, in the principal tenets dear to the age. It was rather his personality, and what they transformed him into by their worship, that had power over them in their search for "liberty;" and truly, though his ideas were incomplete and fragmentary, and inextricably blended, even in their formation, with his impulses and the accidents of his position as a pariah of genius, yet there was a contagion in his spirit, a dash of energy and of abandon, that told as blood tells more than thought.

One advantage, too, Byron had with foreign nations that with his own counts as a defect. He had no form, no art, no finish; and the poet who failed in these things can be read in our day only by a kind of sufferance, and with continual friction with what has come to be our mastering literary taste for perfection in the manner. It has been said that he consequently bore translation better than he otherwise would. His quality is power, not charm; the mood and the situation and the thought are the elements that count in his poetry, while the words are at the best eloquent or witty, but not "the living garment of light." The result was, that he could be given almost completely in a foreign language. This consideration may go far to explain the relative estimate of him by foreign writers in comparison with other English poets; for these others who have the charm that cannot be transfused, the art that will obey no master but its own Prospero, are seen, as one may say, without their singing robes; and their poetry, made prose, loses half its excellence. This, together with the German element in one portion of his work and the strong Italian influence in a larger portion, especially in "Don Juan," must be taken into account in any attempt to understand why he was the best known English poet on the Continent, and perhaps, with the exception of Shakespeare, still is.

In England, Byron's reputation met with rapid decline from natural causes. It is not likely that his misconduct in morals was much against him, and Beaconsfield was wholly on the wrong track when he reminded the Byron meeting that, after half a century, a man's private life scarcely enters into the estimate of his literary genius. It seems rather Byron's lack of orthodoxy that England most resented. Society put up with much libertinism in those days in high quarters; but Byron had attacked the faith, or at least elements of it, which the Church shared in common with Calvinism, and this was too shocking a matter for a society which found hardly more than matter for gossip in natural sons and daughters. This was the reason which a bishop alleged in the House of Lords in answer to Brougham, in the debate on the second refusal of the Abbey. Byron had attacked Christianity, and he should not be interred "in the Temple of our God." The middle classes have always rejected Byron, in like manner, because he scoffed, though, no doubt, his life and the licentious portions of his poetry also offended them. From the first his skepticism was heavily against him, and probably it still remains the strongest objection to his works in the minds of Englishmen generally. In Landor's bitter attack (he had offended Landor by rhyming his name with *gander*) this charge is made the climax, and the passage is brief enough to quote as the best word of Byron's enemies:—

"Afterwards, whenever he wrote a bad poem, he supported his sinking fame by some signal act of profligacy: an elegy by a seduction, a heroic by an adultery, a tragedy by a divorce. On the remark of a learned man that irregularity is no indication of genius, he began to lose ground rapidly, when, on a sudden, he cried out at the Haymarket, *There is no God*. It was then surmised more generally and more gravely that there was something in him, and he stood upon his legs almost to the last. Say what you will, once whispered a friend of mine, there are things in him strong as poison and original as sin." This, with all its excess, is no inapt character of Byron, as English prejudice drew him.

On the other hand, much that was in his favor at first was necessarily temporary. The man had a story. He was one of the picturesque characters of the age, and while he lived he was interesting to his time merely for his personal fortunes. It was to his gain, too, that he identified his own romance with that which he early invented, appealing to the adventurous in men and to the pity and admiration of women. His heroes are strong, and strength succeeds with the sex in fiction as well as in life; and they are, besides, usually faithful in love, while their crimes are taken out of the moral region of deliberate choice by a kind of emotional sophistry, and somehow are charged to their circumstances, so that the unwary and innocent reader commiserates their villainies instead of being revolted by them. These tales (and no part of his work was more popular) are hard to read to-day, but we forget too readily what raw and bloody fiction the world had in the first score years of this century; we cannot conceive how London ran after stories of blighted brigands and sentimental corsairs, in the very thunder of Waterloo. But so it was, and Byron was more interesting in that he was the unhappy and noble original from which the pirates of his imagination were drawn. If he changed the scene and wandered over Europe as Childe Harold, he gained in sentiment; if he wore the mask of Manfred, he gained in tragedy; and if he sneered in Don Juan, there was the jaded man of the world, perhaps more interesting. He was, moreover, a peer; but a dead peer certainly is no better than a dead lion, and when he died, why, — the fashion in collars changed. Other living personalities occupied the stage; England grew steadily more sincere in religion, more strict in the standard of private morals, more exacting of seriousness in thought and of perfection in literary form; and all these influences were adverse to Byron, who made no offsetting gain in his own country from the revolutionary fervor that helped him on the Continent.

What is there left? Some stirring passages of adventure, some eloquent descriptions of nature, some personal lyrics of true poetic feeling, dramas which, it is to be hoped, have finally damned "the unities," and one great poem of the modern spirit, "Don Juan." And what remains of that melodramatic Byron of women's fancies? His character has come out plain, and we are really amazed at it, — proud, sensual, selfish, and, it must be added, mean. Ignoble he was, in many ways, but, for all that, the energy of his passions, his vitality, his masterly egotism, and the splendid force of his genius, made him a commanding name and stamped him upon the succeeding European time. He cannot be neglected by history, but men certainly appear to pass him by. Arnold has endeavored to bring him back by a collection; but Arnold's critical views on poetry seem to be justifications in age for the tastes he had when he was young, — reasons after the act. A late biographer thinks that the decadence of his fame is due to the conservatism of the last half-century, and that in the revolutionary age that ought soon to be beginning, he will retrieve himself. But can this be hoped of a "revolutionary" poet whom Swinburne has cast aside? The prediction does not convince us. Byronism has gone by, and the age of the "enlightenment" in Germany and France; such a mood is not repeated. Goethe outlived Wertherism, but had Byron such good fortune? In his own character there are such defects as forbid admiration in the light of our moral ideas; and in his poems, taken apart from their time, there are other defects, both in their substance, and, unquestionably, in their form, which forbid the sort of approval that would make them in a true sense classic, as a whole, though the qualities that make "Childe Harold" and "Don Juan" great, and preserve here and there passages in other poems, are those that confer immortality. He was a poet; he was a force, also, that spent itself partly in creating a world-wide affectation and partly in rousing and reinforcing the impulse of individual liberty on the Continent; but he is a poet no one can love, and he left a memory that no one can admire, and there is none of his works that receives the meed of perfect praise.

# ON BROWNING'S DEATH

THE death of Browning brings one stage nearer the too plainly approaching end of a literary age which will long be full of curious interest to the student of the moods of the mind of man. Time has linked his name with that of Tennyson, and the conjunction gives to England another of those double stars of genius in which her years are rich, and by which the spirit of an age has a two-fold expression. The old opposition, the polarity of mind, by virtue of which the Platonist differs from the Aristotelian, the artist from the thinker, Shakespeare from Jonson, shows its efficacy here, too, in the last modern age, and divides the poets and their admirers by innate preferences. It is needful to remember this contrast, though not to insist upon it unduly, in order to approach the work of Browning rightly, to be just to those who idolize him without offense to those who are repelled by him. The analysis of his powers, the charting of his life and work, are not difficult; but the value of his real achievement is more uncertain. Interest centers entirely in his poetry, for his career has been without notable incident, and is told when it is said that he has lived the life of a scholar and man of letters in England and Italy amid the social culture of his time. For the world, his career is the succession of books he has put forth, and this is as he would have it; publicity beyond this he did not seek, but refused with violence and acrimony.

In his earliest poem, youthful in its self-portraiture, its

literary touch, and its fragmentary plan, the one striking quality is the flow of language. Here was a writer who would never lack for words; fluent, as if inexhaustible, the merely verbal element in "Pauline" shows no struggle with the medium of the poet's art. This gift of facility was, as is usual, first to show itself. In "Paracelsus" the second primary quality of Browning was equally conspicuous, — the power of reasoning in verse. These two traits have for a poet as much weakness as strength, and they lie at the source of Browning's defects as a master of poetic art. His facility allowed him to be diffuse in language, and his reasoning habit led him often to be diffuse in matter. In "Sordello" the two produced a monstrosity, both in construction and expression, not to be rivaled in literature. Picturesque detail, intellectual interest, moral meaning, struggle in vain in that tale to make themselves felt and discerned through the tangle of words and the labyrinth of act and reflection. But already in these poems Browning had shown, to himself, if not to the world, that he had come to certain conclusions, to a conception of human life and a decision as to the use of his art in regard to it, which were to give him substantial power. He defined it by his absorption in "Paracelsus" with the broad ideas of infinite power and infinite love, which in his last poem still maintain their place in his system as the highest solvents of experience and speculation; and in "Sordello" he stated the end of art, which he continued to seek, in his maxim that little else is worth study except the "history of a soul." His entire poetic work, broadly speaking, is the illustration of this short sentence. Such prepossessions with the spiritual meaning of life as these poems show made sure the predominance in his work of the higher interests of man; and he won his audience finally by this fact, that he had something to say that was ethical and religious. The development, however, of both the theory and practice of his mind had to be realized in far more definite and striking forms than the earlier poems before the attention of the world could be secured.

It would seem natural that a man with such convictions as Browning acknowledged, should be preëminently an idealist, and that his point of weakness should prove to be the tendency to metaphysical and vague matter not easily putting on poetical form. But he was, in fact, a realist, — one who is primarily concerned with things, and uses the method of observation. His sense for actual fact is always keen. In that poem of "Paracelsus," which is a discussion in the air if ever a poem was, it is significant to find him emphasizing the circumstance that he had taken very few liberties with his subject, and bringing books to show evidence of historical fidelity. But little of the dramatic spirit as there is in "Paracelsus," there was much in Browning when it should come to be released, and it belongs to the dramatist to be interested in the facts of life, the flesh and blood reality, in which he may or may not (according to his greatness) find a soul. Browning was thus a realist, and he chose habitually the objective method of art — but to set forth "the history of a soul." Had he been an idealist, his subject would have been "the history of *the* soul;" his method might or might not have been different. This change of the particle is a slight one, but it involves that polarity of mind which sets Browning opposite to Tennyson. He deals with individuals, takes in imagination their point of view, assumes for the time being their circumstances and emotions; and one who does this in our time, with a preoccupation with the soul in the individual, cannot escape from one overpowering impression, repeated from every side of the modern age, — the impression, namely, of the relativity of human life.

This is the lesson which is spread over Browning's pages, with line on line and precept on precept. By it he comes into harmony with the very spirit of the century on its intellectual side, and represents it. The "history of a soul" differs very greatly according to circumstance, native impulses, the needs of life at different stages of growth, the balance of faculties and desires in it, the temperament of its historical period, the access to it of art or music or thought, and in a thousand ways; and Browning devotes himself oftentimes to the exposition of all this web of circumstance, in order that we may see the soul as it was under its conditions, instead of leaping to a conclusion by a hard-and-fast morality based upon the similarity of the soul in all men. The task happily falls in with his fine gift of reasoning, and increases by practice the suppleness and subtlety of this faculty of his. One might say, indeed, without close computation, that the larger part of his entire poetic work is occupied with such reasoning upon psychological cases, in the manner of a lawyer who educes a client's justification from the details of his temptation. Many of the longer poems are only instances of special pleading and have all the faults that belong to that form of thought. "The Ring and the Book" is such an interminable argument, marvelous for intellectual resource, for skill in dialectic, for plausibility. Bishop Blougram, Mr. Sludge, Prince Hohenstiel-Schwangau, and others, readily occur in mind as being in the same way "apologies;" and in these one feels that, while it is well to know what the prisoner urges on his own behalf, it is the shabby, the cowardly, the criminal, the base, the detestable, that is masking under a too well-woven cloak of words, and that the special pleader is pursuing his game at the risk of a higher honesty than consists in the mere understanding of the mechanism of motive and act. Yet this catholicity, which seems to have for its motto, "Who understands all, forgives all," is a natural consequence in a mind so impressed with the doctrine of the relativity of human life as was Browning's. The tendency of the doctrine is to efface moral judgment, and to substitute for it intellectual comprehension; and usually this results in a practical fatalism, acquiesced in if not actively held. Here, too, Browning's mental temperament has another point of contact with the general spirit of the age, and allows him to take up into his genius the humanitarian instinct so powerful in his contemporaries. For the perception of the excuses for men's action in those of low or morbid or deformed development liberalizes the mind, and the finding of the spark of soul in such individuals does mean to the Christian the finding of that immortal part which equalizes all in an equal destiny, however the difference may look between men while the process of life is going on. Browning came very early to this conviction, that in all men, however weak or grossly set this spark may be, it is to be sought for. In this he is consistently philanthropic and democratic, Christian in spirit and practice, comprehensive in tolerance, large in charity, intellectually (but not emotionally) sympathetic. It is perhaps unnecessary to add that his love of righteousness is not so striking a trait.

But what in all this view of life is most original in Browning is something that possibly perplexes even his devoted admirers. Life, he says, no matter what it may be in its accidents of time, or place, or action, is the stuff to make the soul of. In the humblest as the noblest, in Caliban as in Prospero, the life vouchsafed is the means (adequate, he seems to say, in all cases) of which the soul makes use to grow in. He thus avoids the deadening conclusions to which his doctrine of relativity might lead, by asserting the equal and identical opportunity in all to develop the soul. He unites with this the original theory — at least one that he has made his own — that whatever the soul seeks it should seek with all its might; and, pushing to the extreme, he urges that if a man sin, let him sin to the uttermost of his desire. This is the moral of the typical poem of this class, "The Statue and the Bust," and he means more by this than that the intention, sinning in thought, is equivalent to sinning in act, — he means that a man should have his will. No doubt this is directly in accord with the great value he places on strength of character, vitality in life, on resolution, courage, and the braving of consequences. But the ignoring of the immense value of restraint as an element in character is complete; and in the case of many whose choice is slowly and doubtfully made in those younger years when the desire for life in its fullness of experience is strongest, and the wisdom of knowledge of life in its effects is weakest, the advice to obey impulse at all costs, to throw doubt and authority to the winds, and "live my life and have my day," is of dubious utility. Over and over again in Browning's poetry one meets with this insistence on the value of moments of high excitement, of intense living, of full experience of pleasure, even though such moments be of the essence of evil and fruitful in all dark consequences. It is probable that a deep optimism underlies all this;

that Browning believed that the soul does not perish in its wrong-doing, but that through this experience, too, as through good, it develops finally its immortal nature, and that, as in his view the life of the soul is in its energy of action, the man must act even evil if he is to grow at all. Optimism, certainly, of the most thorough-going kind this is; but Browning is so consistent an optimist in other parts of his philosophy that this defense may be made for him on a point where the common thought and deepest conviction of the race, in its noblest thinkers and purest artists, are opposed to him, refusing to believe that the doing of evil is to be urged in the interest of true manliness.

The discussion of Browning's attitude towards life in the actual world of men has led away from the direct consideration of the work in which he embodied his convictions. The important portion of it came in middle life, when he obtained mastery of the form of poetic art known as the dramatic monologue. A realist, if he be a poet, must resort to the drama. It was inevitable in Browning's case. Yet the drama, as a form, offered as much unfitness for Browning's genius as it did fitness. The drama requires energy, it is true, and interest in men as individuals; and these Browning had. It also requires concentration, economy of material, and constructive power; and these were difficult to Browning. He did not succeed in his attempts to write drama in its perfect form. He could make fragments of intense power in passion; he could reveal a single character at one critical moment of its career; he could sum up a life history in a long soliloquy; but he could not do more than this and keep the same level of performance. Why he failed is a curious question, and will doubtless be critically debated with a plentiful lack of results. His growth in dramatic faculty, in apprehension of the salient points of character and grasp in presenting them, in perception of the value of situation and power to use it to the full, can readily be traced; but there comes a point where the growth stops. Superior as his mature work is to that of his youth in all these qualities, it falls short of that perfect and complex design and that informing life which mark the developed dramatist. In the monologues he deals with incidents in a life, with moods of a personality, with the consciousness which a man has of his own character at the end of his career; but he seizes these singly, and at one moment. His characters do not develop before the eye; he does not catch the soul in the very act; he does not present life so much as the results of life. He frequently works by the method of retrospect, he tells the story, but does not enact it. In all these he displays the governing motive of his art, which is to reveal the soul; but if the soul reveals itself in his verses, it is commonly by confession, not presentation. He has, in fact, that malady of thought which interferes with the dramatist's control of his hand; he is thinking *about* his characters, and only indirectly *in* them, and he is most anxious to convey his reflections upon the psychical phenomenon which he is attending to. In other words, he is, primarily, a moralist; he reasons, and he is fluent in words and fertile in thoughts, and so he loses the object itself, becomes indirect, full of afterthought and parenthesis, and impairs the dramatic effect. These traits may be observed, in different degrees, in many of the poems, even in the best. In the dramas themselves the lack of constructive power is absolute. "Pippa Passes" is only a succession of dramatic fragments artificially bound together, and in the others the lack of body and interdependent life between the parts is patent to all. "In a Balcony," certainly one of the finest wrought poems, is only an incident. He is at his best when his field is most narrow — in such a poem as "The Laboratory."

There is a compensation for these deficiencies of power in that the preference of his mind for a single passion or mood or crisis at its main moment opens to him the plain and unobstructed way to lyrical expression. His dramatic feeling of the passion and the situation supplies an intensity which finds its natural course in lyrical exaltation. It may well be thought, if it were deemed necessary to decide upon the best in Browning's work, that his genius is most nobly manifest in those lyrics and romances which he called dramatic. The scale rises from his argumentative and moralizing verse, however employed, through those monologues which obey the necessity for greater concentration as the dramatic element enters into them, up to those most powerful and direct poems in which the intensity of feeling enforces a lyrical movement and lift; and akin to these last are the songs of love or heroism into which the dramatic element does not enter. Indeed, Browning's lyrical gift was more perfect than his dramatic gift; he knew the secret of a music which has witchery in it independent of what the words may say, and when his hand fell on that chord, he mastered the heart with real poetic charm. It was seldom, however, that this happy moment came to him, ennobling his language and giving wing to his emotion; and, such poems being rare, it remains true that the best of his work is to be sought in those pieces, comprehending more of life, where his dramatic power takes on a lyrical measure. Such work became more infrequent as years went on, and he declined again into that earlier style of wordy ratiocination, of tedious pleading as of a lawsuit, of mere intellectuality as of the old hair-splitting schoolmen, though he retained the strength and definiteness of mind which mere growth had brought to him, and he occasionally produced a poem which was only less good than the best of his middle age. The translations from the Greek with which he employed his age stand in a different class from his original poems, and were a fortunate resort for his vigorous but now feebly creative mind. At the end he still applied himself to the interpretation of individual lives, but in choosing them he was attracted even more uniformly by something exceptional, often grotesque, in them, and hence they are more curious and less instructive than the earlier work of the same kind.

The mass of Browning's writings which has been glanced at as the expression of the reasoning, the dramatic, or the lyrical impulse in his genius has attracted attention as wide as the English language, and it has been intimated that this success has been won in some degree on other than poetic grounds. It is fair to say, in view of the facts, that many who have felt his appeal to them have found a teacher rather than a poet. Two points in which he reflects his age have been mentioned, but there is a third point which has perhaps been more efficacious than his sense of the relativity of human life or his conviction of the worth of every human soul: he adds to these cardinal doctrines a firm and loudly asseverated religious belief. It is the more noteworthy because his reasoning faculty might in his time have led him almost anywhere rather than to the supreme validity of truth arrived at by intuition. This makes his character the more interesting, for the rationalizing mind which submits itself to intuitive faith exactly parallels in Browning the realist with a predominating interest in the soul. There is no true contradiction in this, no inconsistency; but the combination is unusual. It is natural that, in a time of decreasing authority in formal religion, a poet in Browning's position should wield an immense attraction, and owe something, as Carlyle did, to the wish of his audience to be reassured in their religious faith. Browning had begun with that resolution of the universe into infinite power and infinite love of which something has already been said, and he continued to teach that through nature we arrive at the conception of omnipotence, and through the soul at the conception of love, and he apparently finds the act of faith in the belief that infinite power will finally be discerned as the instrument and expression of infinite love. This is pure optimism; and in accordance with it he preaches his gospel, which is that each soul should grow to its utmost in power and in love, and in the face of difficulties — of mysteries in experience or thought — should repose with entire trust on the doctrine that God has ordered life beneficently, and that we who live should wait with patience, even in the wreck of our own or others' lives, for the disclosure hereafter which shall reconcile to our eyes and hearts the jar with justice and goodness of all that has gone before. This is a system simple enough and complete enough to live by, if it be truly accepted. It is probable, however, that Browning wins less by these doctrines, which are old and commonplace, than by the vigor with which he dogmatizes upon them; the certainty with which he speaks of such high matters; the fervor, and sometimes the eloquence, with which, touching on the deepest and most secret chords of the heart's desire, he strikes out the notes of courage, of hope and vision, and of the foretasted triumph. The energy of his own faith carries others along with it; the manliness of his own soul infects others with its cheer and its delight in the struggle of spiritual life on earth; and all this the more because he is learned in the wisdom of the Rabbis, is conversant with modern life and knowledge in all its range, is gifted with intellectual genius, and yet displays a faith the more robust because it is not cloistered, the more credible because it is not professional.

The character of Browning's genius, his individual traits, the general substance of his thought, do not admit of material misconception. It is when the question is raised upon the permanent value of his work that the opportunity for wide divergence arises. That there are dreary wastes in it cannot be gainsaid. Much is now unreadable that was excused in a contemporary book; much never was readable at all; and of the remainder how much will the next age in its turn cast aside? Its serious claim to our attention on ethical, religious, or intellectual grounds may be admitted, without pledging the twentieth century, which will have its own special phases of thought, and thinkers to illustrate them. Browning must live, as the other immortals do, by the poetry in him. It is true he has enlarged the field of poetry by annexing the experience that belongs to the artist and the musician, and has made some of his finest and most original poems out of such motives; and his wide knowledge has served him in other ways, though it has stiffened many a page with pedantry and antiquarianism. It is true that there is a grotesque quality in some of his work, but his humor in this kind is really a pretense; no one laughs at it; it arouses only an amazed wonder, like the stone masks of some medieval church. In all that he derived from learning and scholarship there is the alloy of mortality; in all his moralizing and special pleading and superfine reasoning there enters the chance that the world may lose interest in his treatment of the subject; in all, except where he sings from the heart itself or pictures life directly and without comment save of the briefest, there is some opportunity for time to breed decay. The faith he preached was the poetical complement of Carlyle's prose, and proceeded from much the same grounds and by the same steps: believe in God, and act like a man — that was the substance of it. But Carlyle himself already grows old and harsh. The class of mind to which Browning belongs depends on its matter for its life; unless he has transformed it into poetry, time will deal hardly with it.

To come to the question which cannot be honestly set aside, although it is no longer profitable to discuss it, Browning has not cared for that poetic form which bestows perennial charm, or else he was incapable of it. He fails in beauty, in concentration of interest, in economy of language, in selection of the best from the common treasure of experience. In those works where he has been most indifferent, as in the "Red Cotton Night-Cap Country," he has been merely whimsical and dull; in those works where the genius he possessed is most felt, as in "Saul," "A Toccata of Galuppi's," "Rabbi Ben Ezra," "The Flight of the Duchess," "The Bishop Orders his Tomb in St. Praxed's Church," "Hervé Riel," "Cavalier Tunes," "Time's Revenges," and many more, he achieves beauty or nobility or fitness of phrase such as only a poet is capable of. It is in these last pieces and their like that his fame lies for the future. It was his lot to be strong as the thinker, the moralist with "the accomplishment of verse," the scholar interested to rebuild the past of experience, the teacher with an explicit dogma to enforce in an intellectual form with examples from life, the anatomist of human passions, instincts, and impulses in all their gamut, the commentator on his own age; he was weak as the artist, and indulged, often unnecessarily and by choice, in the repulsive form — in the awkward, the obscure, the ugly. He belongs with Jonson, with Dryden, with the heirs of the masculine intellect, the men of power not unvisited by grace, but in whom mind is predominant. Upon the work of such poets time hesitates, conscious of their mental greatness, but also of their imperfect art, their heterogeneous matter; at last the good is sifted from that whence worth has departed.

# MATTHEW ARNOLD

THAT considerable portion of Arnold's writings which was concerned with education and politics, or with phases of theological thought and religious tendency, however valuable in contemporary discussion, and to men and movements of the third quarter of the century, must be set on one side. It is not because of anything there contained that he has become a permanent figure of his time, or is of interest in literature. He achieved distinction as a critic and as a poet; but although he was earlier in the field as a poet, he was first recognized by the public at large as a critic. The union of the two functions is not unusual in the story of literature; but where success has been attained in both, the critic has commonly sprung from the poet in the man, and his range and quality have been limited thereby. It was so with Dryden and Wordsworth, and, less obviously, with Landor and Lowell. In Arnold's case there was no such growth: the two modes of writing, prose and verse, were disconnected. One might read his essays without suspecting a poet, and his poems without discerning a critic, except so far as one finds the moralist there. In fact, Arnold's critical faculty belonged rather to the practical side of his life, and was a part of his talents as a public man.

This appears by the very definitions that he gave, and by the turn of his phrase, which always keeps an audience rather than a meditative reader in view. "What is the function of criticism at the present time?" he asks, and answers — "A disinterested endeavor to learn and propagate the best that is known and thought in the world." That is a wide warrant. The writer who exercises his critical function under it, however, is plainly a reformer at heart, and labors for the social welfare. He is not an analyst of the form of art for its own sake, or a contemplator of its substance of wisdom or beauty merely. He is not limited to literature or the other arts of expression, but the world — the intellectual world — is all before him where to choose; and having learned the best that is known and thought, his second and manifestly not inferior duty is to go into all nations, a messenger of the propaganda of intelligence. It is a great mission, and nobly characterized; but if criticism be so defined, it is criticism of a large mold.

The scope of the word conspicuously appears also in the phrase, which became proverbial, declaring that literature is "a criticism of life." In such an employment of terms, ordinary meanings evaporate; and it becomes necessary to know the thought of the author rather than the usage of men. Without granting the dictum, therefore, which would be far from the purpose, is it not clear that by "critic" and "criticism" Arnold intended to designate, or at least to convey, something peculiar to his own conception, — not strictly related to literature at all, it may be, but more closely tied to society in its general mental activity? In other words, Arnold was a critic of civilization more than of books, and aimed at illumination by means of ideas. With this goes his manner, — that habitual air of telling you something which you did not know before, and doing it for your good, which stamps him as a preacher born. Under the mask of the critic is the long English face of the gospeler; that type whose persistent physiognomy was never absent from the conventicle of English thought.

This evangelizing prepossession of Arnold's mind must be recognized in order to understand alike his attitude of superiority, his stiffly didactic method, and his success in attracting converts in whom the seed proved barren. The first impression that his entire work makes is one of limitation; so strict is this limitation, and it profits him so much, that it seems the element in which he had his being. On a close survey, the fewness of his ideas is most surprising, though the fact is somewhat cloaked by the lucidity of his thought, its logical vigor, and the manner of its presentation. He takes a text, either some formula of his own or some adopted phrase that he has made his own, and from that he starts out only to return to it again and again with ceaseless iteration. In his illustrations, for example, when he has pilloried some poor gentleman, otherwise unknown, for the astounded and amused contemplation of the Anglican monocle, he cannot let him alone. So too when, with the journalist's knack for nicknames, he divides all England into three parts, he cannot forget the rhetorical exploit. He never lets the points he has made fall into oblivion; and hence his work in general, as a critic, is skeletonized to the memory in watchwords, formulas, and nicknames, which, taken altogether, make up only a small number of ideas.

His scale, likewise, is meager. His essay is apt to be a book review or a plea merely; it is without that free allusiveness and undeveloped suggestion which indicate a full mind and give to such brief pieces of writing the sense of overflow. He takes no large subject as a whole, but either a small one or else some phases of the larger one; and he exhausts all that he touches. He seems to have no more to say. It is probable that his acquaintance with literature was incommensurate with his reputation or apparent scope as a writer. As he has fewer ideas than any other author of his time of the same rank, so he discloses less knowledge of his own or foreign literatures. His occupations forbade wide acquisition; he husbanded his time, and economized also by giving the best direction to his private studies; and he accomplished much; but he could not master the field as any man whose profession was literature might easily do. Consequently, in comparison with Coleridge or Lowell, his critical work seems dry and bare, with neither the fluency nor the richness of a master.

In yet another point this paucity of matter appears. What Mr. Richard Holt Hutton says in his essay on the poetry of Arnold is so apposite here that it will be best to quote the passage. He is speaking, in an aside, of Arnold's crticisms: —

"They are fine, they are keen, they are often true; but they are always too much limited to the thin superficial layer of the moral nature of their subjects, and seem to take little comparative interest in the deeper individuality beneath. Read his essay on Heine, and you will see the critic engrossed with the relation of Heine to the political and social ideas of his day, and passing over with comparative indifference the true soul of Heine, the fountain of both his poetry and his cynicism. Read his five lectures on translating Homer, and observe how exclusively the critic's mind is occupied with the form as distinguished from the substance of the Homeric poetry. Even when he concerns himself with the greatest modern poets, — with Shakespeare as in the preface to the earlier edition of his poems, or with Goethe in reiterated poetical criticisms, or when he again and again in his poems treats of Wordsworth, — it is always the style and superficial doctrine of their poetry, not the individual character and unique genius, which occupy him.

He will tell you whether a poet is 'sane and clear,' or stormy and fervent; whether he is rapid and noble, or loquacious and quaint; whether a thinker penetrates the husks of conventional thought which mislead the crowd; whether there is sweetness as well as lucidity in his aims; whether a descriptive writer has 'distinction' of style, or is admirable only for his vivacity: but he rarely goes to the individual heart of any of the subjects of his criticism; he finds their style and class, but not their personality in that class; he *ranks* his men, but does not portray them; hardly even seems to find much interest in the *individual* roots of their character."

In brief, this is to say that Arnold took little interest in human nature; nor is there anything in his later essays on Byron, Keats, Wordsworth, Milton, or Gray, to cause us to revise the judgment on this point. In fact, so far as he touched on the personality of Keats or Gray, to take the capital instances, he was most unsatisfactory.

Arnold was not, then, one of those critics who are interested in life itself, and through the literary work seize on the soul of the author in its original brightness, or set forth the life-stains in the successive incarnations of his heart and mind. Nor was he of those who consider the work itself final, and endeavor simply to understand it, — form and matter, — and so to mediate between genius and our slower intelligence. He followed neither the psychological nor the esthetic method. It need hardly be said that he was born too early to be able ever to conceive of literature as a phenomenon of society, and its great men as only terms in an evolutionary series. He had only a moderate knowledge of literature, and his stock of ideas was small; his manner of speech was hard and dry, there was a trick in his style, and his self-repetition is tiresome.

What gave him vogue, then, and what still keeps his volumes of essays alive? Is it anything more than the temper in which he worked, and the spirit which he evoked in the reader? He stood for the very spirit of intelligence in his time. He made his readers respect ideas, and want to have as many as possible. He enveloped them in an atmosphere of mental curiosity and alertness, and put them in contact with novel and attractive themes. In particular, he took their minds to the Continent and made them feel that they were becoming cosmopolitan by knowing Joubert; or at home, he rallied them in opposition to the dullness of the period, to "barbarism" or other objectionable traits in the social classes: and he volleyed contempt upon the common multitudinous foe in general, and from time to time cheered them with some delectable examples of single combat. It cannot be concealed that there was much malicious pleasure in it all. He was not indisposed to high-bred cruelty. Like Lamb, he "loved a fool," but it was in a mortar; and pleasant it was to see the spectacle when he really took a man in hand for the chastisement of irony. It is thus that "the *seraphim illuminati* sneer." And in all his controversial writing there was a brilliancy and unsparingness that will appeal to the deepest instincts of a fighting race, willy-nilly; and as one had only to read the words to feel himself among the children of light, so that our withers were unwrung, there was high enjoyment.

This liveliness of intellectual conflict, together with the sense of ideas, was a boon to youth especially; and the academic air in which the thought and style always moved, with scholarly self-possession and assurance, with the dogmatism of "enlightenment" in all ages and among all sects, with serenity and security unassailable, from within at least — this academic "clearness and purity without shadow or stain" had an overpowering charm to the college-bred and cultivated, who found the rare combination of information, taste, and aggressiveness in one of their own ilk. Above all, there was the play of intelligence on every page; there was an application of ideas to life in many regions of the world's interests; there was contact with a mind keen, clear, and firm, armed for controversy or persuasion equally, and filled with eager belief in itself, its ways, and its will.

To meet such personality in a book was a bracing experience; and for many these essays were an awakening of the mind itself. We may go to others for the greater part of what criticism can give, — for definite and fundamental principles, for adequate characterization, for the intuition and the revelation, the penetrant flash of thought and phrase: but Arnold generates and supports a temper of mind in which the work of these writers best thrives even in its own sphere; and through him this temper becomes less individual than social, encompassing the whole of life. Few critics have been really less "disinterested," few have kept their eyes less steadily "upon the object": but that fact does not lessen the value of his precepts of disinterestedness and objectivity; nor is it necessary in becoming "a child of light," to join in spirit the unhappy "remnant" of the academy, or to drink too deep of that honeyed satisfaction, with which he fills his readers, of being on his side. As a critic, Arnold succeeds if his main purpose does not fail, and that was to reinforce the party of ideas, of culture, of the children of light; to impart, not moral vigor, but openness and reasonableness of mind; and to arouse and arm the intellectual in contradistinction to the other energies of civilization.

The poetry of Arnold, to pass to the second portion of his work, was less widely welcomed than his prose, and made its way very slowly; but it now seems the more important and permanent part. It is not small in quantity, though his unproductiveness in later years has made it appear that he was less fluent and abundant in verse than he really was. The remarkable thing, as one turns to his poems, is the contrast in spirit that they afford to the essays: there is here an atmosphere of entire calm. We seem to be in a different world. This fact, with the singular silence of his familiar letters in regard to his verse, indicates that his poetic life was truly a thing apart.

In one respect only is there something in common between his prose and verse: just as interest in human nature is absent in the former, it is absent also in the latter. There is no action in the poems; neither is there character for its own sake. Arnold was a man of the mind, and he betrays no interest in personality except for its intellectual traits; in Clough as in Obermann, it is the life of thought, not the human being, that he portrays. As a poet, he expresses the moods of the meditative spirit in view of nature and our moral existence; and he represents life, not lyrically by its changeful moments, nor tragically by its conflict in great characters, but philosophically by a self-contained and varying monologue, deeper or less deep in feeling and with cadences of tone, but always with the same grave and serious effect. He is constantly thinking, whatever his subject or his mood; his attitude is intellectual, his sentiments are maxims, his conclusions are advisory. His world is the sphere of thought, and his poems have the distance and repose and also the coldness that befit that sphere; and the character of his imagination, which lays hold of form and reason, makes natural to him the classical style.

It is obvious that the sources of his poetical culture are Greek. It is not merely, however, that he takes for his early subjects Merope and Empedocles, or that he strives in "Balder Dead" for Homeric narrative, or that in the recitative to which he was addicted he evoked an immelodious phantom of Greek choruses; nor is it the "marmoreal air" that chills while it ennobles much of his finest work. One feels the Greek quality not as a source, but as a presence. In Tennyson, Keats, and Shelley, there was Greek influence, but in them the result was modern. In Arnold the antiquity remains; remains in mood, just as in Landor it remains in form. The Greek twilight broods over all his poetry. It is pagan in philosophic spirit; not Attic, but of a later and stoical time, with the very virtues of patience, endurance, suffering, not in their Christian types, but as they now seem to a post-Christian imagination looking back to the imperial past. There is a difference, it is true, in Arnold's expression of the mood: he is as little Sophoclean as he is Homeric, as little Lucretian as he is Virgilian. The temperament is not the same, not a survival or a revival of the antique, but original and living. And yet the mood of the verse is felt at once to be a reincarnation of the deathless spirit of Hellas that in other ages also has made beautiful and solemn for a time the shadowed places of the Christian world. If one does not realize this, he must miss the secret of the tranquillity, the chill, the grave austerity, as well as the philosophical resignation, which are essential to the verse. Even in those parts of the poems which use romantic motives, one reason of their original charm is that they suggest how the Greek imagination would have dealt with the forsaken merman, the church of Brou, and Tristram and Iseult. The presence of such motives, such mythology, and such Christian and chivalric color in the work of Arnold does not disturb the simple unity of its feeling, which finds no solvent for life, whatever its accident of time and place and faith, except in that Greek spirit which ruled in thoughtful men before the triumph of Christianity, and is still native in men who accept the intellect as the sole guide of life.

It was with reference to these modern men and the movement they took part in, that he made his serious claim to greatness; to rank, that is, with Tennyson and Browning, as he said, in the literature of his time. "My poems," he wrote, "represent on the whole the main movement of mind of the last quarter of a century; and thus they will probably have their day as people become conscious to themselves of what that movement of mind is, and interested in the literary productions that reflect it. It might be fairly urged that I have less poetical sentiment than Tennyson, and less intellectual vigor and abundance than Browning; yet because I have, perhaps, more of a fusion of the two than either of them, and have more regularly applied that fusion to the main line of modern development, I am likely enough to have my turn, as they have had theirs." If the main movement had been such as he thought it, or if it had been of importance in the long run, there might be a sounder basis for this hope than now appears to be the case; but there can be no doubt, let the contemporary movement have been what it may, that Arnold's mood is one that will not pass out of men's hearts to-day nor to-morrow.

On the modern side the example of Wordsworth was most formative, and in fact it is common to describe Arnold as a Wordsworthian: and so, in his contemplative attitude to nature, and in his habitual recourse to her, he was; but both nature herself as she appeared to him, and his mood in her presence, were very different from Wordsworth's conception and emotion. Arnold finds in nature a refuge from life, an anodyne, an escape; but Wordsworth, in going into the hills for poetical communion, passed from a less to a fuller and deeper life, and obtained an inspiration, and was seeking the goal of all his being. In the method of approach, too, as well as in the character of the experience, there was a profound difference between the two poets. Arnold sees with the outward rather than the inward eye. He is pictorial in a way that Wordsworth seldom is; he uses detail much more, and gives a group or a scene with the externality of a painter. The method resembles that of Tennyson rather than that of Wordsworth, and has more direct analogy with the Greek manner than with the modern and emotional schools; it is objective, often minute, and always carefully composed, in the artistic sense of that term. The description of the river Oxus, for example, though faintly charged with suggested and allegoric meaning, is a noble close to the poem which ends in it. The scale is large, and Arnold was fond of a broad landsscape of mountains, and prospects over the land; but one cannot fancy Wordsworth writing it. So too, on a small scale, the charming scene of the English garden in "Thyrsis" is far from Wordsworth's manner:—

"When garden walks and all the grassy floor
  With blossoms red and white of fallen May
    And chestnut-flowers are strewn —
So have I heard the cuckoo's parting cry,
  From the wet field, through the vext garden trees,
  Come with the volleying rain and tossing breeze."

This is a picture that could be framed: how different from Wordsworth's "wandering voice"! Or to take another notable example, which, like the Oxus passage, is a fine close in the "Tristram and Iseult," — the hunter on the arras above the dead lovers:—

> "A stately huntsman, clad in green,
> And round him a fresh forest scene.
> On that clear forest-knoll he stays,
> With his pack round him, and delays.
>
> \*    \*    \*    \*    \*    \*
>
> The wild boar rustles in his lair,
> The fierce hounds snuff the tainted air,
> But lord and hounds keep rooted there.
> Cheer, cheer thy dogs into the brake,
> O hunter! and without a fear
> Thy golden tasseled bugle blow —"

But no one is deceived, and the hunter does not move from the arras, but is still "rooted there," with his green suit and his golden tassel. The piece is pictorial, and highly wrought for pictorial effects only, obviously decorative and used as stage scenery precisely in the manner of our later theatrical art, with that accent of forethought which turns the beautiful into the esthetic. This is a method which Wordsworth never used. Take one of his pictures, the "Reaper" for example, and see the difference. The one is out-of-doors, the other is of the studio. The purpose of these illustrations is to show that Arnold's nature-pictures are not only consciously artistic, with an arrangement that approaches artifice, but that he is interested through his eye primarily and not through his emotions. It is characteristic of his temperament also that he reminds one most often of the painter in water-colors.

## MATTHEW ARNOLD

If there is this difference between Arnold and Wordsworth in method, a greater difference in spirit is to be anticipated. It is a fixed gulf. In nature Wordsworth found the one spirit's "plastic stress," and a near and intimate revelation to the soul of truths that were his greatest joy and support in existence. Arnold finds there no inhabitancy of God, no such streaming forth of wisdom and beauty from the fountain heads of being; but the secret frame of nature is filled only with the darkness, the melancholy, the waiting endurance that is projected from himself:—

> "Yet, Fausta, the mute turf we tread,
> The solemn hills about us spread,
> The stream that falls incessantly,
> The strange-scrawled rocks, the lonely sky
> If I might lend their life a voice,
> Seem to bear rather than rejoice."

Compare this with Wordsworth's "Stanzas on Peele Castle," and the important reservations that must be borne in mind in describing Arnold as a Wordsworthian will become clearer. It is as a relief from thought, as a beautiful and half-physical diversion, as a scale of being so vast and mysterious as to reduce the pettiness of human life to nothingness,—it is in these ways that nature has value in Arnold's verse. Such a poet may describe natural scenes well, and obtain by means of them contrast to human conditions, and decorative beauty; but he does not penetrate nature or interpret what her significance is in the human spirit, as the more emotional poets have done. He ends in an antithesis, not in a synthesis, and both nature and man lose by the divorce. One looks in vain for anything deeper than landscapes in Arnold's treatment of nature; she is emptied of her own infinite, and has become spiritually void: and in the simple great line in which he gave the sea —

> "The unplumbed, salt, estranging sea —"

he is thinking of man, not of the ocean: and the mood seems ancient rather than modern, the feeling of a Greek, just as the sound of the waves to him is always Ægean.

In treating of man's life, which must be the main thing in any poet's work, Arnold is either very austere or very pessimistic. If the feeling is moral, the predominant impression is of austerity; if it is intellectual, the predominant impression is of sadness; he was not insensible to the charm of life, but he feels it in his senses only to deny it in his mind. The illustrative passage is from "Dover Beach": —

> "Ah, love, let us be true
> To one another! for the world which seems
> To lie before us like a land of dreams,
>   So various, so beautiful, so new,
> Hath really neither joy, nor love, nor light,
> Nor certitude, nor peace, nor help for pain."

This is the contradiction of sense and thought, the voice of a regret grounded in the intellect (for if it were vital and grounded in the emotions, it would become despair); the creed of illusion and futility in life, which is the characteristic note of Arnold, and the reason of his acceptance by many minds. The one thing about life which he most insists on is its isolation, its individuality. In the series called "Switzerland," this is the substance of the whole; and the doctrine is stated with an intensity and power, with an amplitude and prolongation, that set these poems apart as the most remarkable of all his lyrics. From a poet so deeply impressed with this aspect of existence, and unable to find its remedy or its counterpart in the harmony of life, no joyful or hopeful word can be expected, and none is found. The second thing about life which he dwells on is its futility; though he bids one strive and work, and points to the example of the strong whom he has known, yet one feels that his voice rings more true when he writes of Obermann than in any other of the elegiac poems. In such verse as the "Summer Night," again, the genuineness of the mood is indubitable. In "The Sick King of Bokhara," the one dramatic expression of his genius, futility is the very centre of the action. The fact that so much of his poetry seems to take its motive from the subsidence of Christian faith has set him among the skeptic or agnostic poets, and the "main movement" which he believed he had expressed was doubtless that in which agnosticism was a leading element. The unbelief of the third quarter of the century was certainly a controlling influence over him, and in a man mainly intellectual by nature it could not well have been otherwise.

Hence, as one looks at his more philosophical and lyrical poems — the profounder part of his work — and endeavors to determine their character and sources alike, it is plain to see that in the old phrase, "the pride of the intellect" lifts its lonely column over the desolation of every page. The man of the academy is here, as in the prose, after all. He reveals himself in the literary motive, the bookish atmosphere of the verse, in its vocabulary, its elegance of structure, its precise phrase and its curious allusions (involving foot-notes), and in fact, throughout all its form and structure. So self-conscious is it that it becomes frankly prosaic at inconvenient times, and is more often on the level of eloquent and graceful rhetoric than of poetry. It is frequently liquid and melodious, but there is no burst of native song in it anywhere. It is the work of a true poet, nevertheless; for there are many voices for the Muse. It is sincere, it is touched with reality; it is the mirror of a phase of life in our times, and not in our times only, but whenever the intellect seeks expression for its sense of the limitation of its own career, and its sadness in a world which it cannot solve.

A word should be added concerning the personality of Arnold which is revealed in his familiar letters, — a collection that has dignified the records of literature with a singularly noble memory of private life. Few who did not know Arnold could have been prepared for the revelation of a nature so true, so amiable, so dutiful. In every relation of private life he is shown to have been a man of exceptional constancy and plainness. The letters are mainly home letters; but a few friendships also yielded up their hoard, and thus the circle of private life is made complete. Every one must take delight in the mental association with Arnold in the scenes of his existence, thus daily exposed, and in his family affections. A nature warm to its own, kindly to all, cheerful, fond of sport and fun, and always fed from pure fountains, and with it a character so founded upon the rock, so humbly serviceable, so continuing in power and grace, must wake in all the responses of happy appreciation, and leave the charm of memory.

He did his duty as naturally as if it required neither resolve, nor effort, nor thought of any kind for the morrow, and he never failed, seemingly, in act or word of sympathy, in little or great things; and when, to this, one adds the clear ether of the intellectual life where he habitually moved in his own life apart, and the humanity of his home, the gift that these letters bring may be appreciated. That gift is the man himself; but set in the atmosphere of home, with sonship and fatherhood, sisters and brothers, with the bereavements of years fully accomplished, and those of babyhood and boyhood, — a sweet and wholesome English home, with all the cloud and sunshine of the English world drifting over its rooftree, and the soil of England beneath its stones, and English duties for the breath of its being. To add such a home to the household-rights of English literature is perhaps something from which Arnold would have shrunk, but it endears his memory.

# COLERIDGE

THE poetic genius of Coleridge, the highest of his many gifts, found brilliant and fascinating expression. His poems — those in which his fame lives — are as unique as they are memorable; and though their small number, their confined range, and the brief period during which his faculty was exercised with full freedom and power, seem to indicate a narrow vein, yet the remainder of his work in prose and verse leaves an impression of extraordinary and abundant intellectual force. In proportion as his imaginative creations stand apart, the spirit out of which they came must have possessed some singularity: and if the reader is not content with simple esthetic appreciation of what the gods provide, but has some touch of curiosity leading him to look into the source of such remarkable achievement and its human history, he is at once interested in the personality of the "subtle-souled psychologist," as Shelley with his accurate critical insight first named him; in experiencing the fascination of the poetry one remembers the charm which Coleridge had in life, that quality which arrested attention in all companies and drew men's minds and hearts with a sense of something marvelous in him — "the most wonderful man," said Wordsworth, "that I ever met." The mind and heart of Coleridge, his whole life, have been laid open by himself and his friends and acquaintances without reserve in many volumes of letters and memoirs; it is easy to figure him as he lived and to recover his moods and aspect: but in order to conceive his nature and define its traits, it is necessary to take account especially of his incomplete and less perfect work, of his miscellaneous interests, and those activities which filled and confused his life without having any important share in establishing his fame.

The intellectual precocity which is the leading trait of Coleridge's boyhood, in the familiar portrait of "the inspired charity-boy" drawn by Lamb from school-boy memories, is not unusual in a youth of genius; but the omnivorousness of knowledge which he then displayed continued into his manhood. He consumed vast quantities of book-learning. It is a more remarkable characteristic that from the earliest period in which he comes into clear view, he was accustomed to give out his ideas with freedom in an inexhaustible stream of talk. The activity of his mind was as phenomenal as its receptivity. In his college days, too, he was fanatical in all his energies. The remark of Southey after Shelley's visit to him, that here was a young man who was just what he himself had been in his college days, is illustrative; for if Southey was then inflamed with radicalism, Coleridge was yet more deeply infected and mastered by that wild fever of the revolutionary dawn. The tumult of Coleridge's mind, its incessant action, the lack of discipline in his thought, of restraint in his expression, of judgment in his affairs, are all important elements in his character at a time which in most men would be called the formative period of manhood, but which in him seems to have been intensely chaotic; what is most noticeable, however, is the volume of his mental energy. He expressed himself, too, in ways natural to such self-abundance. He was always a discourser, if the name may be used, from the London days at the "Salutation and the Cat" of which Lamb tells, saying that the landlord was ready to retain him because of the attraction of his conversation for customers; and as he went on to the more set forms of such monologue, he became a preacher without pay in Unitarian chapels, a journalist with unusual capacity for ready and sonorous writing in the press, a composer of whole periodicals such as his ventures "The Watchman" and "The Friend," and a lecturer using only slight notes as the material of his remarks upon literature, education, philosophy, theology, or whatever the subject might be. In all these methods of expression which he took up one after the other, he merely talked in an ample way upon multifarious topics; in the conversation, sermon, leading article, written discourse, or flowing address, he was master of a swelling and often brilliant volubility, but he had neither the certainty of the orator nor the unfailing distinction of the author; there was an occasional and impromptu quality, a colloquial and episodical manner, the style of the irresponsible speaker. In his earlier days especially, the dominant note in Coleridge's whole nature was excitement. He was always animated, he was often violent, he was always without the principle of control. Indeed, a weakness of moral power seems to have been congenital, in the sense that he was not permanently bound by a practical sense of duty nor apparently observant of what place duty has in real life. There was misdirection of his affairs from the time when they came into his own hands; there was impulsiveness, thoughtlessness, a lack of judgment which augured ill for him; and in its total effect this amounted to folly. His intoxication with the scheme known as Pantisocracy, by which he with Southey and a few like-minded projectors were to found a socialistic community on the banks of the Susquehanna, is the most obvious comment on his practical sense. But his marriage, with the anecdotes of its preliminaries (one of which was that in those colloquies with Lamb at the London tavern, so charmingly described by his boon companion, he had forgotten his engagement or was indifferent to it), more strikingly exemplifies the irresponsible course of his life, more particularly as it proved to be ill-sorted, full of petty difficulties and makeshift expedients, and in the end a disastrous failure. A radical social scheme and an imprudent marriage might have fallen to his share of human folly, however, without exciting remark, if in other ways or at a later time he had exhibited the qualities which would allow one to dismiss these matters as mere instances of immaturity; but where Coleridge's reasonable control over himself or his affairs is looked to, it appears to have been feeble. On the other hand, the constancy of his excitement is plain. It was not only mental, but physical. He was, as a young man, full of energy and capable of a good deal of hard exercise; he had animal spirits, and Wordsworth describes him as "noisy" and "gamesome," as one who

"His limbs would toss about him with delight,
Like branches when strong winds the trees annoy;"

and from several passages of his own writing, which are usually disregarded, the evidence of a spirit of rough humor and fun is easily obtained. The truth is that Coleridge changed a great deal in his life; he felt himself to be very different in later years from what he was in the time when, to his own memory he was a sort of glorified spirit: and this earlier Coleridge had many traits which are ignored sometimes, as Carlyle ignored them, and are sometimes remembered rather as idealizations of his friends in their affectionate thoughts of him, but in any event are irreconcilable with the figure of the last period of his life.

It has been suggested that there was something of disease or at least of ill health in Coleridge always, and that it should be regarded as influencing his temperament. Whether it were so or not, the plea itself shows the facts. If excitement was the dominant note, as has been said, in his whole nature, it could not exist without a physical basis and accompaniment; and his bodily state appears to have been often less one of animation than of agitation, and his correspondence frequently discloses moods that seem almost frantic. In the issue, under stress of pain and trouble, he became an opium-eater; but his physical nature may fairly be described as predisposed to such states as lead to the use of opium and also result from its use, with the attendant mental moods. His susceptibility to sensuous impressions, to a voluptuousness of the entire being, together with a certain lassitude and languor, lead to the same conclusion, which thus seems to be supported on all sides, — that Coleridge was, in his youth and early manhood, fevered through all his intellectual and sensuous nature, and deficient on the moral and practical sides in those matters that related to his personal affairs. It is desirable to bring this out in plain terms, because in Coleridge it is best to acknowledge at once that his character was, so far as our part — the world's part — in him is concerned, of less consequence than his temperament; a subtler and more profound thing than character, though without moral meaning. It is not unfair to say, since literature is to be regarded most profitably as the expression of human personality, that with Coleridge the modern literature of temperament, as it has been lately recognized in extreme phases, begins; not that temperament is a new thing in the century now closing, nor that it has been without influence hitherto, but that now it is more often considered, and has in fact more often been, an exclusive ground of artistic expression. The temperament of Coleridge was one of diffused sensuousness physically, and of abnormal mental moods, — moods of weakness, languor, collapse, of visionary imaginative life with a night atmosphere of the spectral, moonlit, swimming, scarcely substantial world; and the poems he wrote, which are the contributions he made to the world's literature, are based on this temperament, like some Fata Morgana upon the sea. The apparent exclusion of reality from the poems in which his genius was most manifest finds its analogue in the detachment of his own mind from the moral, the practical, the usual, in life as he led it in his spirit; and his work of the highest creative sort, which is all there is to his enduring fame, stands amid his prose and verse composition of a lower sort like an island in the waste of waters. This may be best shown, perhaps, by a gradual approach through his cruder to his most perfect compositions.

The cardinal fact in Coleridge's genius is that notwithstanding his immense sensuous susceptibilities and mental receptivity, and the continual excitement of his spirit, he never rose into the highest sphere of creative activity except for the brief period called his *annus mirabilis,* when his great poems were written; and with this is the further related fact that in him we witness the spectacle of the imaginative instinct overborne and supplanted by the intellectual faculty exercising its speculative and critical functions; and in addition, one observes in his entire work an extraordinary inequality not only of treatment, but also of subject-matter. In general, he was an egoistic writer. His sensitiveness to nature was twofold: in the first place he noticed in the objects and movements of nature evanescent and minute details, and as his sense of beauty was keen, he saw and recorded truly the less obvious and less common loveliness in the phenomena of the elements and the seasons, and this gave distinction to his mere description and record of fact; in the second place he often felt in himself moods induced by nature, but yet subjective, — states of his own spirit, which sometimes deepened the charm of night, for example, by his enjoyment of its placid aspects, and sometimes imparted to the external world a despair reflected from his personal melancholy. In his direct treatment of nature, however, as Mr. Stopford Brooke points out, he seldom achieves more than a catalogue of his sensations, which though touched with imaginative detail are never lifted and harmonized into lyrical unity; though he can moralize nature in Wordsworth's fashion, when he does so the result remains Wordsworth's and is stamped with that poet's originality; and in his own original work Coleridge never equaled either the genius of Shelley, who can identify nature with himself, or the charm of Tennyson, who can at least parallel nature's phenomena with his own human moods. Coleridge would not be thought of as a poet of nature, except in so far as he describes what he observes in the way of record, or gives a metaphysical interpretation to phenomena. This is the more remarkable because he had to an eminent degree that intellectual power, that overmastering desire of the mind, to rationalize the facts of life. It was this quality that made him a philosopher, an analyst, a critic on the great lines of Aristotle, seeking to impose an order of ethics and metaphysics on all artistic productions. But in those poems in which he describes nature directly and without metaphysical thought, there is no trace of anything more than a sensuous order of his own perceptions. Beautiful and often unique as his nature poems are, they are not creative. They are rather in the main autobiographic; and it is surprising to notice how large a proportion of his verse is thus autobiographic, not in those phases of his own life which may be, or at least are thought of, as representative of human life in the mass, but which are personal, such as the lines written after hearing Wordsworth read the "Prelude," or those entitled "Dejection." When his verse is not confined to autobiographic expression, it is often a product of his interest in his friends or in his family. What is not personal in it, of this sort, is apt to be domestic or social.

If we turn from the poems of nature to those concerned with man, a similar shallowness, either of interest or of power, appears. He was in early years a radical; he was stirred by the Revolution in France, and he was emotionally charged with the ideas of the time, — ideas of equality, fraternity, and liberty. But this interest died out, as is shown by his political verse. He had none but a social and a philosophical interest in any case. Man, the individual, did not at any time attract him. There was nothing dramatic in his genius, in the narrow and exact sense; he did not engage his curiosity or his philosophy in individual fortunes. It results from this limitation that his verse lacks human interest of the dramatic kind. The truth was that he was interested in thought rather than in deeds, in human nature rather than in its concrete pity and terror. Thus he did not seize on life itself as the material of his imagination and reflection. In the case of man as in the case of nature he gives us only an egoistic account, telling us of his own private fortune, his fears, pains, and despairs, but only as a diary gives them; as he did not transfer his nature impressions into the world of creative art, so he did not transfer his personal experiences into that world.

What has been said would perhaps be accepted, were it not for the existence of those poems, "The Ancient Mariner," "Christabel," "Kubla Khan," which are the marvelous creations of his genius. In these it will be said there is both a world of nature new created, and a dramatic method and interest. It is enough for the purpose of the analysis if it be granted that nowhere else in Coleridge's work, except in these and less noticeably in a few other instances, do these high characteristics occur. The very point which is here to be brought out is that Coleridge applied that intellectual power, that overmastering desire of the mind to rationalize the phenomena of life, which has been mentioned as his great mental trait,— that he applied this faculty with different degrees of power at different times, so that his poetry falls naturally into higher and inferior categories; in the autobiographic verse, in the political and dramatic verse which form so large a part of his work, it appears that he did not have sufficient feeling or exercise sufficient power to raise it out of the lower levels of composition; in his great works of constructive and impersonal art, of moral intensity or romantic beauty and fascination, he did so exercise the creative imagination as to make these of the highest rank, or at least one of them.

"The Ancient Mariner," apart from its many minor merits, has this distinction in Coleridge's work, — it is a poem of perfect unity. "Christabel" is a fragment, "Kubla Khan" is a glimpse; and though the "Ode to France," "Love," "Youth and Age," and possibly a few other short pieces, have this highest artistic virtue of unity, yet in them it is of a simpler kind. "The Ancient Mariner," on the other hand, is a marvel of construction in that its unity is less complex than manifold; it exists, however the form be examined. In the merely external sense, the telling of the tale to the Wedding Guest, with the fact that the wedding is going on, gives it unity; in the merely internal sense, the moral lesson of the salvation of the slayer of the albatross by the medium of love felt toward living things, subtly yet lucidly worked out as the notion is, gives it unity: but in still other ways, as a story of connected and consequential incidents with a plot, a change of fortune, a climax, and the other essentials of this species of tale-telling, it has unity; and if its conception either of the physical or the ethical world be analyzed, these too — and these are the fundamental things — are found consistent wholes. It nevertheless remains true that this system of nature as a vitalized but not humanized mode of life, with its bird, its spirit, its magical powers, is not the nature that we know or believe to be, — it is a modern presentation of an essentially primitive and animistic belief; and similarly this system of human life, — if the word human can be applied to it, with its dead men, its skeleton ship, its spirit sailors, its whole miracle of spectral being, — is not the life we know or believe to be; it is an incantation, a simulacrum. It may still be true therefore that the imaginative faculty of

Coleridge was not aplied either to nature or human life, in the ordinary sense. And this it is that constitutes the uniqueness of the poem, and its wonderful fascination. Coleridge fell heir, by the accidents of time and the revolutions of taste, to the ballad style, its simplicity, directness, and narrative power; he also was most attracted to the machinery of the supernatural, the weird, the terrible, almost to the grotesque and horrid, as these literary motives came into fashion in the crude beginnings of romanticism in that time; his subtle mind, his fine senses, his peculiar susceptibility to the mystic and shadowy in nature, — as shown by his preference of the moonlight, dreamy, or night aspects of real nature, to its brilliant beauties in the waking world, — gave him ease and finesse in the handling of such subject-matter; and he lived late enough to know that all this eerie side of human experience and imaginative capacity, inherited from primeval ages but by no means yet deprived of plausibility, could be effectively used only as an allegoric or scenic setting of what should be truth to the ethical sense; he combined one of the highest lessons of advanced civilization, one of the last results of spiritual perception, — the idea of love toward life in any form, — with the animistic beliefs and supernatural fancies of the crude ages of the senses. This seems to be the substantial matter; and in this he was, to repeat Shelley's phrase, the "subtle-souled psychologist." The material of his imagination, on the sensuous side, was of the slightest: it was the supernaturalism of the romantic movement, somewhat modified by being placed in connection with the animal world; and he put this to use as a means of illustrating spiritual truth. He thus became the first of those who have employed the supernatural in our recent literature, without losing credence for it, as an allegory of psychological states, moral facts, or illusions real to the eye that sees them and having some logical relation to the past of the individual; of such writers Hawthorne and Poe are eminent examples, and both of them, it may be remarked, are writers in whom temperament rather than character is the ground of their creative work. The intimate kinship between imagination so directed and the speculative philosophical temper is plain to see. In "Christabel," on the other hand, the moral substance is not apparent: the place filled by the moral ideas which are the centers of the narrative in "The Ancient Mariner," is taken here by emotional situations; but the supernaturalism is practically the same in both poems, and in both is associated with that mystery of the animal world to man, most concentrated and vivid in the fascination ascribed traditionally to the snake, which is the animal motive in "Christabel" as the goodness of the albatross is in "The Ancient Mariner." In these poems the good and the bad omens that ancient augurs minded are made again dominant over men's imagination. Such are the signal and unique elements in these poems, which have besides that wealth of beauty in detail, of fine diction, of liquid melody, of sentiment, thought, and image, which belongs only to poetry of the highest order, and which is too obvious to require any comment. "Kubla Khan" is a poem of the same kind, in which the mystical effect is given almost wholly by landscape; it is to "The Ancient Mariner" and "Christabel" what protoplasm is to highly organized cells.

If it be recognized, then, that the imagery of Coleridge in the characteristic parts of these cardinal poems is as pure allegory, is as remote from nature or man, as is the machinery of faëry-land and chivalry in Spenser, for example, and he obtains credibility by the psychological and ethical truth presented in this imagery, it is not surprising that his work is small in amount; for the method is not only a difficult one, but the poetic machinery itself is limited and meager. The poverty of the subject-matter is manifest, and the restrictions to its successful use are soon felt. It may well be doubted whether "Christabel" would have gained by being finished. In "The Ancient Mariner" the isolation of the man is a great advantage; if there had been any companion for him, the illusion could not have been entire: as it is, what he experiences has the wholeness and truth within itself of a dream, or of a madman's world, — there is no standard of appeal outside of his own senses and mind, no real world; but in "Christabel" the serpentine fable goes on in a world of fact and action, and as soon as the course of the story involved this fable in the probabilities and actual occurrences of life, it might well be that the tale would have turned into one of simple enchantment and magic, as seems likely from what has been told of its continuation; certainly it could not have equaled the earlier poem, or have been in the same kind with it, unless the unearthly magic, the spell, were finally completely dissolved into the world of moral truth as is the case with "The Ancient Mariner." Coleridge found it still more impossible to continue "Kubla Khan." It seems a fair inference to conclude that Coleridge's genius, however it suffered from the misfortunes and ills of his life, was in these works involved in a field, however congenial, yet of narrow range and infertile in itself. In poetic style it is to be observed that he kept what he had gained; the turbid diction of the earlier period never came back to trouble him, and the cadences he had formed still gave their music to his verse. The change, the decline, was not in his power of style; it was in his power of imagination, if at all, but the fault may have laid in the capacities of the subject-matter. A similar thing certainly happened in his briefer ballad poetry, in that of which "Love," "The Three Graces," "Alice Du Clos," and "The Dark Ladie," are examples; the matter there, the machinery of the romantic ballad, was no longer capable of use; that sort of literature was dead from the exhaustion of its motives. The great "Ode to France," in which he reached his highest point of eloquent and passionate expression, seems to mark the extinction in himself of the revolutionary impulse. On the whole, while the excellence of much of the remainder of his verse, even in later years, is acknowledged, and its originality in several instances, may it not be that in his greatest work Coleridge came to an end because of an impossibility in the kind itself? The supernatural is an accessory rather than a main element in the interpretation of life which literary genius undertakes; Coleridge so subordinates it here by making it contributory to a moral truth; but such a practice would seem to be necessarily incidental to a poet who was also so intellectual as Coleridge, and not to be adopted as a permanent method of self-expression.

From whatever cause, the fact was that Coleridge ceased to create in poetry, and fell back on that fluent, manifold, voluminous faculty he possessed of absorbing and giving out ideas in vast quantities, as it were by bulk. He attended especially to the theory of art as he found it illustrated in the greatest poets, and he popularized among literary men a certain body of doctrine regarding criticism, its growth and methods; and in later years he worked out metaphysical theological views which he inculcated in ways which won for him recognition as a practical influence in contemporary church opinion. In these last years of his lecturing and discoursing in private, the figure he makes is pathetic, though Carlyle describes it with a grim humor, as any one may read in the Life of Sterling: over against that figure should be set the descriptions of the young Coleridge by Dorothy Wordsworth and Lamb; and after these perhaps the contrast which Coleridge himself draws between his spirit and his body may enable a reader to fuse the two — youth and age — into one. Whatever were the weaknesses of his nature and the trials of his life, he was deeply loved by friends of many different minds, who if they grew cold, had paid at least once this tribute to the charm, the gentleness, and the delight of his human companionship.

# SHELLEY'S WORK

The centenary of Shelley's birth will be duly observed with public ceremonies in England and Italy — the land that bore him and drove him forth, and the land that sheltered him and now guards his grave, both equally his home in the eyes of the world; but in the private thoughts of many single lives the day of his birth will be silently remembered with tenderness, with gratitude, and with a renewal of faith in the things in which he believed. Personal devotion must naturally enter into these feelings, for such days are to commemorate a life, and they bring the man back with peculiar power. To win unknown friends, age after age, is a privilege of the poet; it is his reward — the greater because it can touch him no more — for the open trust in mankind with which he confides, to whosoever will, the secret things of his spirit. Yet, to make a poet's personality the main element in his memory, if he be really great, confines his fame too narrowly. Attractive as Shelley was, his worth did not lie wholly in his charm. Interest in his life may become degraded into ignoble curiosity, and, in time's balance, love's gift is less weighty than reason's award.

Recognition of noble human traits is an important part of justice done to the dead; but it is not thus that Shelley would wish to be judged. Chaucer's question, "How shall the world be served?" was the alpha and omega of his life. It inspired his youthful prose; as his faculties grew and the poet emerged from the thinker, it governed the most intense expression of his soul in manhood; it absorbed him, as he himself said, with that passion for reforming the world which was elemental in his genius. It is true that the artistic and the practical instincts in him worked together imperfectly, and that at times of despair he fell back upon himself, pure poet, pouring his heart out in lyrical effusion, with cadences of pain that fill our eyes with tears. But he took heart again, and returned, though always more wearied, to the large interests of the race. He believed that man is the poet's muse; at the height of his aspiration, singing with the skylark, he still remembered that the poet's "unbidden hymns" are the means by which the world shall be wrought to sympathies with unheeded hopes and fears; in the depth of his dejection he still prayed that the wind might blow abroad the poet's words, "as from an unextinguished hearth ashes and sparks," to be an enkindling prophecy throughout the world — "my words among mankind." What he believed true poets are he told in a familiar passage of his prose — "the hierophants of an unapprehended inspiration; the mirrors of the gigantic shadows which futurity casts upon the present; the words which express what they understand not; the trumpets that sing to battle and feel not what they inspire; the influence which is moved not, but moves."

One hundred years have passed since he was born, and two generations have been buried since his ashes were laid by the Roman wall. It is reasonable to ask whether he had any share in this prophetic power, brooding on things to come, which is the mystical endowment of poetic genius; whether he anticipated time in those far thoughts forecasting hope, which he declared to be the substance of poetic intuition; whether he be one of those who, in his own phrase, rule our spirits from their urns, with power still vital in the chaotic thought and striving of mankind. "Poets," he said, concluding the impassioned words just quoted, "are the unacknowledged legislators of the world." If the phrase seems the mere enthusiasm of eloquence, yet so opposite a mind as Johnson's ratifies it. "He," said the old doctor concerning the poet, "must write as the interpreter of nature and the legislator of mankind, and consider himself as presiding over the thoughts and manners of future generations." To leave, then, Shelley's charm, his character, and all his private life, which the world well knows; to leave analysis and criticism, since any occasion will serve for such examination of the propriety of his moral method in poetry, and its beneficial or injurious effects upon his work, of the truth of his imagination and of its nearness or remoteness in human interest and reality, of his art, the speed and exaltation of his luminous eloquence, the piercing tone of his lyrical song — to leave such matters, I say, of merely personal or literary concern, what has the century past disclosed in regard to Shelley's sympathies with the next ages, and the vitality of his energy in the forces that advance mankind? The influences that blend in progress are many and various; the fore-knowledge of the most clear-sighted is vague and doubtful, and the wisest contributes only his portion to the great result. But, this being allowed, in what sense and how far was Shelley prophetic of the time to come, and an element in its coming?

The spirit of discontent has been a presiding genius in literature since the reflective life of man began. The imaginative creation of ideal commonwealths marks its conquest of political thought, and the dream of the golden age its victory in poetry. So long is it since the inspiration that governed Shelley has been active in minds like his own. The "Republic" of Plato, however, and that eclogue of the young Virgil which won for him a place among the prophets of Christ, though they are the highest reach of literature in such expression, are negative; they condemn what is, by a poetic escape into a world that should be. With the rise of democracy the positive expression of discontent, in those parts of literature which reflect the life of society as distinguished from individual life, has become more direct, comprehensive, and telling. In the last century, in particular, the world was coming to a consciousness of its own misery. The state of man was never more bitterly set forth than by Swift, nor more drearily than by Johnson. Comfortable and self-satisfied as that century is often described, it was the dark soil in which the seeds of time were germinating. It ended in dry skepticism, cold rationalism, and finally in that utilitarian preoccupation of the mind which was a European mood.

The first effort toward better things, as is apt to be the case, was political. The Revolution broke. The hopefulness of that time, when in the year of Shelley's birth Wordsworth said, " 'Twas bliss to be alive, but to be young was very heaven," is perhaps that one of its phases which is now realized with most difficulty. It reminds one of the faith of the early Church in the immediate coming of the reign of Christ on earth. When Shelley began to think and feel, and became a living soul, the first flush of dawn had gone by; but the same hopefulness sprang up in him, it was invincible, and it made him the poet of the Revolution, of which he was the child. So far as the Revolution was speculative or moral, he reflected it completely. Its commonplaces were burning truths in his heart; its ferment was his own intellectual life; its confusions, its simplicities, its misapprehensions of the laws of social change, were a part of himself. It would be wrong to ascribe the crudities of Shelley's thought merely to his immature and boyish development: they belonged quite as much to the youth of the cause; he received what he was taught in the form in which his masters held it. The ease with which genius thrives upon any food, and turns all to use, might be astonishing were it not so commonly to be observed; but its transformations are sometimes bewildering. Like fire from heaven Shelley's genius fell upon the dry bones of rationalism, and they rose up, a spirit of beauty and of power. It was the same change that took place when philosophy went out into the streets of Paris, and in the twinkling of an eye was made a flaming mænad. It was the wand of the Revolution touching the soul of man. Shelley was, in truth, in the whirl of forces which he only half understood, vaster than he knew, with destinies dimly adumbrated in his own spirit, like the poet of his own eloquent description. The Revolution was, in Gray's phrase, "the Mighty Mother" of this child; she showed him the world-old vision of the Saturnian reign that has ever hung over Italy, yet more fair than the fairest of all our lands; she set him in the footprints of Plato; and she filled his heart with many hatreds.

The principles and remedies which Shelley adopted were of the utmost simplicity. Principles and remedies must be simple in order to be capable of wide application in the reform of society. He was not an original thinker. He had the enormous receptive and assimilative power which characterizes high genius, and he made it his function to give lofty and winning expression to the ideas that he felt to be of ennobling and beneficent power over men. He had also a strongly practical temperament; and he wished to apply ideas as well as to express them, and in his own life he was always restlessly doing what he thought, linking the word with an act, carrying conviction to the extreme issue of duty performed. It was this union of the practical and speculative instincts, each highly developed, which, under the breath of his poetic nature, made his sympathies with reform so intense that he might well describe them as a passion. Yet his political, social, and religious beliefs were nothing unusual. They have been called superficial; but they were so, in the main, in no other sense than are the principles of democracy, philanthropy, and intellectual liberty. They were the simple truths whose acceptance by the world goes on so slowly. He adopted the right of private judgment, and with it the right of the individual to put his beliefs in action; the first discredited for him the excellence of the existing order, and brought him quickly into conflict with prevailing opinion; the second, in its turn, occasioned a more serious collision with that existing order itself, which met him in the form of custom, intolerance, and force. These three things he hated, because he hated most of all injustice, of which they were the triple heads. In all this he had the ordinary fortune of the revolutionist. He was face to face with the enemy. The power of custom in society, which Wordsworth had described, "heavy as frost and deep almost as life"; the venom of intolerance, the foe against which Locke had armed him; the supremacy of force, if it be invoked, in which the long history of tyranny had instructed him —

## SHELLEY'S WORK

these stood in his way, and only his own indignant verse can express the violence of the hatred and contempt they excited in his breast.

What were the tenets that had so involved him in opposition to the social opinion of his own country that he went into voluntary exile? His atheism stands first because it caused his expulsion from Oxford. What was this atheism in substance? He had conceived the divine power in terms of the historic Jehovah, and its relation to man under the Christian dispensation in terms of the legal definitions of an obsolescent theology; nor can it be gainsaid that these notions coincided with the ideas then prevalent, but not realized with the same distinctness in the moral consciousness of those who held them as in Shelley's. When he began to think, this conception was antagonized in two ways. In the first instance he acquired some rudimentary metaphysics, and it became necessary to reconcile an anthropomorphic conception of deity with a philosophical definition. In the second instance he developed an ideal of goodness, and it became necessary to reconcile the divine virtue, as shown in the same historic conception of deity, with the voice of his own conscience. He took the short and easy, but natural method, and denied the truth of the original conception. The metaphysical difficulty, however little it may vex mature minds, was a real one to him; and in connection with it Newman's statement may profitably be recalled, that no question is hedged about with more difficulties than the being of God. The moral difficulty, also, was a real one; and Robertson, whose Christian faith and sincerity none can doubt, was right in defending Shelley's decision and saying, "Change the *name*, and I will bid that *character* defiance with you." This was

Shelley's atheism — on the one hand, a philosophical definition, and on the other, the humanizing of a pre-Christian and medieval idea of God in accordance with that moral enlightenment which Christianity itself has spread through the world. Shelley expressed his denial in terms of blasphemy, as the words were then understood; but the "almighty fiend" whom he denounced was as much an idol as Dagon or Moloch.

What has the issue been? The conception which Shelley attacked with such vehemence no longer finds a voice in public discussion. It is as dumb as the ideas which once suggested such picturesquely lurid titles to the sermons under which our fathers trembled and transgressed. Today the philosophical definition would be less difficult to frame, and it would awake no serious hostility; the moral ideal, too, is enthroned in religious conceptions as securely as in the conscience of man. It would be idle to say that advance has not been made, or to deny that it has pursued the lines of Shelley's instincts, his intellectual questioning, and his moral sympathies. Merely as a polemical writer he stood in the necessary path of progress; but as a poet, he vastly strengthened that moral enthusiasm which after his death regenerated religion as it had before inspired politics. He impressed his own moral ideal on those whom he influenced, and the old conception became as impossible for them as for him. Other forces united in the general tendency, for all things spiritual drew that way; nor is it possible to distinguish his share in the change that has passed over English theology in this country. But some sentences of the Rev. Stopford Brooke are apposite, and the opinion of such an observer may be allowed weight upon the question of Shelley's place in this field. "He indirectly made," says this writer, "as time went on, an ever-increasing number of men feel that the will of God could not be in antagonism to the universal ideas concerning man, that His character could not be in contradiction to the moralities of the heart, and that the destiny He willed for mankind must be as universal and as just and loving as Himself. There are more clergymen and more religious laymen than we imagine who trace to the emotion Shelley awakened in them when they were young their wider and better views of God." Whether this be true to the extent indicated is immaterial. It is enough if it becomes clear that Shelley's "atheism" was, by its revolt, the sign and promise of that liberalized thought and more humane feeling in respect to the divine dealing with men which characterized the religious progress of the time; that his denial has been sustained by the common conscience of mankind; and that the affirmations of the moral ideal which he made have been strengthened by years as they passed by, and have spread and been accepted as noble expressions of the conviction and aspiration of the men who came after him. Whether Shelley intended these results in the precise form that they took is also immaterial. It probably never entered his mind that clergymen would thank him for a liberalized orthodoxy, any more than that Owenites would use Queen Mab as an instrument in their propaganda, and thus give the widest circulation to that one of his poems which he would have suppressed. Certainly he had a conscious purpose to destroy old religious conceptions and to quicken the hearts of men with new ideals, not religious, but moral. If both results came about, under the favor of time, and were such as the poet meant them to be, as in some measure was the case, and yet the influence also operated in an unexpected way by the reaction of the awakened conscience on the narrower faith to its liberalization instead of its destruction, this does not affect the reality of Shelley's work; it affords rather an example of that element in the poet through which, as Shelley said, he is an instrument as well as a power, and in neither capacity is wholly conscious of his significance.

The second tenet which immediately drew upon him scandal and obloquy was his belief that legal marriage was not a proper social institution. He had derived the opinion from his teachers, and held it in common with other reformers of the age. It is a view that from time to time arises in minds of an entirely pure and virtuous disposition under the stress of a rigorous and undiscriminating law. The state of women under English law was then one of practical servitude, and in the case of unfit marriages might become, and sometimes was, deplorable. The continuance of forced union, on the side of either man or woman, after affection or respect ceased, was revolting to Shelley, the more so in proportion to the refinement and purity of his own poetic idealization of the relation of love. The helpless condition of woman under such circumstances appealed to him as a violation of justice and of liberty as well as a degradation of love. If since his time the rights of married women have been recognized by important and really sweeping changes in their legal status, and if the bonds of the legal tie have been relaxed, in both instances it was an acknowledgment of the reality of the social wrongs which were the basis of his conviction. If there is less tendency among reformers to attack the institution of marriage, and the subject has ceased to be conspicuous, though still occasionally manifest, it is because the removal of the more oppressive and tyrannic elements in the difficulty has relieved the situation. The belief of Shelley in love without marriage was an extreme way of stating his disbelief in marriage without love, as the law of England then was. There was, too, a positive as well as a negative side to his conviction, but in this he merely repeated the dream of the golden age, and asserted that in the ideal commonwealth love and marriage would be one; and this has been the common theme of Utopians, whether poets or thinkers, in all ages. In other words, it may reasonably be held that, in this case as in that of his atheism, an extreme view was taken; but in relation to the time and to the reforms made since then, his ideas of marriage held in them the substantial injustice of a state of facts then existing and the lines of tendency along which advance was subsequently made. He reflected the age, and he foreshadowed the future; though the results, just as in the case of religion, consist in a modification, and not in demolition, of the ideas which he antagonized.

Shelley's atheism, however, and his views of legal marriage, have had a disproportionate attention directed to them because of their close relation to the events of his own life. These were not the things in his philosophy for which he most cared. In the matter of marriage, though he acted on his belief in taking his second wife without a divorce from his first, in both unions he went through the form of marriage. He would never have so compromised with the world in an opinion which was a point of conscience with him. If it had been a question of the freedom of the press, or of the welfare of the masses, he would have stood by his conviction though they sent him to prison or the scaffold. The affairs which he took an active interest in, and endeavored to make practical, were political. At first the freedom of the press was nearest to him, and he helped with sympathy or money those whom he knew to be singled out for persecution by the Government; then the state of Ireland, Catholic emancipation, the putting of reform to the vote, the condition of the poor, exercised his mind and called out such labors as were open to him; at a still later time the Manchester riots, the revolutions on the Continent, and such larger matters engaged his enthusiasm. He was the most contemporary of all poets. His keen interest in what was going on was characteristic; he lost no occasion which gave him opportunity to use the question of the moment to spread his general principles. His immediate response to the hour is noticeable from the time, for example, of the death of the Princess Charlotte, on which he wrote a pamphlet, to that of the Greek rising, on which he composed a lyric drama. What poet before ever had occasion, as he did in the preface to "Hellas," to beg "the forgiveness of my readers for the display of newspaper erudition to which I have been reduced"? The words are most significant of the spirit of his life. It is also not useless to observe that a share of Shelley's violence, especially in early years, is due to the fact that he was actually in the arena and taking blows in his own person. Such a man does not, between the ages of seventeen and twenty-four, write with the same equable restraint as a student in his library; he is not likely to hold opinions in temperate forms; and if, like Shelley, he is by nature sensitive to injury and resentful of it, his language takes heat and may become extravagant. What he struggled with was not only thought, but fact. It was to his advantage, doubtless, that he removed to Italy, where, being less irritated, he

## SHELLEY'S WORK

was able to express his abstract ideas in the quiet and undisturbed atmosphere of imaginative poetry.

These abstract ideas, his scheme of society, were acquired in his youth, and they were, as has been said, of the utmost simplicity. He adopted the doctrine known as that of the perfectibility of man. It is especially associated with the name of Condorcet. Shelley believed that society could be made over in such a way that virtue would prevail and happiness be secured. He thought that institutions should be abolished and a new rule of life substituted. He did not enter upon details. The present was wrong; let it cease: that was the whole of the matter. It was a form of what is now called nihilism. The state of society that existed seemed to him real anarchy. "Anarchs" was a favorite word with him for kings and all persons in power. His hatred was consequently centred on the established order. It was a government of force, and therefore he hated force; kings and priests were its depositaries, he hated them; war was its method, he hated war. The word is not too strong. Gall flows from his pen when he mentions any of these things. Their very names are to him embodied curses. If the system he saw prevailing in Europe bred in him such hatred, its results in practice filled him with pity. He was susceptible to the sight of suffering and misery, and almost from boyhood the effort to relieve wretchedness by personal action characterized him. He could endure the sight of pain as little as the sight of wrong. The lot of the poor, wherever he came upon it in experience or in description, stirred his commiseration to the depth of his heart. He was one of those born to bear the sufferings of the world, in a real and not a sentimental or metaphorical sense. He had seen the marks of the devastation of war in France; he knew the state of the people under tyrannical rule; he was as well aware of the degradation of the English masses as of the stagnation of Italy. Wherever he looked, the fruits of government were poverty, ignorance, hopelessness, in vast bodies of mankind. There was nothing for it but the Revolution, and heart and soul he was pledged to that cause.

But his hopes went far beyond the purposes of a change to be brought about by force for limited political ends; such an event involved the destruction of forms of power which he wished to see destroyed, and might result in amelioration, since force become popular was better than force that remained aristocratic; but his heart was set upon a change of a far different nature, more penetrating, more universal, more permanent — nothing less than that "divine result to which the whole creation moves." Since Shelley, in common with the thinkers of his time, believed that the world's wretchedness was due to political misrule, and could be obviated by a change of institutions, he was on his practical side in alliance with every expression of revolutionary force; but he had an ideal side, and in his poetry it was this that found expression. He sang the golden age; time and again he returned to the theme, of which he could not weary, from the hour of youth when he poured forth the story of man's perfect state in eloquence still burning with first enthusiasm, to the impassioned moment when he created the titanic forms of his highest lyrical drama, and bade the planetary spirits discourse in spheral music the pean of peace on earth, good will to men. The paradise of "The Revolt of Islam," the isle of seclusion in "Epipsychidion," the echoes of the Virgilian song in "Hellas," like "Queen Mab" and "Prometheus Unbound," show the permanence before his rapt eyes of that vision of heaven descended upon earth which has fascinated the poets of all times. Yet how transform this "world's woe" into that harmony? Shelley's command was as simple, as direct, as Christ's — "Love thy neighbor." No; there was nothing novel in it, nothing profound or original. It is so long now since man's knowledge of what is right has outrun his will to embody it in individual life and the institutions of society, that new gospels, were they possible, are quite superfluous. What Shelley had that other men seldom have was faith in this doctrine, the will to practice it, the passion to spread it. There may be to our eyes something pathetic in such simplicity, as the belief of boyhood in goodness is pathetic in the sight of the man; something innocent, as we say, in such unworldliness, and again we intimate the eternal child in the poet's heart; but it is the simplicity and innocence — the pathos it may be — of what Christ taught. That Shelley believed what he said cannot be doubted. He thought that men might, if they would, love their fellowmen, and then injustice would of itself cease, being dried at its source, and that reign of mutual helpfulness, of the common sharing of the abundance of the earth's harvest, of man's enfranchisement from slavery to another's luxurious wants, would begin; war, poverty, and tyranny, force and fraud, greed, indulgence, and crime would be abolished. It was too obvious to need consideration; man was capable of perfection, and the method to attain to it was love, and this way once adopted, as it could be, by the fiat of each individual will, would enthrone justice and spread virtue throughout the world. It was not reason that withstood this doctrine, but custom, tradition, interested individuals and classes, the active and law-intrenched power of institutions established for the security and profit of the few — a whole order of society resting upon a principle opposite to love, the principle of organized force. If this time-incrusted evil, this blind and deaf and dumb authority of wrong long prevalent, this sorry scheme of accepted lies, could be destroyed at a stroke, a simple resolve in each breast would bring heaven on earth.

This was Shelley's creed. It may be false, impracticable, and chimerical; it may be a doctrinaire's philosophy, an enthusiast's program, a poet's dream: but that it has points of contact and coincidence with gospel truth is plain to see; and in fact Shelley's whole effort may be truly described as an incident in that slow spread of Christian ideas whose assimilation by mankind is so partial, uneven, imperfect, so hesitating, so full of compromise, so hopeless in delay. He had disengaged once more from the ritual of Pharisees and the things of Cæsar the original primitive commands, and made them as simple as conscience; he may have been wrong in the sense that these things are impossible to man in society; but if he was in error, he erred with a greater than Plato.

But it is not necessary to carry the matter so far. Shelley was a moralist, but he used the poet's methods. He declared the great commands, and he denounced wrong with anathemas; but he also gave a voice to the lament of the soul, to its aspirations and its ineradicable, if mistaken, faith in the results of time; and the ideas which he uttered with such affluence of expression, such poignancy of sympathy, such a thrill of prophetic triumph, are absorbed in the spirit which poured them forth — in its indignation at injustice, its hopefulness of progress, its complete conviction of the righteousness of its cause. He has this kindling power in men's hearts. They may not believe in the perfectibility of man under the conditions of mortal life, but they do believe in his greater perfection; and Shelley's words strengthen them in effort. No cause that he had greatly at heart has retreated since his day. There are thousands now, where there were hundreds then, who hold his beliefs. The Revolution has gone on, and is still in progress, though it has yet far to go. What part he has had in the increase of the mastering ideas of the century is indeterminable. He was dead when his apostolic work began. His earliest and unripe poem, "Queen Mab," was the first to be caught up by the spirit of the times, and was scattered broadcast; and wherever it fell it served, beyond doubt, to unsettle the minds that felt it. Crude as it was, it was vehement and eloquent; and the crudities which have most offense in them are of the sort that make the entrance of such ideas into uneducated minds more easy. It was nearer intellectually to these minds than a better poem would have been. Rude thoughts not too carefully discriminated are more powerful revolutionary instruments than more exact truths in finer phrases. "Queen Mab" was certainly the poem by which he was long best known. The first revival of his works came just before the time of the Reform Bill, and they were an element in the agitation of men's minds; but his permanent influence began with the second revival, ten years later, when his collected works were issued by his widow. Since then edition has followed edition, and with every fall of his poems from the presses of England and America new readers feel the impulse of his passion, blending naturally with the moral and political inspiration of an age which has exhausted its spiritual force in pursuit of the objects that he bade men seek. Democracy, of which philanthropy is the shadow, has made enormous gains; the cause is older and social analysis has gone farther than in his day; his denunciation of kings and priests seems antiquated only because the attack is now directed on the general conditions of society which make tyrannical power and legalized privilege possible under any political organization, and in industrial and commercial as well as military civilizations; his objects of detestation seem vague and unreal only because a hundred definite propositions, developed by socialistic thought, — any one of which was more rife with danger than his own elementary principles, — have been put forth without any such penalty being visited upon their authors as was fixed upon him. This advance, and more, has been made. The consciousness of the masses, both in respect to their material position and their power to remedy it, has increased indefinitely in extent and in intensity in all countries affected by European thought; socialism, anarchism, nihilism are names upon every lip, and they measure the active discontent of those strata of society last to be reached by thought except the *bourgeoisie*. Whatever revolutionary excess may unite with the movement, the stream flows in the direct course of Shelley's thought with an undreamt vehemence and mass. That he still implants in others that passion of his for reforming the world is not questioned; his works have been a perennial fountain of the democratic spirit with its philanthropic ardor. As in the other phases of his influence, so in this its grand phase, his work has been in modification instead of demolition of the social order; it has been only one individual element in a world-movement issuing from many causes and sustained from many

## SHELLEY'S WORK

sources; but here too he fulfils his own characterization of the poet, imperfectly conscious of his own meanings, dimly prophetic of what shall be, belonging to the future whose ideas come into being through his intuitions, sympathies, and longings.

Shelley's genius, then, it must be acknowledged, had this prescience by which it seized the elements of the future yet inchoate, and glorified them, and won the hearts of men to worship them as an imagined hope, and fervently to desire their coming. If one thing were to be sought for as the secret of his power on man, I should say it was his belief in the soul. No poet ever put such unreserved trust in the human spirit. He laid upon it the most noble of all ideal tasks, and inspired it with faith in its own passion. "Save thyself," he said, and showed at the same time the death in which it lay, the life of beauty, love, and justice to which it was born as to a destiny. Virtue in her shape how lovely, humanity throughout the world how miserable, were the two visions on which he bade men look; and he refused to accept this antithesis of what is and what ought to be as inevitable in man's nature or divine providence; it remained with man, he said, to heal himself. He was helped, perhaps, in his faith in the human spirit by the early denial he made of religion as interpreted by the theology of his period; for him salvation rested with man, or nowhere. In later years he made love the principle, not only of human society, but of the government of the universe; it was his only conception of divine power; but he never reconciled in thought this mystical belief with the apparent absence of this divine element from its lost provinces in human life. He promised men in their effort no other aid than the mere existence, in the universe, of beneficent laws of which mankind could avail itself by submitting thereto. The doctrine of the power of the human spirit to perfect itself, and the necessity of the exercise of this power as the sole means of progress, remained in unaffected integrity. This fundamental conviction is one that has spread equally with the democratic idea or the philanthropic impulse. The immediacy of the soul as the medium of even revealed truth is a conception that clarifies with each decade, and it is in harmony with Shelley's most intimate convictions, with those tendencies and dispositions of his temperament so natural to him that they were felt rather than thought. But in such analysis one may refine too much. It is meant only to illustrate how completely, in the recesses of his nature as well as in definite manifestation of his thought, he was the child, intellectually and morally, of the conquering influences implicit in his age, so readily apprehensive of them that he anticipated their power in the world, so intensely sympathetic that he embodied them in imagination before the fullness of time, so compelled to express them that he was their prophet and leader in the next ages.

By his own judgment, therefore, of what great poets are, he must be placed among them, and the office of genius, as he defined it, must be declared to be his. The millennium has not come, any more than it came in the first century. The cause Shelley served is still in its struggle; but those to whom social justice is a watchword, and the development of the individual everywhere in liberty, intelligence, and virtue is a cherished hope, must be thankful that Shelley lived, that the substance of his work is so vital, and his influence, inspiring as it is beyond that of any of our poets in these ways, was, and is, so completely on the side of the century's advance. His words are sung by marching thousands in the streets of London. No poet of our time has touched the cause of progress in the living breath and heart-throb of men so close as that. Yet, remote as the poet's dream always seems, it is rather that life-long singing of the golden age, in poem after poem, which most restores and inflames those who, whether they be rude or refined, are the choicer spirits of mankind, and bring, with revolutionary violence or ideal imagination, the times to come. They hate the things he hated; like him they love, above all things, justice; they share the passion of his faith in mankind. Thus, were his own life as dark as Shakespeare's, and had he left unwritten those personal lyrics which some who conceive the poet's art less nobly would exalt above his grander poems, he would stand preeminent and almost solitary for his service to the struggling world, for what he did as a quickener of men's hearts by his passion for supreme and simple truths. If these have more hold in society now than when he died, and if his influence has contributed its share, however blended with the large forces of civilization, he has in this sense given law to the world and equaled the height of the loftiest conception of the poet's significance in the spiritual life of man. Such, taken in large lines and in its true relations, seems to me the work for which men should praise Shelley on this anniversary, leaving mere poetic enjoyment, however delightful, and personal charm, however winning, to other occasions.

# CERVANTES

Cervantes, noble by blood, was born poor. An infancy at Alcalá de Henares, boyhood at Valladolid, youth at Madrid; from such early years he emerges into the half lights of biography in the two worlds of arms and letters. He was certainly the poet of his school, for his master praised and printed the verse of his "dear and beloved pupil"; and why should we not believe he was that same Miguel de Cervantes, page at court, who for ruffling there in an affair of gallantry was condemned to ten years' exile and to have his right hand cut off, and escaped to hiding? 'Tis as easy as deer-stealing. But whether as a cavalier in flight, or as a protégé more peacefully picked up, Cervantes left Madrid at twenty-one in the train of the Papal Ambassador, Monsignor Acquaviva, a fortunate Italian youth two years his senior and a patron of art and letters; and, as a gentleman in attendance upon him, traveled to Rome.

There in a city which was still the world's high capital the young Spanish provincial, half poet, half gallant, came into touch with life in the large. He learned Italian, then the master tongue of literature; in the palace he mingled with the most cultivated society of the world and heard much high-bred discussion; he came to recognize that something barbarous and belated which foreign nations found in the literature of his own land. Cervantes had a soul capable of great enthusiasms. At Rome, in 1570, a great cause was in the air. It was one of the oldest of great causes. "A Crusade! A Crusade!" was the cry. The Turks were storming Cyprus; they threatened Venice; they filled the African coast; they held the sea. Was the Mediterranean to be a Turkish lake? It appealed to Cervantes because it was a Christian cause, and he was of the "old Christian blood" that for centuries had waged the duel with the Moors, to whom the Turks were heirs. It appealed to him because it belonged to the glory of Spain, with her vice-royalties strewn in Italy and on the islands, to crush the infidel. And it appealed to him because he was young. Don John of Austria, whose figure stood out in Southern Catholic chivalry with a brilliancy of knighthood not unlike Sidney's in the Puritan North, in its power to awake the imagination of the generous and the jealousies of the cold and mean, was the leader of the cause. Cervantes's choice was a foregone conclusion. If by the spirit he was a writer, by the flesh he was a soldier. In that adventurous age a Spaniard, though a genius, was born for roving and for arms. When his young patron, Acquaviva, following the pleasant Italian way, put on the Cardinal's hat at twenty-four, Cervantes left the antechamber and enlisted in the Spanish ranks.

A year later, the sun of Lepanto breaking, October 7, 1571, the young recruit, sick and weak with fever, lay below on the galleon, "Marquesas." At noon, the fight being on, he pleaded his duty against the remonstrances of his comrades, came on deck, and was stationed by the long boat in command of twelve men. At night, the fight over, he lay there with two gun-shot wounds in the breast and his left hand shattered. It was a fruitless victory, men say to-day; then it was the greatest sea-fight of the world. To Cervantes it remained his "one crowded hour of glorious life." Five years he was in these wars, in barracks and on campaigns. He served at Navarino, Corfu, Tunis, Sardinia, Sicily, and in Italy — one fair last year at Naples. Don John himself and the Sicilian viceroy bore testimony to his good conduct. He sailed for home, was captured, taken to Algiers, and fell to the spoils of a Greek renegade as a Christian slave. Five years more he was in these bonds. Once he was sold to the Dey, Hassan, for five hundred ducats, an interesting fact, the price of a world-genius as a slave not being often quoted.

His character now shone conspicuous. Two things marked him out among thousands: He was first in the eyes of the captives — to plan, to encourage and to undertake. He was the central plotter of daring escapes for himself and his comrades, by twos and threes, and by scores, by land and by sea. He even dreamed of a general rising and a Spanish rescue of all the sufferers. Hassan said, "could he preserve himself against the maimed Spaniard, he would hold safe his Christians, his ships and his city." He was first also in the respect of his masters. Repeatedly detected, he refused to abandon his attempts; often threatened and with the noose about his neck, in the full peril of such atrocities as he frequently saw inflicted, with unbroken constancy he shielded others and took all danger on himself. Yet he was never once struck. A certain readiness of jesting speech — helped perhaps, like Lamb's, by his stammer — seems to have served him at such times. His security, nevertheless, is inexplicable. A wilder tale than this of his captivity one does not read in books of reality. He was already on board ship for transportation to Constantinople, when the long efforts of his good mother, together with the aid of a subscription in Algiers among the merchants by the hands of a Redemptionist Father, bought his freedom. So the decamping court page of twenty came back to Spain at thirty-three, a crippled soldier and a ransomed slave.

He became a king's officer, a commissary to collect stores for naval adventures, like that great one of the Armada, and a tax-gatherer. He got embarrassed with courts and officers, a trusted agent defaulted, and he was more than once in prison. He had married a wife, Dona Catalina, not a fortune, but she brought him — here opens the domestic interior — besides some vineyards, "two linen sheets, one good blanket and one worn, tables, chairs, a brazier, a grater, several sacred images, one cock, and forty-five pullets." His house was the general refuge of the women of the family; there, in 1605, were living his wife, his natural daughter, two sisters, and a niece; the women took in needlework, and Cervantes himself by that time had become apparently a general business agent and made out papers for customers who called on him.

The jail, the tax collectorship, the long-suffering poverty — are they not the familiar marks of that other profession, the career of letters? "Pen never blunted lance, nor lance the pen," he said; one failing, he took the other. Strong by nature, he cared for success, and with good sense he sought it in the beaten track. He obeyed occasions, he followed the fashion and the market, he tried all kinds. It was the age of artificial sentiment; and he wrote a shepherd book, like Sidney's "Arcadia," a tangle of intrigue, rhetoric and love-plaining verse. It was the age of the rising drama; and he tried the play, staging realistic scenes from his life in Algiers. It was the age of the European short story; and he tried the tale, creating that variety of it which springs from direct observation of manners. Twenty years of such labors, a range from the finished whimsies of fashionable courtly fancy to the hard realism of the thieves' market, and he had not yet succeeded; but his mind comprised the theater of life, and he was trained in all the modes of literary art. "Don Quixote," when it appeared in his fifty-eighth year, was the book of a wise old man. Its popular success did not bring him friends or money. Ten years later the second part was issued.

The grave old man, on the verge of seventy, was near his end; a figure of medium height, an oval face, with chestnut hair, a Roman nose, vivid complexion, and "the silvery beard that twenty years ago was golden" — so he describes himself. Though he mingled much with men all his life, he appears in the retrospect singularly solitary. Not bred in the university, he had never been accepted by those of the schools; he had led an independent career, frank of speech, careless of enmity, aloof from every clique, acquainted with the strength and weakness of all, soberly judging even his young rival, Lope de Vega, the darling of the age. No one who saw him moving with the stooped shoulders and the slow gait, thought how future ages would have prized some living portrait of that face, nor guessed that this stammerer was the world-voice of Spain; none of the religious brotherhood he joined to secure his funeral rites, as they followed him "with his face uncovered," a little unnoticed company, knew that the greatest Spaniard was there consigned to an obscure and now forgotten grave.

Cervantes himself could not have foreknown the nature of his fame. He did not perceive the relative importance of "Don Quixote" among his works. Not recognizing that he had broken out the modern path, he went back to the old ways. He again sought the honors of the poet in his "Journey to Parnassus." He fell in with the opinion of his friends that his "Persiles and Sigismunda" would reach "the extreme of possible goodness," and be "the best composed in our language, of books of entertainment"; he died still projecting a sequel to his first pastoral romance, "Galatea." He was in no haste to take up and finish the second part of "Don Quixote." Literature was in those days, by the standard of taste and in tradition, a thing of refinement, elevation, style, in matter noble, in manner conventional; and the conscious ambition of Cervantes clung to this dying classicism for true reputation. "Don Quixote" was never planned to be a great book. It was "engendered in a prison," perhaps a by-thought of his mind, as a parody of the romances of chivalry. Cervantes was apt to have a purpose in his writings. In his realistic plays he meant to bring home to men's bosoms that cause of the freeing of Algiers which was his only practical dream in life and lingered long; in his novels he professed that they were exemplary or moral tales; and in "Don Quixote" he declared that his only aim was to destroy the popular chivalric romance which he looked on as a false and harmful mode of fiction. In his first sketch he found it, perhaps, vulgar in matter and barren in topic, too slight a theme to bear his genius; he tried to heighten it by introducing independent tales either wholly foreign or loosely connected, and episodes of gallantry more closely yet carelessly interwoven with the main plot. The book grew under his hand, and almost changed its nature in the second part, where there is nothing extraneous; it displayed a depth of type and a reach of discourse equal to the power of any genius for creation or reflection, and gathered to itself with infinite variety the universal significance of life. Though Cervantes grew conscious of its intimacy with his own spirit, it is only on the last page that he declares the identity of the work with himself. He had gradually put into it, substantially, all he was — all he had seen, all he knew — without being aware of what he had done till it was done; and, like Columbus, he was never fully aware of what he had done. "Don Quixote" announced a new age.

Cervantes was not in advance of his age. A great book greatens with time; and the seed-vessels which it contains Time rifles, and scatters its germinal forces throughout the world and ripens them in the bosom of a broad humanity; but the vitality of these belongs to the human spirit and is a thing apart from the individuality of the original author. Men have found in Cervantes a reformer, a free-thinker, a censor of Church and State, a modern pessimist — all the vexed brood of restless spirits of the latter days. He was none of these. He was a man of his country and age, and accepted the world as it was about him. He observed its elements, its operations — summed the general result of life; but he had no thought of changing what was. The idea of change, the revolutionary idea, was out of his ken. Cervantes was part and parcel of the present, whole with his time; a loyal subject, a true Catholic. He approved of the expulsion of the Moors. He had a liberal outlook on the foreign world, shown especially by his fair words for England, Spain's foe; and at home he saw the political and even the ecclesiastical organization as human institutions subject to defect in persons, means and all their temporalities; if divinely instituted, they were humanly constituted. Institutional life he saw in its right proportions as a part of fixed mortal routine, belonging essentially in the material sphere — the body politic, the body ecclesiastic. He was concerned with life in other phases. He was a natural critic; judgment was one of his principal gifts, shown not only in minor literary notices that stud the way, but in the large in those discourses which richly interweave the narrative or arise out of the dialogue, turning eloquently to monologue under the flame of thought; and in the creative parts he was a critic of life. He was a great critic of life just because he had no ulterior aim either reformatory or humanitarian. Not the practical modification of life, not life in the prospect, but its imaginative contemplation, life in the retrospect, was his sphere. It is an old man's book. To him life was externally a spectacle, and in himself a function; as a function it had been a gradually disillusioning enthusiasm; as a spectacle it had become an increasing irony. An enthusiastic youth is apt to be followed by an ironical old age. In the South, especially, young passion begot these pleasant ironies of later years, and the Mediterranean literature, except in the greatest, is well divided between young passion and old irony, whose blend in "Don Quixote" attains to greatness. Its chance "engendering in a prison" is in itself ironical; its destiny to enthrall the world is the very fatalism of the grotesque in life. A madman and a fool, a horse and ass, seeking adventures in a world as it is, go faring forth on the great empty Spanish plains: what mortal interest can there be in their doings or their fate?

"Don Quixote" is the book of Spain. Its theater is the Spanish land. It is a book of the open air and the broad world. It has for landscape the burning plains, the desolate romantic mountains, the strip of blue by the coast; its outlook is along the Mediterranean world by the highway of the islands that Cervantes had traveled in youth, whence men came back with tales of sea-fight and captivity; on the long Northern edge lay Protestantism like a high mountain range, and its over-sea horizons stretched away to Peru and the Indies. It is a book written in Spain as from the center of the world, and this Spain was filled with its own folk; the race-mark of "the old Christian blood," of dark-skinned Moor and gipsy was stamped on them; they came forth in all their variety of life, hidalgo, bourgeoise, picaresque, ducal, provincial, intellectual, young and old, good and bad, soldier, student, and priest, innkeepers, criminals, players, peasants, lovers, highwaymen, barbers, carriers, judges, officials, doctors, menagerie-men, damsels, duennas — an endless list. Scarce any book has so many people in it. This mass is put in constant movement which gives unwearied liveliness to the scene. It is a book of life on the road. All the world is *en voyage*. The galley slaves are there; even the dead are going a journey. The delineation of manners is on the national scale. Only the high dignitaries of Church and State are exempt from the general conscription. The Court and the great ecclesiastics are not seen, but their absence only proves how small a part exalted officials have in constituting the character of a people. The Spanish folk is represented in its racial life without them, and the portrayal is nationally complete. Cervantes deals with this multitude easily, taking them individually and a few at a time. It is a book of short flights, of incidents lightly dovetailed, of scenes strung together, of combinations rapidly formed and dissolved.

The characters are seized like Holbein's in the "Dance of Death," only here the dramatic moments are as various as the manifold situations of the living range of human affairs; the pictures and groupings are nevertheless on a similar limited scale, momentary and shifting, and each person is characterized with his own habit of life, caught in his own world, and shown completely in a few strokes. How many such small scenes crowd to the memory! The muleteer trolling the snatch of Roncesvalles in the dark morning of El Toboso; the student singing on his way to the wars, the puppet-show, the lion, and in low life, the disasters of the night at the inn; innumerable vivid sketches! Thus the book is, by its surface, representative of all Spain, of the look of the land, the figures of the people, the daily event and business of life. But it exceeds the mere flat pictorial method. It is more richly bodied forth.

About all this panorama there is what gives wholeness to life. There is a world-perspective of the larger present, that secular environment of contemporaneity found in Shakespeare's plays, and here signified by means of the continuous inroad of the Turkish power into the story. There is a historical background, most clearly reflected in the popular knowledge of chivalric romance, and in the fact that every one knows of chivalry and each character, no matter how humble, takes up a natural and instantaneous attitude towards Don Quixote almost as if he were an expected guest. The blend of ballad history with this romance helps the effect. This whole Spanish folk inhabits knightly ground, and preserves its tradition and sentiment. There is also an emotional *fond*, a part of national character, interpreted here by the incessant gallantry of love in operatic episodes, by the shepherds, the serenades, the runaways, the youthfulness of love, its sentimental sufferings, the folly of its escapades, all its charms and senselessness. And there are in the Spanish nature of the book qualities more abstractly felt — intrigue and trick, ceremonial, grandiloquence, boasting, gullibility, mendacity, coarseness, cruelty — human qualities all, but here with their Spanish physiognomy. "Don Quixote," even in its national aspects, is a book that has all the dimensions of life, personal, geographical, historical, emotional, moral. It sweats Spain as an olive does oil.

But all this is only the environment of the action and the means of its operation in the tale. Cervantes knew a more admirable way of setting forth the soul of Spain. It is not merely because Don Quixote and Sancho are always on the scene that they surpass the other characters in power of interest; they have a higher life. Cervantes stamped the genius of the race by a double die, on the loftier and the humbler side; noble and peasant, the mad hidalgo and the deluded boor, divide between them the spiritual realm of Spain. The illusion of the one, the duping of the other only intensify their racial traits and perfect them. Character is deeper than circumstance, and owns a superiority over all the world of appearance. If Don Quixote is at first interesting for what happens to him as is the way of life, he becomes of interest for what he is; and the same, though in an inferior degree, is true of Sancho. Don Quixote achieves his ideal in his soul, however badly he fares with fortune in the outer world. He is complete in true knighthood, and when his madness leaves him it cannot take away the nobility of nature which it has brought the poor gentleman whom it found nameless and unoccupied on his little estate and made one of the world's heroes. The vocabulary of moral praise cannot exhaust his virtues. He is brave, resolute, courteous, wise, kind, gentle, patient; and, not to continue the enumeration, he possesses these traits with a distinctive Spanish excellence. What tenacity there is in his resolution, what recklessness in his courage, what fatalistic sweetness in his resignation, what endurance in a land of lost causes, what sadness of defeat accepted in the quiet of adversity! If these are not the most obvious, they are perhaps the deepest Spanish traits in the noble natures of that birth and soil. In Sancho, faithful, affectionate, dubious, nationality has lower relief, since he shares more simply the universal peasant nature of the South, but he is as abundantly Spanish in his peasanthood as Don Quixote in his sublimated chivalry. Both were fooled to the top of their bent; but destiny did not mistake her way; by comedy she perfected them, each in his own kind. It does not matter what happens to the battered body of Don Quixote any more than to his crazy armor; in him the soul's the thing, and Cervantes keeps his soul invulnerable and undishonored. The dignity of the virtue of the great qualities of the Spanish ideal is preserved as well as set forth, and is seconded by the humbler virtue of the life near to the soil. No nation has cast ideal types of itself more summary, exemplary and real.

Later ages have seen in Don Quixote a typifying power even more profound, and far beyond the reach of Cervantes to know, as no one can know the depths of his own personality. Don Quixote was a man of the past, bringing outworn arms against a changed world. Spain is a backward nation, ill-furnished for modern times. Other lands have persisted in seeing in Spain the Don

Quixote of nations, whose life was a dream of past glory, whose thoughts and appliances were antiquated, whose career in the modern world must be foredoomed. So they saw her set forth lately in full tilt in the lists against the best equipped, the most modern, the youngest of the nations of the earth. But what unconscious penetration there was in that man's genius, what depth of truth, whose embodiment of the Spanish ideal has become the synonym of his country's fate!

As the book of Spain, in the external and to some extent in the internal sense, "Don Quixote" was fed from the active life of Cervantes in his goings up and down in the country as a tax-gatherer and his journeys as a young soldier on the sea. He had, however, another and perhaps more engaging life in the world of books. He was as full of ideas as of experience. He was a scholar; and using this side of his nature he made his work as expressive of the literary power of Spain as it was representative of her active genius. "Don Quixote" was literary in its origin, a crusade by parody against a particular kind of literature; and, besides, the hero became a knight-errant through the reading of books, and he retained on his adventures that interest in literature of all kinds which makes the book as much one of letters as of arms. All varieties of literature used in Spain are to be found in it either in examples or by allusion and criticism, and not only those of native growth but some of foreign extraction, Italian and Arabic. The chronicle, the romance, the pastoral are everywhere present; verse in many forms, comic and serious; the tale of the Boccaccio type, and the realistic tale; the old Renaissance debate between arms and letters, and those discourses which are little highly finished essays of a not unlike sort; drama and poetry are also present in elaborate examination of their theory and practice, and the whole question of diction both by example and precept; and there is much specific criticism of authors and books. The ballad and the proverb, characteristically Spanish kinds, underlie the book, and the style includes all the scale from the homeliest and coarsest to the most artificial, ornate and resonant known to fancy and conceit. Cervantes's interest in all these forms, methods and questions is of the liveliest. Literature was in an unsettled state, a period of experiment, change and learning. He was himself two-natured. On the one hand he was breaking out new ways by sheer impulse, coming near to life in his plays, nearer in his novels, nearest of all in "Don Quixote," and using plain prose with perfection for directness, vividness and truth; on the other hand he was charmed by the academic traditions of the Renaissance in topic, sentiment, imaginative method, language, poetry, and in the greater part of his writings emulated it. His entire works exhibit the whole range of literature in his time; "Don Quixote" shows it substantially, in epitome.

"Don Quixote" thus comes to have one of the high distinguishing traits of literary greatness; it is one of those remarkable books which are watersheds of literature. It looks before and after. Toward the past it slopes back on the forests of chivalry and the glades and hills of the pastoral, and it is clothed with the power of poetry in one or another mode of its various magic; and it rolls on to the land of the future in its realism, its humor, its direct contact with life as it is, its recognition of the popular lot, of common-sense, of positive things, and here it is clothed with the power of prose in one or another mode of its modern efficiency. Cervantes could not know this; his conscious ambition, unable to emancipate itself from the bonds of the long-loved and still glorious tradition, harked back to the ways of the past, but his genius always struck out for the future with the instinct of a wild creature that has mysterious knowledge of its own paths; his genius struck for realism, for humor, for prose, out toward the modern world. The poetic irony of chivalry had been attempted in the old way and successfully accomplished by Ariosto, and other Italians, and their work ended an age; they belong to the Renaissance past. The solvent which Cervantes applied to chivalry was another irony, the irony of the living and actual world, the irony of prose; hence "Don Quixote" is said to begin modern literature, and the greatest of our Northern novelists, Fielding, Scott, Victor Hugo, to name no others, have taken alms of Cervantes's genius.

Notwithstanding the brilliancy of the exploit — Cervantes, like Columbus, finding the new world that men of another race and nations of a later destiny were to possess — the Spanish literary genius in "Don Quixote" is mainly reminiscent. Though the modern child was born, it lay in an antique cradle, in an environment of the past. Cervantes loved the old romances which he destroyed as Plato loved the poets whom he exiled. He had a soul that felt the swell of great enterprises; he knew the spell of the lonely deed of high emprise appealing to individual prowess, the call of the adventure reserved for the destined knight. Who doubts that in that passage where, the priest speaking of Turkish troubles, Don Quixote makes his dark suggestion, Cervantes is smiling at his own heart? "Were they alive now," says Don Quixote "(in an evil hour for me — I will not speak of any else), the famous Don Belianis or some one of those of the innumerable progeny of Amadis of Gaul! If any of them were living to-day, and were to confront the Turk, i' faith, I could not answer for the consequences. God understands me, and I say no more." This had been Cervantes's dream — the freeing of Algiers; and had Philip given him a fleet, doubtless he could have done it; but Philip had other thoughts, and Cervantes shrugged his old shoulders, and smiled at his self-confidence of earlier days. Cervantes loved the pastoral, too, and the serenade and all the dear old-fashioned pleasures, the guitar and the high-sounding words; though set in a humorous situation the eloquent discourse of Don Quixote on the golden age gives the true note of the literary heart. Cervantes was pouring himself into his book, and all these loves went along with him — a poet's, a scholar's, a lover's, as well as a humorist's loves. He was no young novice, without a past and life-affections of the mind; the wine ripening in his temperament was mellowed from the stock of the world's old books. If he had clothed Don Quixote with some shadows of Amadis, he knew that Sancho, too, had his literary ancestry in Italy and remote Provence. Spain was not only a body of contemporary manners and events; it had a soul of poets dead and gone, a various and rich literary tradition, gathered and exemplified in these flowing pages. "Don Quixote" is a book of arms and the active life, but it is also a book of letters and the scholarly life; either alone had been but half the man; together, body and soul, they make up the world's most wonderful national book in prose — the one that is all Spain.

"Don Quixote" was welcomed by foreign nations, but

## CERVANTES

not altogether as a foreigner. It is a European book. Cervantes, besides what the genius of his race and country gave him, received a gift from destiny. He embodied a great moment of time, the passing-hour of the old European ideal. It was a living ideal, that of chivalry. It was sprung from real conditions, and greatly ruled the minds and somewhat the lives of men through a long era. It belonged to a world of social disorder, the thinly populated, scarce reclaimed wilderness of feudal Europe; it belonged, too, to a world of marvel, where the unknown even in geography was a large constituent element, and magic, superstition and devildom were so rife as to be almost parts of the human mind; but such as it found the world, there this ideal moved with power. The military spirit never took form more nobly than in this chivalric type. It combined and reconciled two of the greatest motive powers in the human spirit; the idea of sacrifice and the force of self-assertive personality. The perfect knight would die for his faith, his loyalty and his love, but he died in battle. The reality of this ideal is shown by the depth, the richness and the long continuance of its appeal to the bosoms of men. The idea of rescue, generated from medieval misery and helplessness in an environment of brutal physical force, is its ethical core; but its efflorescence in the imagination of men was as many-colored as a sun. Beginning in the British waste marshes and the Frankish Court, it annexed the farthest Orient to the forests, deserts and seas of its adventures; it re-made the genealogies of history and drew all the great, emperors and saints alike, into the lives of its parentage; it absorbed into its own tradition all past heroic excellence. It developed a ceremonial ritual; it gathered to itself the mighty power of symbolism in its most august and passionate forms; it gave forth a great legendary literature, one of the richest products of human effort and faith, written in every European tongue and splendid with the deeds of every soil. In the fullness of time, Arthur and Roland receding, it was Amadis who was the star of chivalry. Amadis's tale, though now out of the way, was once the book of Europe. It had a spell to hold the finest spirits, like Sidney's, and appealed to them directly and intimately as the mirror of their hearts and hopes. It contained the European mood of knighthood in its last beauty before its near eclipse and sudden dimming. Cervantes loved and honored it, and its hero was Don Quixote's ideal man, as he had been of thousands of the dying cult. Such was the nature of the literature which Cervantes "smiled away." For that had happened to the burning faith of chivalry which is the fate of all the gods; at first men are overawed by them and worship, then they lift equal eyes to them and find them companions of life; and last they laugh at them. The laughter of men at chivalry had already filled the world from the lips of Italy before Cervantes came. In his day chivalry was dead and buried. The madness of Don Quixote was but its ghost, wandering in the staring daylight of a new age, forlorn, ridiculous, without place or use in the world.

The pastoral, which was a later growth, was complementary to the chivalric romance, and by its means feminine elements entered into the simple manhood of the knightly type and softened its humanity. Its affiliations were Renaissance, as those of chivalry were medieval, and it appropriated easily the grace, the sentiment and the emotional luxury of the reborn classic ideal. It survived the true chivalric mood, and lingered; in "Don

Quixote" it is not less omnipresent than chivalry, but is less obviously ridiculed, more lightly satirized, more tenderly treated; it is related to chivalry, in the composition, as sentimental to comic opera, but both are alike out of date and discarded moods living only in parody, which is in literature the last stage of extinction. The passing of the pastoral dream, however, is subordinate and not comparable to the death of the chivalric ideal; in "Don Quixote" it is the latter that strikes the tragic note. Whether Cervantes was himself conscious of this note of tragedy in his work must remain forever obscure; if he was aware of it, he very successfully concealed his knowledge. He began with pure comic intention and made fun of the chivalric tradition, and very rough fun it was, nor did it grow less rough. His treatment of the knight is not free from coarseness, and is unremitting in cruelty; here are the standards of the practical joker and the buffoon-stage; but it may be usefully remembered that Cervantes's scale of cruelty in life was one familiar with the ways of the Turk and the pains of the Christian victims in Algiers. Primarily a comedy by its conception and unflinching conduct, "Don Quixote" gave out the note of tragedy only in our own latter days. In this aspect, it is a myth of the modern mind, which has taken on new meanings and disclosed fresh phases of significance with time, as is the way of myths; with this Cervantes had nothing to do. As he did not see in his hero the incarnation of his country's fate, neither did he see in him the last and greatest of knight-errants. He did not look with our eyes; and it is only through the perspective of centuries that we recognize the historic moment, and discern the famous knight, a great-hearted gentleman, standing in his travesty at the grave of chivalry.

The unconscious element, or what seems such, in the works of the highest genius, is their most immortal part. There is a mystical union of the race with these great works; they are humanized as much by the adoption of mankind as by their original creation. The general human spirit enters into them; they blend with it and become impersonal; in the large results of time — in mythologies, in the legend of chivalry, in the masterpieces of culture — they become racial products, unindebted to individuals. It is thus that "Don Quixote" is enfranchised from being the book of a country or of a historic moment merely, and becomes a great book of the modern spirit. It rises with the vigor of world-life in it, and bears the supreme title of a book of humanity. It contains the experience, the thought, the doubt of man. This comedy is found to be the tragedy of all idealism. If this is not the aspect under which it has most widely spread as a book of popular amusement, it is thus that it has most profoundly affected the mind of modern times. Mephistopheles and Don Quixote are the two great myths that the modern world has generated out of itself, as characteristic as Achilles in Homeric time or Roland in the middle ages or Amadis in the Renaissance. They are forms of its deepest consciousness, types created in its own image, planets cast from its own orb. The modern world is psychological, and this book contains a psychology seemingly as elementary and comprehensive as a law of nature; it is sceptical, and this book utters, as no other does, the *double entendre* of life; it is pessimistic, and this book makes the most destructive impeachment of life. Doubtless one goes far from Cervantes in such thoughts; but if he did not fathom, we may well believe that he felt the deeper meanings of his book, for

CERVANTES 149

even in the eyes of the comedian it is a book of much sadness.

The double nature of life is put to the fore. There is an opposition in human nature, and this is set forth by the contrast of Don Quixote and Sancho. It is rendered in them by divers ways as the antithesis of the imagination with the senses, of the life of thought with the life of fact, of illusion with reality, of the eloquent discourse with the proverb, of the poetry with the prose of life; but, essentially, this polarity is in the double aspect of life as soul and sense. Cervantes decides for neither; he presents both as liable to error. He portrays Don Quixote with the characteristic defect of the soul, imaginative illusion; and he gives to Sancho the characteristic defect of the material man, self-interest. The higher nature betrayed by its own nobility, the lower duped by its own baseness — that is the two-edged sword of life. That is the human comedy.

It is in the madness of Don Quixote that the heart of the book beats. It is a very singular madness. The invention manifested in the narrative is generally thought to be its prime literary trait; but its verisimilitude, the skill with which it keeps the quaking edge of truth and fiction, is as marvelous; and nowhere more than in Don Quixote's madness are the shades made subtle. It is a very normal madness. Don Quixote does not differ much from other men in his mental processes. He interprets the sights and sounds of the actual world by his past experience; only, as he has lived in the world of books a life of imagination, his experience is unreal, his memory is inapplicable to the world about him, or, as is said, his inferences are all wrong. His illusions have an origin from without, and are misinterpretations of the external world, due to an expectancy in his own mind which has arisen from his absorbed reading of romances. His senses are overlaid with thought, and he sees what he expects to see. It is impossible, too, to acquit him of a certain complicity with his own madness. He shows it when he refrains from testing his second helmet; in the fact that he was not fully persuaded he was a knight-errant till the Duke treated him as such; and unmistakably in his tale of what happened in the Cave of Montesinos, where Sancho frankly charges him with making it up; at the end, too, his recovery seems, in part at least, self-willed. The history of his madness, also, has a method in it; in the first part he is his own victim; in the second he is the victim of others; beginning with self-deception, he ends as the butt of the deception of all from Sancho to the Duke and the Bachelor. His madness is intermittent; if his mind is in fact diseased, it is by a capability of going mad under certain exciting causes, but on all other occasions he is as remarkable for judgment as for learning and eloquence.

This strange madness of Don Quixote is comic in its accidents, in its circumstantial defeat, in its earthly environment; but in itself it is tragic. Its seat is in the very excellency of the soul; its illusions take body in the noblest human aims, the most heroic nature and virtue of the purest strain. A madman has no character; but it is the character of Don Quixote that at last draws the knight out of all his degradations and makes him triumph in the heart of the reader. Modern dismay begins in the thought that here is not the abnormality of an individual but the madness of the soul in its own nature. That high aims may be ridiculous; that heroism may be folly; that virtue may be insanity; that the ideal which was the spiritual wealth of the fathers may be the farce of the children; that the soul in its exaltation, its gentleness and sacrifice, has no necessary wisdom and in its own vision no warrant of reality; that the good cast down, the kind trampled on, the brave broken, become the laughter of the world; these are the truths which make "Don Quixote" such sorry reading for the idealist. He thought to make the reality of things curtsey to the lie in his mind; but that lie was itself the substantive virtue of his soul. This is the paradox of idealism.

Don Quixote, so far as the Knight of the Rueful Feature is concerned, would indeed be a pitiful farce to modern feeling, were not his madness typical of the partial sanity of mankind. Still as in old time a man finds what he goes out to seek; a man sees his own face in the world; and man is still a victim of past greatness. These are capital truths. Imaginative illusion, the soul's vice, is common in life, and affects most the best of men, and especially those of great emotional capacity, and since emotional imagination is the principal feeder of the religious and moral energies of men, this illusion most characterizes men of ideal temper possessed with the ideas of rescue, sacrifice and battle, and arises most frequently in the field of the reform of the world. A man of one or few ideas does not differ from Don Quixote psychologically, except in degree. Whether his experience is bookish or real, he confines his attention to a specially selected and usually narrow theme, neglects the correctives that life furnishes, and becomes absorbed in his mastering preconception of life; he is infatuated. Often he exhibits a like complicity with his own partial madness, suppresses irreconcilable facts, and refuses to think in their direction. Often, too, he passes on from the stage of self-deception, in which he is only his own victim, and becomes the victim of others practising on him, whom they profess to take at his own estimate, for gain, convenience, or amusement. The parallel is easily followed out, and the fact is recognized in the word Quixotic, which has become a familiar term in all languages. Such Quixotism is inherent in the social ideal, especially as held in youth, which having necessarily an inaccurate idea of life indulges those hopes natural to the human breast which can have no accomplishment in reality; and it is imbedded in inherited beliefs and the tradition of education, which contain an element of the past inapplicable to the changing present; the outworn creed, the lost cause, all shells of past faith and passion are its strongholds. In this lies the permanent truth of the book to life. Illusion, and specifically the illusion of the noble mind inheriting a great past, is the original mark of Quixotism; and the moral which men have read into it is, the finer the soul, the more utter its earthly defeat. The hero from whom it took its name marked a break in the moral ideas of the race as things of practice; and in the futility of his high behavior, reaching the height of the ridiculous, seems too clearly to exemplify the earthly defeat of the ideal; a defeat so absolute that the best one can say is — he was wholly mad.

The point of view is that of a dying age. So Demosthenes felt on the eve of the Hellenizing of the Mediterranean world, and Brutus on the eve of its imperialization; so, on the scale of personal life, an old man feels. "Don Quixote" is an old man's book. Cervantes applied a destructive criticism to the higher nature of man, in its aims, methods, and intelligence; the waste of noble nature, the practical inefficiency of virtue did not disturb him; sceptical in that he saw the fallibility of the soul, as such, in its own vision, and pessimistic in that he recognized the impotence of the soul as such in action, he remains serene; the governing factor in human life is its mortal condition, not its spiritual motive, he concludes. Passion, how sublime it is! but oh, the irony of it at last! and no form of it so ironical as the passion for reforming the world, the will to serve mankind!

Cervantes is disillusioned; he has accepted the disillusionment; he smiles at it. The peculiarity of "Don Quixote" is that all this is set forth with loud laughter, with frank and overflowing sympathy with the world as it is, with delight in all its various material life and people. It is the world of Maritornes, of Ginés de Pasamonte, of Roque Guinart, of the innkeepers and muleteers, of the graceless duke and his duchess, of real people; it is not Don Quixote's world. It is this acceptance of life as it is, of the lower element in life, that is the complement in the book to the denial of the old ideal. Here is the victory of realism, of the positive spirit, of the oncoming age, of prose and sense and actuality, the modern time. Don Quixote closes a period, and in all that relates to him there is the pathos of death, the hopelessness of failure, the despair of the end; in all he is, the eye is reverted to the past and sees its dissolution, the death of aristocracy in its ideal as it was to die in its person on the French scaffold. Faith in the ideal is dead in the book to the last spark. The key of ideal faith had passed into the hands of the new genius of the changing world, democracy, of which Cervantes knew nothing; he saw and helped to mold the body of the new real world, but its spirit was not yet born. It is because the ideal in "Don Quixote" has no spiritual future that its outworn and lifeless forms are such a mockery of the soul. It brings, too, the immortal doubt. Will the democratic ideal in its evolution prove as inapplicable to the enduring life of man as have the other great historic ideals of the race? Is there nothing absolute in the soul? Is "Don Quixote" finally greatest in its philosophy, as a book of that relativity which the modern spirit finds in all things and most dearly loves?

"Don Quixote" is the book of the one great defeat, but also of many victories, and especially those of prose, realism, and humor in modern literature. Of all the victories which it embodies, however, the greatest is that of Cervantes over himself. The unfailing cheerfulness of its spirit is the temperament of Cervantes playing through it. He had lived and toiled, he had felt the full passion of life, he had dreamed and planned and striven, both as man and writer, in arms and letters, and he had met for the most part only the blows of fortune; wounds and slavery, neglect and poverty, the well-known wages of genius, had been paid him in full measure. Yet every indication of his personality that survives shows him unspoiled and still companionable, pleasant, patient. It was in this spirit that, being about to die, he bade farewell to all. Scott at the end of his days, with Wordsworth and others about him in the library at Abbotsford, asked Lockhart to read the scene. Allan, the painter, "remembered nothing he ever saw with such sad pleasure as the attitudes of Scott and Wordsworth as the story went on." It was a scene that recalls that other death of Tennyson, lying with his open Shakespeare in the moonlight. "Good-by, humors; good-by, pleasant fancies; good-by, merry friends, for I perceive I am dying, in the wish to see you happy in the other life." These were Cervantes's last words in his world. The most profound master of the irony of life preserved his heart uncorroded by that knowledge, as he had kept it sweet against the enmity of man and fortune.

# SCOTT

Sir Walter Scott, the prince of prose romancers, should be reckoned among the great benefactors of mankind. Of the works of prose in the nineteenth century, which have contributed to human happiness on the universal scale, the "Waverley Novels" hold a place by virtue of their millions of readers; and now, coming into the hands of the fourth generation, they are still one of the principal effective contemporary possessions of the English race in literature. Criticism, which sooner or later, assails all works of great fame, has the most trifling effect upon them; they are invulnerable in the hearts of the people. They contain so much humanity in its plain style; they disclose such romantic scenes, such stir of gallantry, such a high behavior, in connection with events and personages otherwise memorable; and they are, besides, so colored with the hues of the mind arising from local association, imaginative legend, historic glamor and the sense of the presence of fine action, that their reception by the heart is spontaneous. Especially, they contain Scotland as Don Quixote contains Spain, only upon a broader and more diversified scale. Cervantes, indeed, comes into one's mind in connection with Scott in many ways.

Scott's descent was like that of Cervantes. He was of the old blood, but born in a modest station. If the changes of time had not reduced his family stock to the condition of the poor hidalgo, they had much tempered its original border strain. Scott was as much attached to his ancestors as a New Englander, and was continually harking back in his anecdotes — and he had a full repertory of such tales of the house — to "Auld Watt" of Harden and "Beardie" of Teviotdale, while through these worthies and otherwise he could trace the affluents of his blood to the great Scotch houses, among which he took particular pride in Buccleugh. His father was a simple lawyer, whose portrait is exactly drawn in Saunders Fairford, in "Redgauntlet," a plain citizen, shrewd, formal, practical, well exemplifying the fixed type of the profession at Edinburgh. Perhaps the literary strain, which does not appear in the paternal ancestry, came from the mother, the daughter of an eminent physician, Dr. Rutherford, and herself well-educated; certainly, although Scott had several brothers and a sister, the genius of the family was wholly allotted to him. Owing to a lameness, which developed in his right leg in childhood and was an impediment to him throughout life, the boy was in early years country-bred and much encouraged in physical exertion, for which indeed he had a natural inclination, being full of animal vigor and spirits. He said late in life — "from childhood's earliest hour I have rebelled against external circumstances"; and in combatting this physical disadvantage he first exercised his courage and pertinacity. His deficiency did not interfere with his good comradery as a school-boy. He walked and rode a good deal, and he bore perhaps more than his share in the rough fighting of the schools and the town then in vogue. As he passed from master to master, each of them characteristic examples of the old discipline, he did his tasks and won their interest and favor, but it was rather by his sympathetic understanding of literature than by any brilliancy of mind. He had the education of the schools as a thing of course, and it was valuable to him; but he illustrates the fact that to turn a boy loose in a library is to give him the best of all opportunities — the opportunity for self-education. He read from childhood widely and well, and while yet a boy had such an acquaintance with great literature as would now seem phenomenal, though it was precisely the same as that which a generation later New England boys had at the same age, if they were so inclined. More than in his childish verses or the tales composed with his schoolmates there is the feeling of instinct in Ballantyne's school anecdote: "Come, slink over beside me, Jamie, and I'll tell you a story." Plainly in his boyhood Scott was as full of literature as he was of fight. If one could have discerned it, however, the true sign of the future was not in the literary tastes which Scott shared with others of his kind, but in the historic sense which he possessed in a peculiar degree. He was from the start deeply interested in his own country and his own people; he was an insatiable listener to the tales of "Sixty years since" and their like, to the border ballads, the legends, all the romantic growths of the Scotch memory; he had the zeal of an antiquary in seeing the places where events had happened, the old fields of battle, the ruined castle, the border-wall, or whatever spot or object history had left its mark upon. This was the gift that, like Aaron's rod, was to swallow up all the others.

It is impossible to trace in Scott, in early life, any of the self-consciousness that is apt to accompany such precocity and intensity, any sense of a call from the future. His father tolerated and indulged these tastes, but to his practical mind a literary career for his son would hardly have occurred. The youth was docile, was apprenticed in his father's office, and at twenty-one was called to the bar. Meanwhile he maintained his literary pursuits as a matter of course. Intellectual interest at that time was still a part of men's life, and in the clubs of good fellowship, where Scott delighted to make one and was often a leading spirit, literature had its share with other topics. Thus it happened that he was among the first of his contemporaries to feel the attraction of German literature, then reaching England, and to acquire some knowledge of it; the kinship of its ballad and romance with the spirit of the border, which was already growing incarnate in Scott, prepared a ready welcome for it in his sympathies. Nothing is more remarkable in Scott's life than its entire naturalness. He never made an effort, hardly a choice; he merely did the next thing; so now he did not think of adopting literature as a career, but it was natural for him to try his hand at a translation. Life went on as naturally, too, in other ways. The course of true love not running smooth, he was left with a memory of early devotion which diffused a pathetic tenderness over his recollections of youth; and in the lapse of time — not too long a lapse — he married happily an English-bred lady of French birth, being speedy in both the wooing and the wedding. In his cottage at Lasswade and afterwards on the little estate of Ashestiel he had a characteristic home, filled with his personality, and in both he showed that passion for making the place his own which was later displayed on the grand scale at Abbotsford. He made no great progress at the bar, and as time went on he habitually ascribed something of this slowness to the unfavorable effect of his literary avocations on his professional reputation. Tenacity, however, was characteristic of him. He never let go of anything while it would hold. He knew the ways of his world, too, and was not averse to them; and in this case wisdom was justified of her child. At twenty-eight he was made sheriff of Selkirkshire, and five years later obtained the additional post of clerk to the Court of Session; and although he did not at once come into the emoluments of the latter, the two places secured him for life an ample independence and honorable station. His position in the working world was that of a gentleman of the law with clerical and executive duties.

It may be that this security of tenure as a practical man contributed something to Scott's attitude toward the profession of literature — a view exceptional among authors — as a mode of life like any other, and consequently to his remarkable freedom from literary vanity. He was always a man of many affairs, of which literature was only one; and it took its place as a normal part of life. It is likely, however, that the slowness of his development as an author was the fundamental cause of his taking so sober a view. His precocity never took the form of immature publication. In the case of no genius is the gradual hiving of the material on which it was to work so marked, the unhurried ripening of faculty so like a process of nature; and Scott seems all the time as ignorant of what was to be the outcome as the seed and blade are of the full corn in the ear. He was an out-of-doors man as he had been a tramping boy. It is impossible to think of him without his horses and dogs. His duties as sheriff took him across country continually, and he always had more months out of Edinburgh than in it notwithstanding his clerkship. He was thus in constant contact with Scotch life and country, and he never lost or relaxed his first impulse, to know and see with his eyes, so far as his eyes could see it, all the local history. He was also in love with the genius of Scotland as it was stamped in the people of all sorts and conditions. Human nature, the rough hard article free from its alloy of the town, was treasure-trove to him. On those annual "raids into Liddesdale," and on many another journey, he made himself master of this book of truth out of which came so much of the character, anecdote and phrase that are most sterling, real and humorsome in his books. For all such actuality in the country-side he had the same tenacity of mind that Lincoln showed in his circuit-riding, and he was as full of genuine telling anecdote gathered from the living lip. He was, too, most companionable; "he met every man," it was said, "like his blood relation." In these "raids" and journeys there was much roughness, but it was welcome to him as having some taste of the old border life. The country people were fond of him; to them he was to the end of his days "the Sheriff." In Edinburgh, also, he held a vigorous and social life with men. In the times of the fear of Napoleonic invasion, he had been a live patriot and cavalryman, quartermaster of the Light Horse, and took his share of camp and drill with great zest, while still in the late twenties of life; and he was always a fearless horseman, preferring the turbulent ford to the safe passage and never "going round" for anything in the way. If he "broke the neck of the day's work" before breakfast, as was his lifelong habit, it was a matter of necessity; for a man who spent the greater part of the day in physical activity and exercise could have a fresh mind only in the morning. It was in those early hours that he accomplished his literary work; and if there was much mechanical routine in the practice, perhaps his youthful experience as a writer of legal foolscap had accustomed him to the drudgery of the desk. In a life of such variety and scope, so full of work of all kinds, with many active interests, overflowing too with hospitality and rich in friendships, genius less abundant and powerful than Scott's would have been overwhelmed, but he had the knack to turn it all into new resources.

Until Scott was past thirty he may well have thought of literature as only the busiest and most delightful part of his leisure, and have seemed to himself as to others the son of the old lawyer treading in his father's footsteps to a like mediocre fortune. He was of a more generous make, it is true; he was not at all a precisian; there was much freedom for human nature in Edinburgh life, and he took his share; in the careless cheer of his youthful days and in the hearty sociability of his manhood there was something that would now be thought boisterous; boy and man, conviviality was warm in his blood. He was one of those men who diffuse a physical glow about them. But also, it is plain, there was something in him that set him distinctly apart; the unlikeness which isolates genius, felt before it is recognized, like the electric air of the undischarged cloud; in every company, however varied, though never too much the leader, he was the interesting man. There was a glow in his mind as well as in his blood. It was not literary ambition exactly; though he says that when he wrote the song of Young Lochinvar he was "passionately ambitious of fame," it was more the flash of a young man's feeling than the awakening of resolute ambition. Though so widely and well read in literature and with a real bookishness in his tastes, his genius was not at all bookish. The glow in his mind was vital, and nourished on life, and it flowed almost entirely from that historic sense, that absorbed interest in his own country and people, which was the master-light in which he saw life. He attracted all Scottishness to himself as by the necessity of a fairy gift. If any delver in the old literature was in the neighborhood, such as the marvelous Leyden, he was close in his company; if there was a kindred scholar across the border, like Ellis, he was in correspondence with him; and with such men he began that growing circle of friendships by letter, reinforced with occasional visits, which is one of the most agreeable and peculiar pleasures of the literary life and in Scott's case was so large and interesting a part of his biography. He had, for the time, concentrated his antiquarian interest in the endeavor to collect and edit the ballads which he finally issued as the "Minstrelsy of the Scottish Border," and in particular attention to old metrical romances. This work was really a stage in his preparation to write, a stone that marks his progress in that absorption of Scotland into his own genius which he was unconsciously accomplishing without a thought of its ulterior end. He was so far, in the line of his true development, only a literary antiquary.

The beginnings of his literary career, which antedated the "Minstrelsy," did not grow out of his true material, but in a curiously opposite way were distinctly bookish. His faculty of imagination was stirred independently and apart from the subjects it was to operate upon habitually. He made some translations from the German ballads, and also a version of Goethe's "Goetz von Berlichingen"; and in connection with these studies he tried some original ballads of his own. He was then twenty-eight years old and he describes these as his first "serious attempts at verse." Two years later when he published the early volumes of the "Minstrelsy," the idea that he might make literature an important part of his life seems to have been distinctly formed, and it had found its true roots. The close tie, the natural birth indeed, of his first poem, "The Lay of the Last Minstrel," out of the deepest prepossession of his mind, is obvious. He wrote it, perhaps, with as little self-confidence as ever any distinguished poet felt in composing his first work, and was as much surprised by its reception as the world was at its appearance. He won at once a popular crown which no hand feebler than Byron's was to wrest from him. He had then already reached his thirty-fourth year. "Marmion," and "The Lady of the Lake," which quickly followed, confirmed his poetic fame; on these three tales in verse, together with a score of lyrics, his permanent vogue as what he might have called "a rhymer" rests.

The merit of Scott's poetry has been much attacked by latter-day critics; but there is a reasonable view to be taken of it, and within its limitations its worth is still unimpaired. Its survival, notwithstanding the immensely greater work of the poets who followed him — men who were purely poets — shows life at the root. It had originality, and retains its force. Scott broke new ground; he discovered material which had natural poetry, and he treated it in a novel manner, appropriate to the subject and stimulating to the mind. If he borrowed his metre from Coleridge, he applied it in a manner and on a scale that Coleridge was incapable of. He was an experimenter in a new kind, and in it was wholly self-educated; such real defects as there are in the verse are incidental to its being tentative work. There is more power than craft, more life than skill; he succeeds by spontaneity more than by art. The careless cross-country gallop of the metre is in keeping with the verve and unevenness which characterize the whole; but the blood is kept awake. His great power of narrative tells the tale, but the interest is less in the individuals than in the kind of life depicted, the baronial hall, the border battle, the Highland romance; he revivified the times he treated in enduring colors, which replace history in the memory for his district equally with Shakespeare's plays for the kingdom. He gave especially to the Highlands an imaginative memory which annexed them to the lands which have a meaning to the general heart of man; he alone gave that charm to Loch Katrine and its environs which lifts the scene above the savagery of nature. It is not due only to his description, but he placed action there. It is an error to think of nature-poetry as lying in the sphere of contemplation, merely because that was Wordsworth's way; out-of-doors poetry, such as Byron's tales, often contains more of nature in the mingling of the great scene with the action than any number of addresses to flowers of the wayside and lonely weeds on the rocks. In Scott, fair as the landscape is, nature is more than landscape; it is the place of the action, the breathing air of life itself. The action, moreover, which is the main interest, is unsurpassed in the quality of gallantry, in the stirring moment and the personal adventure. He is the most martial of English poets; excepting a half-dozen lyrics and ballads by Campbell, and one or two others, there is nothing in our poetry to rival him in this respect. This is the Homeric fighting quality that some find in his verse, and there is truth in the remark. It is said that he "pleases boys"; that is not against him. The obviousness of his meaning, the fact that his ideas, images and language are within easy reach of the average mind, the presence of much ordinariness in the substance, as they partly account for his ready popularity and its wide spread, also denote his permanent appeal; for with all this, which is called his commonness, there goes that most uncommon power to stir the blood, to send the soul out of doors, to revivify lost romantic modes of life in all their picturesque color, their daring spirit, their emotional reality. He makes his reader live the life, and it is not only the life of a past age but it is one of the great permanent types of life. It appeals to all freemen; the echo of it, the desire for it, are in their blood. I have referred to the sneer that Scott "pleases boys." He does. It was "many and many a year ago, in a kingdom by the sea," that my own fourteenth summer was made happy with this delight. I remember that I read every line of his verse with eagerness and poured out my admiration in a longer essay than this is likely to prove. The experience was not a bad one for a boy who, at the yet more tender age of twelve had been deep in Byron and melancholy. It is thirty years and more since then; but to this day the clang of the verse of Branksome Hall turns all the iron of my blood to music, and the sight of the falling standard on Flodden Field is the most I shall ever know of the heart of Sidney "moved more than with a trumpet." This is the sort of mastery in which Scott is great, for both boy and man. The personal reminiscence only gives emphasis to what is broadly true. Poetry, in the mold which Scott commanded, could not give expression to his whole genius; it is not in verse that he did his great work; but he had set the fashion and showed the way for Byron — in itself surely no small thing — and when Byron "beat" him, as he said, he turned to prose fiction and came into his own. It is not the least of his honors as a man that after Byron had surpassed him, and in fact dethroned him in the popular breath, Scott made and kept his friendship and, notwithstanding their profound difference in character, defended his name and fame against the bitter storm of English enmity. He did not, however, give up the tale in verse at once, just as he had not given up the law. It was not in his nature, as has been said, to let go. He continued to write metrical romances, but none of them have the same boldness of execution or the same cling to the mind that belonged to the earlier efforts. In these poetic years, too, he had done what in any other man would in itself have seemed abundant labor, in massive editorial work and other miscellaneous literary ways. His poems represent, after all, but a fragment of his immense energy; and now, feeling the need of appealing to the public in a new line, he solved the situation by taking up a new and unfinished task.

The entrance of Scott on the field of prose fiction bears a close resemblance to his début in poetry. It has the same tentativeness, the character of an experiment. He had long had in mind an attempt to depict the manners of his country in prose. He had read Miss Edgeworth's Irish tales, and he thought something like that could be done for Scotland. He had for some years been privately interested with Ballantyne in the printing business; and the fact had turned his mind to the problems of publishing and kept him keenly alive to the opportunities of trade, as if he had been — as essentially he was — a publisher's adviser. He was always interested in "bringing out" something, and the usefulness of his own faculties in feeding the press was a constant element in the business. Like Cervantes, again, he tried all kinds; but his first experiment in fiction had not seemed promising. He began "Waverley" in 1805, just after the publication of the "Lay of the Last Minstrel"; he resumed it five years later and was again discouraged; after another interval, finding the manuscript while he was hunting for fishing tackle, he wrote the last two volumes in three weeks, in 1813, and it was published anonymously early the next year. Its success, which is one of the legends of literature, was as far beyond expectation as that of "The Lay" had been in its time; and he followed it up, just as he had done in poetry, with that rapid succession of triumph after triumph which made him in the end one of the leading figures of contemporary Europe and the national glory of his own country.

The "Author of Waverley" was forty-three years old when he began the great series; but though the discovery and application of his powers have the semblance of accident, both his success and his fertility were the direct result of slowly maturing causes. That long hiving of material and ripening of faculty had gone on without any consciousness of the end to which they were to be applied; but the preparation was complete, and Scott had now found the work — a necessity of genius — into which he could put the whole of himself. His primary endowment was the historic sense, in which he excelled all other English imaginative writers, and in him it was bred of such love of country as to be an impelling passion of patriotism. His love of Scotland was as close to him as his family pride, and his life was a thing of direct contact with what he loved. His tenacity, remarkable in all its manifestations, became genius when applied to anything Scottish. He had an ocular memory of the places he had seen; probably there is no local spot described in his Scotch novels that is not a direct transcript from nature; and the native landscape had so filled his mind that, at the end, in the soft environs of Naples he could see only Scotland; "on proceeding," says his companion there, remarking on this, "he repeated in a grave tone and with great emphasis:

> "Up the craggy mountain, and down the mossy glen
> We canna gang a-milking, for Charlie and his men."

There was the same prepossession of his mind with the historical and living characters of the land, its feuds and legends, its past and present. In truth, in these years of unconscious preparation he was not unlike Don Quixote reading the romances of chivalry; his mind was charged with Scotland, and when he went forth into the world as a novelist spent itself in the things of fiction, in a Quixotic enthusiasm. He lived much of the time in an imaginary world, as he said, not only when he was actually composing but in his mood of mind; it had been so from childhood; he had partly realized this world in poetry, he completely embodied it in prose. His active professional duties, which were of a routine nature, and his out-of-doors life with men and practical affairs were, no doubt, a means of keeping the balance of sanity, of actuality, in his life; but, for all that, he had built up a world of his own in which his mind lived. It was this world which came to birth in the "Waverley Novels," primarily in the Scotch tales, which are the core of the series, and secondarily in the foreign tales, including the English, which often have large Scotch elements and are all created on the same ground principles. As on the ideal side, like Don Quixote, his mind was imbued with a past age that gave its colors to his waking life, so too on the side of actuality, like the Knight of La Mancha's author, he had gone up and down in the land and knew all its people, high and low, noble and peasant and cateran, its professions and trades, its servants, its castaways and poor scholars, the whole range of its human types; for the ideal and the actual, and they were homogeneous and not opposed in his case, he was equally well furnished; his representation of Scotland would be as complete as Cervantes had made of Spain, and vaster.

The oneness of his genius — the fact that the same power is here at work that produced the poems — is shown by the identical way in which he approached his task. The defects of "Waverley," as an experimental trial, are the same as those of "The Lay"; "The Antiquary" is better made in the same way as "Marmion." He owed little, if anything, to example in either case; he was self educated both as poet and novelist. The virtues of mere craft do not count for much in his success in prose any more than in verse. Construction is loose, composition is rapid and careless; art is secondary to matter. Sheer power of genius, however, is there with its inevitable and brilliant mastery of the situation. It takes the same direction as in the poems; the novelist does not aim at a tale of individual fortunes, but he endeavors to represent a kind of life. It is this that gives him breadth of meaning. It is social not private life that he sets forth. In a novel there may be many elements — the plot, the hero, situation, dialogue, tableau, atmosphere and the like; and these may be subordinated or emphasized separately in infinite combinations. The faults which criticism charges to Scott's form largely proceed from a too limited and rigid conception, from the point of view of construction, of what narrative art consists in. In fact his novel bears, in its relation to the more unified type, some resemblance to the chronicle play in its relation to the more organized drama. He seeks, under the impulse of his historic sense, a broader effect than any tale of individual life can give — a social effect. He is apt to set his particular story in a stream of general events, to which the fortunes of the individuals are related, but the interest is less in the plot than in the stream of events. He thus gives a truer perspective to life and greater significance to his matter. The control of the plot, and its issues, are apt to lie at a distance, in what may be called a kind of machination in the background, as the affair of the house of Osbaldiston in "Rob Roy," or old Elspeth's secret in "The Antiquary." The encompassing of a larger world is round about the story. Like all the greatest writers, Scott gives the great scene of life always; it is a crowded stage, a world full of people. In such a scene the hero may occupy an unimportant place; the interest is not primarily in him. It is a feudal, commercial, political world, filled with fixed types; there is an abundance of stock characters; to set forth the manners and concerns of this world largely in a vivid human way, to be, as it were, a public historian, not a writer of private memoirs, is Scott's scope. The fortunes of the individuals being inserted in this environing world, much as the dialect is inlaid in the English, the progress of the tale is managed by a succession of scenes. Scott's greatest talent of execution lay in the depicting of these scenes; if he was not a dramatist, there was something theatrical in his faculty, and though he could not write a play, no one could better stage an incident. These scenes are of all kinds; indoor scenes with the fidelity of Dutch masters, such as the hut in "Rob Roy" or Norna's dwelling; out-of-door scenes of infinite variety like the vengeance of Rob's wife or the drover's foray at the end; scenes of all degrees of spirited action and emotional play, or simple instances of noble behavior like the farewell of the prince in "Redgauntlet." Scott has an unrivalled power of realizing life at such times, and here he centers human interest, while about this incessant stream of incidents conducted by persons suffering and doing there is constantly felt the play of great forces, social, political, hereditary, the sense of life as an element in which lives exist and here presented especially and most powerfully as a thing of history and nationality.

Such a presentation of national history and manners, maintaining a permanent hold on the people whom it depicts, must necessarily have great veracity. Imagination could not part company with fact in such a case. The basis of reality in the "Waverley Novels" is one of their most distinguishing qualities, and underlies their endurance in literature. It is not merely that particular characters are studied from life; that George Constable and John Clerk sat for "The Antiquary," that Scott himself is Mr. Mannering, that Laidlaw or another is Dandie Dinmont; nor is it that other characters, like Meg Merrilies and the gypsies are suggestions from living figures that had arrested the author's passing glance. It is not that the scene of "Castle Dangerous" is governed by what his eye beheld on his visit there, or the whole landscape of "The Pirate" transcribed from his voyages among the islands of the north. Still less is it what he gained from books, either of ordinary history and records of events or such sermons as those from which he transferred the dark and intense eloquence of "Old Mortality." He had such a marvelous memory for whatever bore the national stamp, he was so brain-packed with the ocular and audible experience of his converse with the people, so full of their physiognomy, gesture and phrase, that he fed his narrative incessantly with actuality; and such was his surplus of treasure of this sort that in his general edition he continued to pour out an illustrative stream of anecdote, reminiscence and antiquarian lore in the notes and prefaces. A keen friend was confirmed in his belief of Scott's authorship by the presence of a striking phrase that he had heard him once use. The Scotch novels are, as it were, an amalgam of memory. When he came to write them all his love of tradition and the country-side with which his mind was impregnated was precipitated in an unfailing flow. It was because Scott was so much alive with Scotland that he made his imaginary characters live with that intense reality, that instant conviction of their truth, in which he is to be compared only with Shakespeare. It is true that it was a man of letters who wrote the "Waverley Novels," a mind fed on the stuff of medieval romance and on the tradition of the English drama, the "old play" of which he was so fond; but the literary element in the tales is a thing of allusion, like Waverley's studies, or episodical as in the character of Bunce or on a more important scale of Sir Percie Shafton, or else its rambling antiquarianism serves to set forth Scotch pedantry appropriately. The "Waverley Novels" are not a development out of older literature, they are an original growth, a fresh form of the imaginative interpretation of the human past, a new and vital rendering straight from the life. Even in the tales whose scene is laid in England and the continent, where Scott was more dependent on printed sources, the literary element is little more perceptible than in the Scotch novels themselves; the sense of reality in them is not appreciably less. But Scott already had the best historical education as a living discipline in assimilating his own country and he came to the interpretation of history in other lands with trained powers of understanding and imagination in that field. A distinguished historian once expressed to me his admiration for "Count Robert of Paris," and I was glad to find such unexpected support for my own liking of this novel, which is generally regarded, I believe, as a pitiable example of Scott's mental decline; but my friend had been struck, he said, by its remarkable grasp of history, its brilliant adequacy in that way. It was the same power with which Scott had grasped "Ivanhoe," and told the tale of "Quentin Durward," and made Richard Lion-heart like one of Shakespeare's kings. He had learned the way by making history alive on his own heath in the most living contact with the past that ever man had.

Veracity is the first great quality of the "Waverley Novels." The second is emotional power. Scott was a man of strength; he liked strong deeds and strong men; and he liked strong emotions. I do not mean the passion of love, in which he showed little interest. The way of a man with a maid was not to him the whole of life. In the national temperament in its action in history he found two great emotions: the passion of loyalty, which was incarnate in the Cavaliers and clans, and the enthusiasm of religion which filled the Covenanters. These were social forces and supported a lifelong character in men. They gave ideal elevation to the tragic and cruel events which belong to Scotch history, and made an atmosphere about the actors which glowed with life. Scott shared to the full the national capacity for enthusiasm, and was in his own imaginary world as much a Jacobite as he was a border-raider; and he put into his representation a fervor hardly less than contemporary. He was master, too, on the scale of private as opposed to public feeling, of all the moods of sorrow and especially of that dark brooding spirit, frequent in the Scotch character, which he has repeatedly drawn. Such emotion, in the people or in individuals, is the crucible of romance. He used its fires to the full. Whether the scene be battle-broad or dungeon-narrow, whether the passion involves the fortune of a crown or burns in the single breast of Ravenswood, he finds in these deep-flowing and overmastering human feelings the ideal substance which makes his romances so charged with power over the heart, with the essential meaning of human life, in its course in character, and at its moments of personal crisis. The homogeneity of this power of passion with the events of Scotch history and with the character of the people is complete, the unity of the whole is reinforced by the romantic quality of the landscape, which is its appropriate setting. The state of society, its stage in civilization, is also in keeping. It is, in fact, a kind of Homeric world, without any fancifulness; or if, when the parallel is stated, the difference is more felt than the likeness, it is a world of free action, bold character, primitive customs, as well as of high feeling and enterprise, such as has fallen to the lot of no other author since Homer to depict with the same breadth and elevation. It was good fortune for Scott, too, that he could follow Shakespeare's example in relieving the serious scene with humor. It is humor of the first quality, which lies in character itself and not in farcical action or the buffoonery of words. It centers in and proceeds from eccentricity, in which the Scottish character is also rich; nor in general is the eccentricity overstrained or monotonously insisted on. Scott is very tender of his fools, whose defectiveness in nature is never made a reproach or cruel burden to themselves; and the humorous side of his serious characters only completes their humanity. All parts of life thus enter into his general material, but harmoniously. His share of artistic power was instinctive; he was never very conscious of it; but it was most remarkable in the perfect blend he made of the elements used. "The Pirate" is an admirable example. It is a sea story, and takes its whole atmosphere from the coasts where its action lies. The struggle with the elements in Mordaunt's opening journey is like an overture; the rescue of the sailor-castaway, the cliff-setting of Mertoun's house, the old Norse of the patriarch's home, and the life of the beach there with its fishing fleet, the superstitious character of Norna, the weird familiar of the winds, the bardic lays of Claude Halcro, the sentimental pirate-father and the son with his crew, the secret of the past which unlocks the plot — all these make a combination of land, character and story, each raised in power by imaginative treatment to a romantic height and echoing the same note of the sea one to the other in a blend as naturally one as sky, cliff and weather. As a sea piece, given by character and event as well as by description, it is an unrivalled work, and this is due to its artistic keeping. This power of blend was an essential element in Scott's genius; by it his romance becomes integral in plot, character and setting; and this felicity of composition achieves in its own way the same end in artistic effect that is sought in another way by construction in the strict sense. Scott never fails in unity of feeling; it was a part of his emotional gift.

The third commanding trait of the "Waverley Novels" is creative power. It is this that places Scott among the greatest imaginative prose writers of the world, and makes him the first of romancers as Shakespeare is the first of dramatists. He had that highest faculty of genius which works with the simplicity of nature herself and has something magical in its immediacy, in the way in which it escapes observation and in its instant success; he speaks the word, and there is a world of men, moving, acting, suffering in the wholeness of life. These masters of imagination, too, have as many molds as nature; whoever appears on the scene of Homer or Shakespeare, no one is surprised; and Scott was as fertile as any of his kind. He is a master of behavior, for both gentleman and peasant, and of the phrases that seem the very speech of a man's mouth. The world of gentlemen is represented in its motives and interests, its sacrifices and ideas for both age and youth, with a sympathetic comprehension that makes it seem the most just tribute ever given to the essential nobility of that kind of life, aristocratic in ideal, warring, terrible in what it did and what it suffered, but habitually moving in a high plane of conduct and having for its life-breath that passion of loyalty, which however unreasoning, or mistaken, is one of the glorious virtues of men. The world of humble life, likewise, is rendered with vivid truth in its pursuits, trials and submissions, the virtues welling from the blood itself in peril, sorrow, natural affection, for man and woman, for every time of life and in every station of the poor. It is in the language of these characters that the life lies with most efficacy; only nature makes men and women who can speak thus; and the solidity of their speech is a part of the simplicity of their lives. Cuddie's mother in "Old Mortality," the old fisherman, Macklebackit, in "The Antiquary," Jennie Deans in "The Heart of Midlothian" are examples; but Scott's truth of touch in such dealing with the poor is unfailing. If the behavior of his gentlemen appeals to the sense of chivalry in every generous breast, the words of his humble persons go straight to the heart of all humanity. In both classes there is a vitality that is distinguishable from life itself only by its higher power. He creates from within; he shows character in action so fused that the being and the doing are one; he achieves expression in its highest form — the expression of a soul using its human powers in earthly life. This is the creative act; not the scientific exhibit of the development of character, not the analytic examination of psychology and motivation, for which inferior talent suffices; but the revealing flash of genius which shows the fair soul in the fair act, be it in the highest or the lowest of men, in good fortune or bad, triumphant or tragic, or on the level of all men's days. It belonged to Scott's conception of life that character and act should be in perfect equipoise; to find them so is the supreme moment of art. It was the moment of Shakespeare and Homer, in drama and epic; and it is the moment of Scott in the novel. The living power of his men and women by virtue of which once in the mind they never die out of it, but remain with the other enduring figures of imagination, "forms more real than living man," proceeds from this union of passion, truth and creative power with the form and pressure of life itself. The material is always noble, and the form into which Scott throws it is manly. The impression of all he creates is of nobility; not the nobility that requires high cultivation or special consecration to supreme self-sacrifice, but such nobility as is within the reach of most men, to be honest and brave, tender and strong, simple, true and gallant, fair to a foe and faithful to our own. Scott was not greatly interested in intellect; it plays no part in his work as a governing principle; but in this neglect of it he kept the true perspective of human life; indeed — though this may seem a hard saying — his unconscious subordination of the intellectual to the active virtues and powers is one great cornerstone of his sanity and wholesomeness.

The "Waverley Novels" made Scott one of the famous men of Europe; he held a place of distinction unshared at home, the idol of his own country, and honored and beloved in every English-speaking land. He also, as is well known, made a great deal of money by them; and Scott was glad to make money. He spent it in a magnificent way, and here the trait of Quixotism is very obvious. Abbotsford, his most human monument, may be described as a romantic work, the material counterpart to his estate in imagination. Don Quixote sought the chivalric past which was the life of his brain, in contemporary Spain; and with a touch of the same madness Scott desired to realize on the banks of the Tweed something of that old baronial life which was so large a part of his memory and imagination; he added farm to farm till he had obtained a considerable domain, he built a mansion, he gathered there the museum of relics of crown, battle and clan which is still intact, and there he dispensed hospitality with ancient generosity, as the representative of his country as well as to his friends and dependents with a shadow at least of feudal state. It was a dream that almost came to pass. But at the moment of its realization the crash in his fortunes occurred which condemned him to spend the remainder of his days in a heroic effort to die an honest man. The secret of the authorship of "Waverley" was well kept on the whole; at first it was probably merely a means of guarding his reputation which he did not wish to expose to the risk of failure as a novelist; afterwards, it was useful as a means of exciting interest and there was no particular reason to change. There was another secret, however, that had been much better kept — the fact that he was a commercial partner with the printer, Ballantyne; and the occasion of his secretiveness in this case was that an interest in trade would have been regarded as inconsistent with his professional position as a lawyer. The secretiveness, the willingness to go into trade, the love of money can be turned against Scott; but, to my mind, they only make him more human, a natural man. Scott's practical attitude toward life, and also toward literature itself as a profession like any other, seems not unlike that of Shakespeare; it is the mortal side of the immortal genius which in its own realm was loosened from the sense of reality and lived in an imaginary world. Scott met the situation that confronted him with courage, an unwearied labor, a reckless expenditure of mental power and physical health which again illustrates the marvelous tenacity of his nature. He held on till he died. The story of the last days and the voyage to Italy is well known. He was a failing man. He still held the place of honor which he had won in men's minds, the love of his own and the respect of foreign nations. Goethe saluted him almost from his death-bed; and soon after Scott himself passed away at Abbotsford.

The fruit of Scott's life is an immeasurable good. There is the life itself, as full of kindliness as of energy, of duty as of honor, incessant in activity, many-sided, patient in official routine, with country loves, with refinement, blameless in the relations of son, brother, husband, father and friend, with room for the affections of dogs and horses and all God's creatures; a life, not saintly as we wish the lives of women to be, not without weakness, but a source of strength to others, with the right humilities and the right prides, unshaken in its loyalties, a man's life. There are the works, which have been the delight of millions of homes through four-score years. I remember one summer seeing a boy of six enacting Rob Roy, and not long after hearing Lowell tell me just before he died that he had lately read the "Waverley Novels" through again with much happiness; genius with a reach like that will defy time long. I have read them myself repeatedly in the passing of years, and always with a greater admiration of their literary power, their sheer creative faculty, their high strain of feeling and human truth, and their wholesomeness for the daily sympathies and moral ideals of the democracy. They are a great feature in English literature. They lie massive, like Ben Nevis and Loch Lomond, in the geography of the soul's country, where she builds her earthly mansions. One takes leave of them, for a time, but he closes the volume, whatever it may be, with Tennyson's exclamation in his heart:

> "O great and gallant Scott,
> True gentleman, heart, blood, and bone,
> I would it had been my lot
> To have seen thee, and heard thee, and known."

# MILTON

In the old American mind there are some books that neighbor the Bible in their appeal to the affections. Milton, Bunyan, and Cowper have this distinction. They were the books which in my boyhood I was allowed to read on the Sabbath day — old New England Sundays, days of halcyon memory, true bridals of the earth and sky, brooded on by an unshared peace that no desert solitude or mountain beauty ever knew; the yellowing pages of the worn books still exhale odors of those old summers. It is, perhaps, not over-curious to think that the honor of literature, in our earlier age, owed much to the fact that the living faith of the people was the religion of a book; and in times when, as we learn from many a pious memoir, the child in the cradle was sometimes "dedicated to God," on both sides of the water the thought might well grow up in the boy's mind, unconsciously flowering, that as God had once spoken through a book, the spirit might still use the forms of high literature as its vehicle; the idea of the inspiration of the literary life was not far off from him. Milton and Wordsworth both felt this sense of consecration, of being men set apart, and what from the birth of Apollo has been known to the poet as the enthusiasm of the god in him, they felt in their breasts, Milton more definitely and Wordsworth more abstractly and vaguely, as a divine prompting and motion. Milton's addresses to the Muse are too passionate to be merely imaginative flights; they are poetic prayers to a real presence. The singular thing is that this is the view of posterity also toward Milton. He lives as a great and lonely figure, one of the chosen of Israel, with an almost hieratic solemnity; the blind old man who had seen heaven and its angels, the Creation and the Fall, as none other had ever beheld them, in universal vision. Even in his secular life, he seems an apostle of liberty, not a statesman or a politician or anything merely executive and official, but the impassioned preacher of freedom because his own soul was free, a great declarer of the self-evident truths of man. But it is the "Paradise Lost" that gives him his sacred character. It is a poem on the highest levels of art, derived from ancient and foreign sources, panoplied in severe scholarship, wrought in the inspiration of classicism, academic, intellectual, austere; and yet it made, and continued to make, and still makes such a wide popular appeal as to constitute it one of the greatest monuments of English literature, without regard to the judgment of scholars. It is not only a book; it is a part of English history, of the history of the English race. This is the marvel — and no critical problem is more difficult — what are the grounds of this broad appeal in a poem which appears in many ways so far from the people?

Milton was born a Londoner in that class of society which was the backbone of the movement for popular rights and independence in religion, in whose onward course, during his mature life, the throne fell and English liberties were secured. Little survives to inform us of his childhood except the head of the fair boy which is one of the treasures of English portraiture. He was well-bred in a Puritan home of means and taste, and though there is no sign of rigor in his bringing up, in that home must have been implanted in him in early days those finer elements of Puritanism which seem already instinctive in his first youth. His father who was a scrivener had some merit as a musical composer, and was in prosperous circumstances. He had masters for the boy and sent him to a public school, St. Paul's, where he made one deep and tender friendship with a half-Italian schoolmate, Charles Diodati. At sixteen he went up to Christ's College, Cambridge, where tradition says he was called "the Lady of Christ's," his fair hair and bright cheeks and his slender youth confirming a nickname that he appears to have owed really to the purity of his life and manners and a virginal mind. He remained seven years at Christ's, and won the place of a first scholar, showing plain traces of that saving egotism which is the single trait that brings him humanly before the eye now: "performed the Collegiate and Academical exercises to the admiration of all, and was esteemed to be a virtuous and sober person," says old Anthony Wood, "yet not to be ignorant of his own parts." At Christ's he had written verses, Latin and English, among them the famous ode on the morning of Christ's Nativity; and he showed from the first touches of his hand that feeling for rich words and their melodies, the sense of the molding that beauty of language gives to thought itself, which belongs so often to the poetic precocity of great masters of expression. There was never any immaturity in his style. He wrote perfection. Yet then, of course, no one knew that he had written one of the great lyric poems of England, singular for its majesty of thought and manner in a youth of twenty-one years, and a sonnet — that on arriving at the age of twenty-three — which, in his works, is one of the best remembered where all are memorable.

He retired from the University to Horton, near Windsor, where his father had now removed from London to live at ease; and there, the church, his original destination, being closed to him by the aspect of the times, without seeking another profession, he obtained his father's leave to pursue literary studies undisturbed. "At my father's country residence, whither he had retired to pass his old age, I was wholly intent," says Milton, "through a period of absolute leisure, on a steady perusal of the Greek and Latin writers, but still so that I occasionally exchanged the country for the city, either for the purpose of buying books, or for that of learning anything new in mathematics or in music, in which I then took delight." For the six years that remained till he was thirty, he thus enjoyed a secure and quiet period, comparable to Virgil's ease, during which he perfected himself in a studious knowledge of past literature. It was an accumulative and assimilating rather than an original period; his production of English verse was hardly greater in amount than Virgil's in similar circumstances; yet in its small body are comprised all Milton's minor poems of fame, and among them are "L'Allegro" and "Il Penseroso," the best idyllic poems in the classical Italian manner; "Lycidas," the first of English elegies in rank; and "Comus," the only English masque that the world has cared to remember. These poems are the finest flower of the great literary movement that had swept up the north from Italy for more than a century, and brought to England its great burst of genius in the reigns of Elizabeth and James; the crest of the Renaissance had broken in the turbulent dramatists, but here the golden flood of humanism was still at the full, with Italian serenity, purity, and beauty; the burning noon of passion had gone by, but a finer art, a softer mood were present in Milton's genius in its youth, simple, lucid, melodious, suffused with the perfect beauty of an age of art about to die. In these country years Milton probably looked forward only to a literary career; he was a youthful, humanist poet seeking to write as his Greek and Italian masters had done before him; perhaps such a life as Virgil's, he thought, might lie in his future. These were the first happy fruits.

The figure of Milton at this age is full of "sweet attractive grace." He was handsome in manly beauty, his mind set on high and serious thoughts, and with a strain of uncommon purity in his soul. He led a simple life in his father's house, plain in its habits; he wandered about the well-watered and well-wooded country, making his mind "a mansion for all lovely forms — a dwelling place for all sweet sounds and harmonies," or in his chamber at home moved "in the still air of delightful studies;" a natural, intellectual, poetic life, free from all disturbance. One hears that "music" in which he "then took delight" as its perpetual undertone. It is reflected crystal-like in the "L'Allegro" and "Il Penseroso," with a selective power of art, an idyllic brevity and clearness in the scenes, an evenness of unemphatic beauty, for which there is no parallel except in classical and Italian masterpieces. This poetic softness and clearness mirrors Milton's temper then; there is not a trace of the harsh traits that later came into his life, the sternness of his middle years and his aging into austerity. He was still a pure poet; full of a sweet sensuousness that took delight in all beautiful things; he was a lover of beauty. "What besides God has resolved concerning me I know not, but this at least": — he is writing to a friend — "He has instilled into me at all events a vehement love of the beautiful. Not with so much labor as the fables have it, is Ceres said to have sought her daughter Proserpine, as I am wont day and night to seek for this idea of the beautiful through all the forms and faces of things (for many are the shapes of things divine) and to follow it leading me on as with certain assured traces." This is Plato's voice on the lips of the young Puritan disciple of the "Phædrus," but it denotes the enthusiasm of his soul and its poetic direction. This Platonic vein, this emotional color of beauty in his virtue sets Milton's Puritanism somewhat apart. So also his love of the drama removes him from the historical type of the sect. He could not, being a scholar of classical breeding, fail to look on the drama as a noble form, and its Greek examples fed his genius from the Euripidean passages of "Comus" to the "Samson Agonistes" at the very end. But while yet a student at college he had written the tribute to Shakespeare that was first printed in the Second Folio; and in connection with his friend, Lawes, the musician, he tried, though with an anonymity which he endeavored to preserve, the masque form of the drama, then its popular or at least fashionable phase, in the "Arcades" and on the great scale in the "Comus." This last was really a piece of private theatricals written for the Lord-President of Wales, who had employed Lawes, and acted by his children in the great hall at Ludlow Castle on his inauguration into his office. The substance of the poem, however, which was the praise and defense of chastity, was a very noble form of Puritan feeling in the high sense. It, too, is alive with Platonic philosophy, but this is so inwrought in the poetry that it is not felt by the reader except in its results. The praise of chastity also denotes something exceptional in Milton's temperament, in disclosing which it is necessary to use his own words, but with the more happiness since the passage opens with that remarkable sentence which is the most famous that came from his pen:

"And long it was not after, when I was confirmed in this opinion, that he, who would not be frustrate of his hope to write well hereafter in laudable things, ought himself to be a true poem; that is, a composition and pattern of the best and honorablest things; not presuming to sing high praises of heroic men, or famous cities, unless he have in himself the experience and the practice of all that which is praiseworthy. These reasonings, together with a certain niceness of nature, an honest haughtiness and self-esteem, either of what I was or what I might be (which let envy call pride), and lastly the modesty whereof, though not in the title-page, I may be excused to make here some beseeming profession; all these uniting the supply of their natural aid together kept me still above low descents of mind. . . . Next (for hear me out now, readers), that I may tell you whither my younger feet wandered; I betook me among those lofty fables and romances which recount in solemn cantos the deeds of knighthood founded by our victorious kings, and from hence had in renown over all Christendom. There I read in the oath of every knight that he should defend to the expense of his best blood, or of his life if it so befell him, the honor and chastity of virgin or matron; from whence even then I learnt what a noble virtue chastity sure must be, to the defence of which so many worthies by such a dear adventure of themselves had sworn. . . . So that even these books, which to many others have been the fuel of wantonness and loose living, I cannot think how, unless by divine indulgence, proved to me so many incitements, as you have heard, to the love and steadfast observation of that virtue."

In these matters, perhaps, silence is as golden in a Galahad as in a Launcelot, but the openness of Milton in this and other passages, is a part of his nature and belongs to his essential character. The personal feeling is only an instance of the purity that is elemental in his entire genius which in the end became a genius for austerity. But that time was far off, beyond the barrier of twenty years of the fighting that makes all men stern. The gentler Milton of the earlier day, the youth with the passion for purity, the passion for beauty, the passion for perfection in poetry, had no premonition of what was to be, what truly "God had resolved" concerning him; he looked, it can hardly be doubted, for that Virgilian future, while he pursued his studies of the most mellowed art of civilization in the books of Athens, Rome, and Italy, and dreamed the dream of travel, fearful that he had been rash in allowing his friend Lawes to publish the unripe fruit of "Comus."

It was in this spirit that Milton, when thirty years old, made the journey to Italy where he remained more than a year. He must have been heartened by the praise of Sir Henry Wotton, who gave him letters of introduction, saying of "Comus" — "I should much commend the tragical part, if the lyrical did not ravish me with a certain Doric delicacy in your Songs and Odes, whereunto I must plainly confess to have seen yet nothing parallel in our language." He met famous men, Grotius and Galileo, lingered especially at Florence, Rome, Naples, and Venice, made numerous friends among the men of letters and taste, and had the great happiness to be favored with the acquaintance and warm interest of the aged Manso, the befriender of Tasso in his sad life, and the patron of Marini. It is plain that Milton not only made a good impression, as Manso says, with his "mind, form, grace, face, and morals," but he was socially attractive; notwithstanding his strength of natural reserve and what he calls "haughtiness" in his character, his familiar relations with comrades and elder associates betray real humaneness, and the affectionateness of his single close friendship with Charles Diodati intimates perhaps the sweeter quality of nature by which he bound his Italian acquaintances. He followed Wotton's wise and famous advice — "a tongue and an open face will go safely over the whole world" — indifferently, it is to be feared; but he came out of Italy safe to Geneva, and so home. One wonders what he brought away really from the Italian beauty of scenery, the ruins and the galleries, but it is a vain curiosity; so far as appears, his life in Italy was essentially social, he was interested in the men and their academies, and wrote Italian and Latin verses in their midst, like a dilettante youth; but the great result seems to have been the stir of his mind in response to the appreciation of his talents about him and the forming of a solid and resolved ambition to produce a great poetic work. His own words are important: "Much latelier," he writes, "in the private academies of Italy, whither I was favored to resort, perceiving that some trifles that I had in memory, composed at under twenty or thereabouts (for the manner is that every one must give some proof of his wit and reading there) met with acceptance above what was looked for; and other things, which I had shifted in scarcity of books and conveniences to patch up amongst them, were received with written encomiums, which the Italian is not forward to bestow on men of this side the Alps; I began thus far to assent both to them and divers of my friends here at home, and not less to an inward prompting which now grew daily upon me, that by labor and intent study (which I take to be my portion in this life) joined with the strong propensity of nature, I might perhaps leave something so written to aftertimes as they should not willingly let it die." An epic poem or a tragic drama was to be the form of this attempt, and he listed nigh a hundred subjects for choice, the chief being the British story of Arthur's Knights and the Hebrew myth of Paradise. It might be thought that this width of topic consorts but ill with any theory of "God's resolve" concerning him, and certainly Apollo in his inspiration was not wont to give the priestess a hundred oracles to pick and choose; but if the academic and reflective nature of Milton's muse is thus superficially clear, the selection of the subject of "Paradise Lost" was not really arbitrary, but the choice along which the character of his life and learning and the spirit of the man were felt in self-commanding ways.

Milton had come home because of the threatening aspect of public affairs in the same spirit in which many of our own countrymen returned at the outbreak of the Civil War because it is not fit that a citizen should be abroad (save in her service) when his country is in arms. But he was a private person with no opening into state affairs; so he says very sensibly, "I betook myself to my interrupted studies, trusting the issue of public affairs to God in the first place, and to those to whom the people had committed that charge." Up to this time Milton had depended on paternal support, and his father had been a very good Augustus to him; now he began to earn something, and from undertaking the care of his sister's two young boys, he set up gradually a little private academy of a half-friendly character for the children of families in his acquaintance. A few boys in a house big enough for himself and his books, many of which he had collected and sent from Venice, and with a garden — he always kept a garden near in his many changes of London residence — and with the schoolmaster's task for his useful employment; this was the outward look of the life which within was brooding the work that the world "would not willingly let die." Milton also signalized his entrance on every-day affairs by taking a wife; strangely enough she was of a broken-down worldly Cavalier family, which was much in debt to his father, and she was but just past seventeen. There was a brief two months of festivity in the house, after which the young bride returned to her family for a visit, and would not come back to her husband till two years later when, in the declining fortune of both the Cavalier cause and the family, a reconciliation was arranged. Meanwhile Milton had found an entrance to the life of the public cause as a pamphleteer; he published in swift succession several of the tracts on the times by which for twenty years he was to be mainly known at home, and to become famous abroad as the chief defender of the English nation in the forum of Europe, and in the composition of which he expended his intellectual energy till the last moment of the lost cause.

The golden age of Milton's life had gone by; the happy home where he had been the light of the house — and how dearly he was cherished is humanly indicated by his father's having two portraits of him in boyhood and youth — was broken up; Charles Diodati, his first and only bosom friend, was dead. Life had entered on a new scene, in which domestic unhappiness, conflict with men, the indignation and bitter edge of prose were in sharp contrast with that early felicity, peace and poetic musing. The change was as deep as life, and in fact amounted to a substitution of intellectual for poetic force as the element of its being. Up to now Milton's thinking had been subsidiary to his art, but henceforward it was for its own sake; he had been a man of letters, he became a man of politics. His interest in ideas was immense, though now it was first apparent. He had a greater intellect than commonly falls to the share even of great poets, and it was of that active sort that makes the practical idealist. The passion for perfection in art which makes the poet, and for purity in life which makes the man, are matters of the private life, but the application of analogous ideas of perfection to the lives of other men and to the state necessarily throws the asserter of them into opposition, and in so far as he strives for their victory he finds oftenest a thorny path. Milton now entered on this career. His practical instinct working through ideas is most simply seen in the things nearest to him. It was no common school that he kept, no humdrum routine that he mumbled over to his boys; there was a curriculum of his own devising and noticeably he saw to it that his boys read more books that had life in them and with a broader reach of modern power, as it then was, than other schoolboys had any chance to get, and he put speed into their acquisition of Latin; quicker work and a wider and more contemporary round of study, and in general the Renaissance ideal of the development of personal power in manifold ways, characterized the education he strove to give. It was, no doubt, the most modern school in Europe, though its pupils were only half a handful. His domestic life was, like the school, a near concern; and he no sooner realized that his young wife had deserted him after two months than he at once declared the extreme heretical doctrine of liberty of divorce and re-marriage in case of the incompatibility of the parties. It was a shocking position to take, in those days, and first brought obloquy upon him, but he stuck to his opinion, and indeed among the hundreds of the sects of those days one may still read of the Miltonists or Divorcers. The key to Milton's intellectual life lies in his Renaissance training, though the fact is obscured by the Puritanical matter of his tracts; personal force, such as he raised to heroic proportions in "Satan," was his ideal; personal liberty in all its forms was the thing nearest to his heart. It gave great individuality to his own life. Thus he belonged to no communion, attended no church, and had no prayers at home; his religion must have been very sacred to him, and it suffered no profaning hands; he was true Puritan, full grown, not in the sense of the sectaries of his age but in that which is for all time, the man free from all forms who needs no intermediary with his God except the spiritual Christ. The same proud assertion of individual dignity is the core of the great essay in behalf of a free press, the "Areopagitica," in which he set forth the doctrine of the public toleration of thought and speech, the right of the intellect to be heard, with undying eloquence. Liberty, in one form or another, is the watchword of all his prose; it was then, as it continues to be, the shuttlecock between statecraft and priestcraft, but Milton saw the old Priest in the new Presbyter, and in all ways stood for independence in the individual; by so much the more did he stand for independence in the nation, the liberty of the people to call their rulers to the bar and send the violator of their rights to the block; with the vehement and unabated directness of Demosthenes against Philip, he too thundered against the Stuart line. The name of Cromwell only was known so far and widely abroad as that of this Defender of the People of England. It is this office that gives grandeur to his figure; and no one, not of the race itself, has so much in the thoughts of men the sublime character of a Hebrew prophet, the rebuker of Kings, the declarer of the eternity of truth, the companion of the thoughts of God. This loftiness felt in Milton's prose is what preserves it; if it is not studded with sentences of abstract wisdom, like Burke's, where ripeness of thought and breadth of phrase combine to make memorable political sayings, it is strewn with passages of high and sublime flow in which ideal principles flame at their whitest heat of conviction. To be the voice of England on a great occasion, such as the death of her king by the judgment of her people, was a memorable destiny; but what makes Milton more remembered is that a hundred times liberty spoke by his lips. He was that man, hateful to all tyrants, a Republican; though under the powerful presence of Cromwell, "our chief of men," he swerved slightly from the line, he came home true and belonged with Vane. He was not a democrat; he was too much imbedded in the Renaissance for that, and valued men for their personal distinction; for the honor and force in them that makes for inequality:

> "Nor do I name of men the common rout
> That wandering loose about
> Grow up and perish as the summer fly,
> Heads without name, no more remembered."

That is the very trick of aristocracy in thought and accent. Equality, fraternity, were not yet risen stars. Milton's "Ready and Easy Way," which he sent forth as the last arrow when Charles II was almost on the coast, proposed a kind of permanent Grand Council, like that of the Republic of Venice, as the ruling body of the state. Nevertheless, Milton's republicanism, though it was not the democracy of to-day, was the high tide of the principle of freedom in that age; and when the dying roll of the retreating storm was heard in that last passionate remonstrance of Milton, on the eve of the King's landing, there was to be silence till the Marseillaise.

In these years Milton's life took on that harshness of feature, which it retains in tradition, owing to his invective against the enemies of the State, his unhappiness in his children, and perhaps the color of the name of Puritan. In outward ways it was one of plain habits and personal dignity. He had given up teaching after seven years, and when in a short period the Commonwealth was established he became Foreign Secretary to the Council; it was a good post, well paid, and he held it till the Restoration from his forty-second to his fifty-second year. He received and wrote foreign despatches and was the official intermediary for all ambassadors and envoys, and was thus brought both at the Council Table and in the Hall into habitual association with the heads of State and persons of distinction from abroad. His private fame and character were also such as to attract visits and attention upon his own account. In his appearance and demeanor there must have been the ripened breeding of the scholar and poet whose social art is attested by his Italian travels, together with the matured handsomeness of the man and the personal dignity of the representative of State. His wife had died and he had married again; but after a year of happy wedlock, in this instance, he lost her whose memory he made sacred in the sonnet tenderly recalling her veiled face:

> "Yet to my fancied sight
> Love, sweetness, goodness, in her person shined
> So clear as in no face with more delight."

He may never have seen her face, for before this he had become totally blind in his forty-fifth year. He had continued to perform the duties of his Secretaryship, being led to the Council Room, and there listening, dictating, and composing he went through the necessary business as before. Except for a few sonnets at wide intervals he had entirely discontinued poetry during these twenty years. Dr. Johnson described these sonnets as "cherry-stones," and it has been well said that this "marks the lowest-point imaginable in criticism of verse." They are rather stones of David's sling. That on the massacre in Piedmont is noteworthy as the first blaze of the English muse over the violated liberties of Europe, which Byron and Shelley learned the lightning use of, and whereof Swinburne in our own day flings the revolutionary torch. The sonnets, few as they are, would be a mighty monument for any genius; they have the quality of Michaelangelo. Just before the downfall, Milton seems to have reverted in mind to the predestination of his genius to poetry and that great hope he had indulged on returning from Italy: "that what the greatest and choicest wits of Athens, Rome, or modern Italy, and those Hebrews of old did for their country, I, in my proportion, with this over and above of being a Christian, might do for mine." Now the end had come; blind and in hiding, in those months of unloosed revenge, none, the Regicides excepted, was more likely than he to fall a victim; and indeed few who have escaped it came so near as Milton to being hanged. The peril of this shame to England — and such shame there has been in all literatures and nations of civility — was near, but it passed. The "blind old schoolmaster," as he is known from Dryden's lips, lived on in obscurity and humbleness, though a few friends still remembered him and showed him attention, and distinction still clung to his figure. Life, it must have seemed, was done for him. Then he turned to the unbroken meditation of that poem which for two years had employed his thoughts at times, and in three years more of lonely musing carried it to completion. A new age of literature had come in, and new men, strangers to all that had fashioned the men of old in greatness and him, the last of them; but the old age should yet lift one towering peak to heaven, before it subsided to the levels of the eighteenth century. "Paradise Lost" was this last and belated birth of the greatest English age.

The opposition between the earlier and the later poetry of Milton is very great, and is the more marked because of the barrenness of his middle life in verse. The liquid flow, the beauty of surface locking in mosaic sweet sights and harmonies of the natural world, the mellowness of idyllic and elegiac art, the crystal purity of the air of garden and grove as in some northern Italian night — all these and the like are the traits of his poetic youth; but in the works of his age there is something that dwarfs such qualities and makes natural the designation of the earlier verse as his minor poems. The reason of the difference is, I think, the expansion of Milton's intellectual powers which took place on his entrance into public debate, and the strength they acquired in that Herculean labor of the mind stretched to its utmost of practical force and mastery for twenty years of unremitted strain. "Paradise Lost" is a great poem of the intellect as well as of the imagination. Milton, after a period of wavering, had finally chosen the form of an epic, built on the lines of classical tradition, with the myth of Eden for its central story; the origin and destiny of the soul and the meaning of its course in history was the real theme. The subject was well chosen, and fulfilled the desirable though not essential condition for a work of national appeal in that it was and had long been familiar to the people; the material was at least as well known to the English, in its main outlines, as the myths of the gods on which the Attic tragedians had wrought had been known to the Athenians. Yet it is the decadence of interest in the subject-matter which is now most pointed to as impairing the permanent appeal of the poem. An epic which is in the third century of its victorious power need not fear any displacement. Its childhood myth of the race, its crude science, its antiquated theology, may all be granted, and it is easy to find in its necessary conventions, which belong to it as a work of limited art, something awkward and irrational, even petty and ridiculous to the mind's eye; but the attack along these lines is successful only when conducted against details; the poem in its wholeness retains an overwhelming power. It is conceived in three movements; the first is the Titan struggle of the rebellious angels; the second is the Eden bower; the third is the creation of the world with its pendent panorama of human history. Of these three subjects the first yields the most majestic sight of that other world of Hades which the tragic imagination of man in the greatest poets has essayed to picture in all times; the second gives the most charming rendering of that Bower of Bliss which has also been so often attempted, and the third presents the most nobly impressive story of the birth of our universe that is to be found in poetry. It is not necessary that the mind should cling to the actuality of these scenes and events any more than to the siege of Troy or the voyage of Æneas; if they have imaginary reality — even if they have only that — it is all the truth that poetry seeks and is sufficient to interest men forever. If Adam be as real as Deucalion, and Satan as Enceladus and Prometheus, the only question that remains is with respect to the relative dignity and power of the myth to satisfy the mind in its effort to picture by a symbol — since it cannot know — the secret of its birth, suffering and destiny. If "Paradise Lost" be looked at in this way as only a hypothesis of the imagination, it yet remains the loftiest flight of the mind of man in that region of what is to be only spiritually conceived. It is here that it makes its long and powerful appeal to masses of readers, and remains a poem of the English nation; critics endeavor to empty it of the content of meaning of which it is full, and to leave only the style by which alone, they will have it, the poem survives; but my own mind, I know — and in this I cannot be singular — still holds to the substance as the true poem, indifferent to the fate of the Hebrew myth, of Puritan theology or Darwinian descent, or any other of those matters of contemporaneity which are forever tossed in men's minds. It is possible, perhaps, to trace the operation of some of the elements in the poem, which are not for an age, but for all time.

One of the most salutary uses of great poetry is to give a scale of life. Wordsworth was led by the character of his genius to observe how the continual presence of grand natural features in the landscape and the habitual sight of the processes of nature's life fulfil this function for those who live in communion with them, and give to human life a setting and perspective. The reflection of the Greeks that the dramatic representation of tragic changes of fortune in the lives of the great and powerful imposed on the spectators a truer estimate of their own share of trial in life, is an analogous thought. But the soul grows in knowledge of itself not only by these humbling influences of contrast with the grandeur of nature and tragic calamity; it expands through all ideas that raise its sense of power however excited, and especially that power which is lodged in its own being. "Paradise Lost" performs this service, with great efficiency and in diverse ways. In what poem is the infinity of the universe so sensibly present, merely in the physical sphere? It is true that Milton conceives it on the ancient Ptolemaic system instead of the Copernican; but there is the sense of infinity in either, and so unimportant is this scientific error in the effect that the ordinary man has to be told it before he finds it out, while the localizing of heaven and hell beyond gives the impression of unlimited spaciousness and the endless reach of the world of being quite in the modern manner. In comparison with Shelley's scientifically orthodox representation of the stellar universe in "Queen Mab," Milton's is more sublime, more true to the idea of infinity, in that it is bordered on by the eternal world and held within the compass of human comprehension with no loss to its majestic beauty as a cluster of celestial orbs without number for multitude. What poem, again, so succeeds in realizing to the mind superhuman power, personal force raised to the utmost imaginable height, not only in the magnificent example of

Satan, but in his angelic peers, Uriel and Gabriel, even in the young angels, Ithuriel and Zephron, whom the fiend found invincible? But the infinity which most shines in the poem is not material or personal, not in the universe or the protagonists of the battle that was fought "out of space, out of time;" the infinity is that of man himself as a soul in which issues of eternity converge, about which play mysterious agencies of evil and good, for which in its unknown course celestial powers care; that infinity which in the soul itself is the very ground of being of the Christian religion. The soul, weaving this legend of itself from its far prehistoric dawn, fashioned this wonderful Eden dream; the scenes and events, imbedded in tradition and the life of historical ages, long and continuously in the human consciousness, must have deep affinities with the nature of the soul which in them has incarnated its intuitions, cast its sense of spiritual fact, pictured its beliefs; in a word, this myth embroidered on the hem of the seamless garment of truth is all the memory the soul has of its own unearthly history. The particular actuality of the links of the legend, and even the form of the elements of thought it uses, are immaterial; for the things of the spirit can only be symbolically shown. Genesis and Geneva may be alike disregarded; science and dogma wholly apart, there remains in the myth the long enduring substance of past experience and conviction stored in the race, however to be more broadly interpreted in the future. If the tenet that "in Adam all men sinned" loses its ancient power, it is at least an earlier reading of that solidarity of humanity which is one of the master-truths of the democracy; if the damnation of the angels is repulsive to humanitarianism, it no less reflects the sense of struggle with the Evil Principle which is a fact of the universal consciousness of mankind, and affirms the final triumph of the Good which is an element unshaken in human faith; if the angelic guard round a pre-doomed Paradise seems folly to the reason, it yet does shadow forth the strange double-sense in man of a heavenly guardianship and its mysterious failure to protect the soul in life. But few readers need to consider the matter so curiously as this. Every one, who opens the poem, finds mirrored there the soul in its infinite and eternal nature, and the mystery of its source and destiny set forth with an imaginative definiteness of vision, as nowhere else. The story is displayed with unexampled grandeur in the scenes, in the wasted gloom of hell, in the abyss of chaos, in the freshly created universe of light, upon the battle-plains of heaven; the characters are ennobled to the height of what is possible in faculty and prowess, in form and moving not inferior to the gods, eloquent in speech, majestic in action, each great in his own resolve; every element of epic power and loveliness, that the practice of elder poets had handled, is employed — whole armies in array, individual conflict, the bower of love, the tale of creation, the panorama of history, the pit, the council, set forth in all modes of oratory, dialogue, narrative, apostrophe and idyl, and all in an unrivaled balance and harmony of the parts. The Hebraic solemnity and directness, the Pindaric loftiness of flight, yet so absorbed into Milton's inspiration as to be his own and personal to him, give to the poem that quality that it holds unshared with any other epic — sublimity; this is the instinctive and also the deliberate judgment of all men — it is a sublime poem. If I were to sum up in a single expression the immediate power of "Paradise Lost" over men, I should say that no poem so dilates the mind; by so doing it gives a scale to life — the scale of infinity.

"Paradise Lost" is not a modern poem; and I have dwelt elsewhere, perhaps too exclusively, on the important ways in which it departs from modern sympathy; like all great works of imagination in literature it looks on human affairs with a reverted gaze, for such works are climaxes of past thought and passion in centuries and civilization. But neither is it a Renaissance and Reformation poem, any more than the "Divine Comedy" is a medieval poem. There are cantos of Dante, quite as theologically dead and more unintelligible than Milton's dry tracts. Such elements of hardened matter from which the fire has gone are found in all the greatest compositions. The poem remains universal, not for an age but for all time, because it is thus a poem of the soul and its mystery, and sets forth under an intelligible formula of thought and history and in images of becoming grandeur and splendor that particular legend of the soul which has been the historical framework of spiritual piety in Christian ages and still appeals by countless tendrils of memory, custom and aspiration to men born Christians; it fills imaginatively what is otherwise a void, "peoples the lone infinite," as no other secular work has done. It is thus that, as I said, it neighbors the Bible in men's thoughts; and not only does it do this by its matter, but also by its style. The Bible is the standard of perfection in English writing; but the same influence which flows from it upon the listening mind, and is felt as the unapproached perfection of prose speech in language and cadence by the host of the common people in congregations, also flows from Milton's verse in the region of poetry; every one, however unlearned in literature, feels that here is a standard of perfection. It is a fit and crowning excellence; but the style is no more all of Milton than it is all of Isaiah or St. John. The people cannot escape great style, as all oratory shows; neither can they escape great poetry. The power of the highest is always greatest upon the lowest; it is this which makes a national poem possible; this sent Homer with all Greek ships, Virgil with all Roman eagles, Milton with all English Bibles through the world.

"Paradise Lost" is the greatest of Milton's works because his powers are there in true balance, intellect and imagination in equal fellowship, with the lesser graces of poetry (such as distinguished his early verse) not in neglect. As he grew rapidly old, his expression became bare and austere; in "Paradise Regained" and "Samson Agonistes" intellectual power seems to transcend and perhaps depress the imaginative — the balance is disturbed. They have the severity of outline and surface that belong to the peak. They were the work of the last years, when one thinks of Milton and sees him in the most human way, comes near to him as a natural creature, an old man. One youth there was who came to him now, like the boys he used to teach, and had lessons from him and talk, in return for which he wrote at Milton's dictation. His daughters had left him; a third wife, whom he married late, took kindly care of him; friends visited him. He would sit outside the door in the sun, wrapped in a coarse grey cloth coat. The undying portrait of him is that reported by the painter, Richardson, from an aged clergyman who called on him. "He found him in a small house, he thinks but one room on a floor. In that, up one pair of stairs, which was hung with a rusty green, he found John Milton sitting in an elbow-chair, black clothes and neat enough; pale but not cadaverous; his hands and fingers gouty, and with chalk stones. Among other discourse he expressed himself to this purpose, 'that, was he free from the pain this gave him, his blindness would be tolerable.'" This was the old age appointed for the fair youth of forty years before, in whom the beauty of the Renaissance seemed to have taken on ideal form, on the eve of the Italian journey; to this end he had brought his boyhood passion for beauty, purity and perfection through a life of intellectual conflict to a consummation that gave him kinship with the sterner rather than the softer brothers of his art, with Pindar and Æschylus and the prophets of old rather than Euripides and the mild Italian genius; it is hard to reconcile the two, to find in the old man the youth. It is commonly thought that in the tragedy of "Samson" he had his own fortune in mind, and doubtless he drew sympathetic inspiration from his own position in realizing that of Samson in defeat. But his worn spirit seems to have accepted defeat without that despair of life which in so fiery tempered a soul, so great in faculty, might well be feared. It may be that his faith was equal to that birth of patience, which is the crown of life long lived, and the capacity for which he showed in promise in his birthday sonnet in youth and in thought in his sonnet on his blindness. It is at least noticeable that the last lines of "Samson" look to fuller life, not death, and are words of promise and submission, of growth as well as of faith:

"All is best, though we oft doubt
What the unsearchable dispose
Of highest wisdom brings about,
And ever best found in the close.
. . . . .

> His servants He, with new acquist
> Of true experience from this great event,
> With peace and consolation hath dismissed,
> And calm of mind, all passion spent."

In this high mood, one hopes, Milton took farewell of the world as of the Muse; he died at almost sixty-six years of age, leaving to mankind a life that has been the inspiration of liberty, and these few rolls of immortal verse.

# VIRGIL

Virgil is that poet whose verse has had most power in the world. He was the poet of Rome, and concentrated in his genius its imperial star; so long as that ruled the old Mediterranean world, with the great northwest and eastern hinterlands, Virgil summed its glory for the human populations that fleeted away in that vast basin; in a world forever mightily changing his solitary pre-eminence was one unchanging thing, dimmed only as the empire itself faded. His memory illumined the Dark Ages. He rose again as the morning star of the Latin races. He penetrated the reborn culture of Europe with the persistency and pervasiveness of Latinity itself; not only was knowledge of his works as wide-spread as education, but his influence on the artistic temperament of literatures, the style of authors and even the characters of men in their comprehension of the largeness of life, was subtle and profound, and was the more ample in proportion to the nearness of the new nations to the direct descent of civilization. He, more than any other poet, has been a part of the intellectual life of Europe alike by length of sway and by the multitude of minds he touched in all generations; and, among the Latin races, he is still the climax of their genius, for charm and dignity, for art and the profound substance of his matter, and for its serious inclusiveness of human life. Of no other poet can it be said that his lines are a part of the biography of the great, of emperors like Augustus and

Hadrian, of fathers like Jerome and Augustine, of preachers like Savonarola, churchmen like Fenelon, statesmen like Pitt and Burke; and among the host of humble scholars, of schoolmasters, the power he has held in their bosoms is as remarkable for its personal intimacy as for its universal embrace. No fame so majestic has been cherished with a love so tender. Virgil thus blends in a marvelous manner the authority of a classic with the direct appeal to life.

It belongs to the sense of familiar companionship which Virgil's verse exhales that some shadows of his personality survive, slight but sufficient for memory and affection. He was the son of a small farmer, in the province of North Italy, of whom no more is known than that he wished to give his child the best education then to be had. We first see him, who was to be so great a poet, as the slender tall schoolboy at Cremona and Milan, with the rusticity of manner which he never laid aside. He studied also at Rome, in his youth, and found patrician friends among his mates. He made his way later with men of great affairs, and notwithstanding the shyness of his heart and the awkwardness of his manners they found something to prize in him by some charm the Muses shed, loved him, petted and praised him, and gave him a fortune, a house at Rome, near Maecenas' garden, which he seldom used, and two country homes at Naples and Nola, where he loved to live in the soft Campanian air; there, except for sojourns in Sicily and pleasant travel in the Greek cities and along the islands, he passed those meditative years of privacy in which his self-distrustful and long-brooding genius slowly matured its eternal work; there, too, as he desired, at Naples, over by the hill of Posilipo, his ashes were laid to rest in that pleasant city's soil, which still keeps the tradition of his tomb. He was happy in the protecting affection of his friends, and also in the honor of the world which rose to him as to Augustus when he entered the theater, and in the power of lifelong labor in his art undiminished by an hour wasted on inferior things. In all outward ways his life was the most fortunate recorded in literature; and it is good to know that the world was gentle to one of those delicate spirits who, usually with how different a fate, bring it gifts from eternity. In the memory of Virgil there is no bitterness of regret for the words of unkindness or the blows of adversity; he lived peacefully and in the habitual enoyment of some of the fairest gifts of life.

Nowhere so much as in those works which seem most independent of the power of time, which escape from their own age, their native country and race, and enter upon a cycle of memory so vast that they are fitly named the stars of the intellectual firmament, is it needful to define their moment, to understand the nest of their conception, the law of their creation, the nature of their first appeal to men, in a word their contemporaneity. The moment of Virgil is declared plainly in the "Eclogues." They are little poems, the labored trifles of his 'prentice hand; but in them, like the oak in the acorn there is in miniature all Virgil; both the man and his work are there like a preconception. The teachableness of Virgil is his prime character, and shines in his youth. He woke to the past as simply as a child opens its eyes to the dancing sunlight of the world, and he took it in directly as something belonging to him. He made speed to enter on his inheritance; and for him this heritage in its special form was the glory of Greek literature. The imaginative interpretation of the world stored in a thousand years of Greek poetry was the food of his heart. Thus it came about that he did not begin to write in a way discovered and worked out merely by himself, but imitated, as it is said, Theocritus the Syracusan, the chief Greek master of pastoral verse. He could not have had better fortune. For a youth unacquainted with experience the artificial mode of life which the pastoral presents as its framework of incident and song is itself favorable, since its requirements of accurate representation of reality are less stringent; and, especially, its small scale enforces attention to detail and encourages perfection of phrase, line and image in the workmanship and condensation in the matter, while its variety of description, dialogue and inserted song and its blend of lyric and dramatic moods give scope to a mind experimenting as it learns. It is for this reason that so many of the world's great poets in their youth have tried their wings in these numbers, brief, composite, academic, so well fitted for the exercise of growing talents, already touched with scholarship, in a world not too real to be lightly held nor so fantastic as to preclude truth of feeling. Virgil derived the proper good from the imitation of a great master by developing through it his native power. Theocritus remained the master-singer of the idyl; but before the different genius of Virgil passed on to its own toils, he had left the sweetness of his youth here in the pastoral like a perfume forever.

The poetic life of Virgil, however, in these years was more profound than this. He was not merely training his genius in certain external modes of expression; he was unfolding his soul. Form was the Greek gift to Virgil; not only that form which exists in the outer structure of line and melody or within the verse in its logic of emotion and event, but form which has power to cast the mind itself in predetermined lines of feeling and action, of taste, of choice, of temperament, and finds utterance in that beauty of the soul which is precedent to all verse. Form in its religious moods has this power to possess and shape the souls of men, as is familiarly seen; and so artistic form, alive and bodied in the lovely and ancient Greek tradition, seized Virgil in the spirit and fashioned him; he was its child as the novice is the spiritual son of St. Francis. The opposition between Theocritus and Virgil lies in this: in Theocritus, life puts on the forms of art; in Virgil art puts on the forms of life. In the Syracusan idyls there is objective beauty — pictures idealized and detached from life; in the Mantuan "Eclogues" one feels rather the presence of a beautiful soul to which art has given the gift of tongues to speak to all men. This deep intimate compelling mastery of the Greek spirit over all that was artistic in Virgil shaped him almost in his essential being; he was Hellenized as by a second birth. It was characteristic of him to yield to the will of life, and he yielded happily to the Greek forms of imagination, for he found in this obedience that yoke in which alone everlasting freedoms lie and the power of a free soul; it released his personality as if by some divine and creative touch. This presence of Virgil in his verse is elementary. He was a lover, and through love disengaged from life its moment of beauty, of sentiment, of millennial hope; but this beauty, sentiment and hope are seen under that almost atmospheric charm which has coined for itself the name Virgilian and is breathed from himself. It is not for what these eclogues contain of Theocritus that they have been dear to the poets of all lands, any more than it is for what the youthful lines of Spenser and Milton contain of these eclogues that the English breathings of the pastoral are dear; it is because they express with great purity and sweetness the genius of Virgil in its tender age.

If any one finds in the eclogues only the echo of Theocritus, he is wide of the mark; his ear is not set to the ringing of the master-melody in their song. The poets used the same instrument, and the younger learned its use from the elder; but each employed it with a difference, and this difference is a gulf of ages between them and an opposition in the spring and impulse of poetry. Art is not life, but is evoked from life. Theocritus held the mirror to life, but its image in his verse though more beautiful is still a thing of the external world; he stands outside what he depicts and renders it for its own sake. Virgil projected himself into life, and is the center of the world he expresses; he uses it to illustrate his own personality, to body forth his own various loves of beauty, nature, sentiment, romance, aspiration, to clothe with the forms of life that soul which art had shaped in him. He was still, though thirty, only a half-boyish lover of books and nature and a few friends, and the world he lived in was but little known to him; the eclogues with the personality of autobiography disclose this young scholar in his world. Virgil's world, too, like the temperamental drift of his art, is different from that of Theocritus; it is one more diversified, more actual and contemporaneous even; it is a Roman, Italian, proconsular world. He thinks of Actium and Parthia as we to-day think of Santiago and the Philippines. His landscape has the face and profile of familiar haunts; his shepherds have the features of his own rustics; his interests are his own local and temporal affairs. The pastoral Arcadia is a convention by means of which the encumbrances of time and place and persons and much matter of fact are gotten rid of; but under its clear veil which softens the unimportant, stand undisguised the men and events, the sentiment, the friendships, the scenes, the recreations, all the loves of the young poet from the humblest and tenderest up to the hope of all the world which he in those first years sounded for eternal memory as none before or since has sung the strain. Such is the Roman substance, personal, Italian, imperial, of it all, notwithstanding the superficial artifice of the poetic form.

Roman, too, was the seriousness of the young poet in his art. He and his fellow poets of the age were in literature provincials whose metropolis was Greek letters. They set themselves to the patriotic task of bringing the Greek muses to Latium where Aeneas had brought the Trojan gods, and creating in Latin something as near the Greek poetry as they could accomplish, and by very obviously, often direct, imitative means. They were zealous in the work; all were serious in it, however light the touch or the topic they strove to transplant to their own language and world. Virgil was such a provincial, though Greek art was itself refined in passing through his temperament; and he had such seriousness of mind. To compare great things with small, he was not unlike the young Longfellow in America who was avid of all the literatures of Europe and assimilated the poetic tradition of the thousand years preceding his birth, and who also strove with like seriousness to compass something like that in his own new land; and like Virgil, he too, in after life created for his country its native romance and primitive sentiment, giving to its desert nakedness an ascribed and imputed poetry. The Roman moment, also, in the largest way, was not unlike our own. Virgil was born in a dawning age; for him, as for us, life had been long lived in the world, there was antiquity, the thousand years of literature, and vanishing religions; Egypt was, perhaps, even more a monument of the Unknown Death than to-day; but with the spread of the power of Rome, which was then what the spread of liberty now is, a new age was at hand. Law and peace, which were the other names of Rome, had the world in their grasp, and were conquering far outward along its dark barbaric edges even to Britain "sundered once from all the human race." It was then that Virgil, "in the foremost files of time," sang in his youth that eclogue, the "Pollio" which is the greatest hymn of antiquity, if not of all time, and won for himself, though a pagan, a place among the saints of the Church:

*Magnus ab integro saeclorum nascitur ordo.*

The line has the swell of the "Gloria." Thus early, thus fundamental by virtue of its earliness, arose in him and mingled with his genius that temperament of world-hope, not the diminutive Arcadian dream of a valley or distant islands of the blessed, but world-hope mighty as the world, on the great scale of universal sympathy for mankind, which was one of the authentic signs of a new time. It was the secular hour of the founding of the Empire; it was the spiritual hour of the birth of Christ; and its presence was in the young poet's heart. A mighty voice, too, had before now been heard in Rome, the voice of one crying in the wilderness of the dethroned gods, a man so great that he could endure the longest probation of any of the poets of mankind and wait nineteen centuries for the fullness of his fame — Lucretius. Virgil heard the voice, and stored it in his heart, and meditated upon it; but the time was not yet come. It was the eve of a great past, the dawn of a great future; and the further one penetrates the verse, the more clearly stands out this youthful figure with the radiance of the world's new morning in his face.

The "Eclogues," obeying the law of all beautiful things, have gathered beauty from the lapse of time. Some light streams back upon them from the later glory of Virgil, and they have that increase of charm which belongs to things that have been long loved; the lines, too, like shells, are full of vocal memories. For one who knows them well and knows the poets, they are a nest of the singing birds of all lands; as he reads, voices of Italy, France and England blend with the familiar lines, and a choiring vision rises before him of the world's poets in their youth framing their lips to the smooth-sliding syllables; for the eclogues have been deeply cherished. They are loved chiefly, however, because the young Virgil is seen in them, as in the palaestra of his art before he had put on his singing-robes, with that sweet teachableness, that yielding and hospitable mind, out of which was to come, to bless him and the world, the wide receptivity of his spirit, the rich assimilation, the accumulated power of imagination in the race, already held in the grasp of his genius like Ithuriel's spear. Rome and Athens, the light and majesty of the world, were married in his blood; and though he bore as yet only the rustic reed, here in the adolescence of genius was the form of him who was to hand down by descent the antique vigor to the modern world. Virgil became the great reconciler in his own inherited world, the great mediator between antiquity and Christendom; he maintained in poetry, equally with Plato in philosophy, the unbroken continuity of the human spirit; but before entering on these great offices and preliminary to them he was first of all and by instinct a great lover — a greater lover than Dante — and here in the first friendly affections of the senses melting with the world, of the heart blending with other lives, of the mind breathing the universal hope of all, is this lover in the bud — he, who was to be the greatest lover in all the world of all things beautiful, strong, tender, pitiful, sad, and fated.

There was another scope, a different fiber, in the "Georgics," the fruit of his seven years' toil in early manhood. His genius had been powerfully condensed; the matter of the song was as firmly organized as it was richly diversified; the whole, scarcely two thousand lines in all, was a great single poem. The sense of nationality, no longer diffused and dispersed, burns at the center as its nucleus and feeding flame. The work, though small in scale is monumental in effect; it bears the Roman birthmark in its practical purpose to share in the restoration of the agricultural life, and in the author's dedication of his powers to public spirit. It was characteristic of Virgil to require reality in his subject-matter, and a present hour; contemporaneousness presided in the inception and purpose of all he did; however far he might range, he brought all home to amplify that moment of Rome in which he lived. More than any other of the poets of mankind he used the poetic art to idealize, to exalt and to enrich the nation's consciousness; and, through singleness of mind and comprehensivenenss of effort, he became the most national of all poets. As the world had been given to Rome to rule, Rome had been given to him to be the Empire of his song; this was his destiny. His genius did not expand suddenly and at once to so vast a sphere; but as is the case with all men who accumulate greatness as if by a process of nature, humbler impulses and lesser tasks conducted him upon his way. He would tell the story of Italy — that was the phase under which Rome first appealed to him. It was as if some one of our own poets had chosen to write an idyl of the old free life of New England, in the days before national unity and American destiny had come to fullness in his heart. With unerring instinct, in choosing his theme, he struck straight at the fundamental Roman interest, the land, the soil; but not yet imperializing, he seized this interest not in its foreign form of land-hunger which is the impulse of all empire, but in its primitive form of the home-domain, "the mighty mother of men and fruits," that Italy which was Rome's birthright. He thought of the land, too, not as our nature-poets do in modern days as a description of contour and color and changes of the weather, the magic of the senses, but primitively as the dwelling place of the race and the element of its labors. Toil; that, too, was a Roman idea, and he yoked it with the land in a Roman way; for he saw human life on the soil as an arduous and unremitting warfare with the stubborn obduracy of nature, who being subdued, nevertheless, became beneficent, rejoicing in her captivity, and rewarded her conqueror with the harvest of the earth and its loveliness, with the external blessings of the gods and with moral boons of inward excellence stored in the characters of men by this discipline of the perennial task of life.

The "Georgics" is the story of this perennial task. In its original and parent form no more than an almanac, a manual of the planting of crops, the raising of cattle and the tending of bees, it grew in Virgil's mind to be a poem of the sacred year. Virgil was by instinct and temperament a ritualist. The regularity inherent in times and seasons and all ceremonial, the solemnity belonging to all rites, the presence of the abstract and hidden in their significance, were things profoundly Roman and responded to what was by race deeply implanted in his nature. The round of the seasons in their connection with agricultural life was in his eyes a ritual of the year, the presence and action of a natural religion. The dependence of man on nature always plays a great part in religious life; even now when that dependence is less definitely felt than in primitive times it is at birth, marriage and death, the great moments of nature, that religion has its common and vital impact on the general life; and in the primitive conditions, set forth in this poem, nature might seem herself to appoint the sacred days of the gods both for prayer and for thanksgiving, to order the festivals in their course and to prescribe the peculiar service for the hour, month after month, in annual revolution. The needs of each season and the pursuits appropriate to it determined the active duties of man, and these drew after them the due religious practices consecrated by use and wont; and, in the issue of all, the blessings of the divine gods crowned the labor with a present reward. Natural piety could not have a simpler being than this. The mystery of the world which envelops all life-processes on the earth has always overhung the out-of-doors people with some grandeur in the elements, with stars and winds and waves; in living near to nature, they seem, by virtue of being lost and unprotected there, to reach out to the unknown in habitual ways. Virgil felt this mystery after a different fashion; he knew it in the forms of old mythology that Greek imagination had put on in the divine presence, and also in the forms of new science that Greek intellect had put forth in attempting a rational conception of nature as a thing subject to human knowledge. He was not disturbed by this double possession of imagination and rational intuition; that teachable, that yielding and hospitable mind, by its own nature made him in his self-expression a representative poet; he gave out life in its wholeness. This sacred year, with its ritual of work and worship, drew his eyes upon it, as a thing of outward beauty, and first gave up to his gaze, first of men, that enveloping charm of the land and its life which is now the world's thought of Italy; this year, too, with its antique usages, as old, perhaps, as the tilled soil itself, recurring in their seasons as the sun rose in the zodiac, engaged his affections by which he was bound to all things of reverence, age and piety, and none more than he realized in his heart both their divine and human appeal; and, with all this, awoke, too, the philosophic mind, fed from later fountains, and he flung round this ancient Italy, humanized by long life upon its soil, that large horizon of the intellect, in which his own time was beginning to live.

In such ways as these the poem which was begun as a manual of the farm's task-work came from Virgil's hands so touched with visible beauty, old religious association, the mythology and science of the Mediterranean world and his own loves for all these, that it was, without fiction, an incarnate Italy. He had embodied in his verse the land itself with all its loveliness, then as it is to-day, a land long lived in, with history, legend and ruins of a storied past reaching back into the unknown ages; he had set forth its characteristic life, the human product of the soil, as a thing so sharing in the simplicities of nature and what is divinely primitive as to make it seem the eternal model of what the life of man on earth should be, under the dispensation of labor, yet enveloped in the kindly agencies of sun and rain, springtide and summer heat and mellowing falls, the birth and rebirth of all things in the revolution of the year — a life which was itself religion, a round of duty, prayer and praise; and he had evoked from this land and the life there lived in the plains and uplands that abstract Italy, the eldest of the modern nations, in unveiling whom he may almost be said to have created the mother-land. It is the same Italy, then and now; the stream of Italian patriotism still mounts to the hymn of the second Georgic as its fountain-head. There Italy is first seen clothed with the divinity that a land identified with a race and a renown takes on in the hearts of its children. Virgil seized the fact in its moment, with that revelation of the actual which the highest poetry exists to achieve. He sees Italy as the center of the world, with other lands antique or barbarous lying on the sea about and beyond her, each with its just distance and coloring and place in the Mediterranean world, which is her sphere, but subject and tributary to her unenvious supremacy in fertility and men and fame. The miracle is the perfection with which Virgil expresses this security in happiness, beauty and power, this unclouded felicity of fortune, this ordered peace, while distant clouds of war and menace whirl only on the far confines of the scene.

He had prepared himself with wonderful thoroughness for the work; a broad base of scholarship lies under it, and for the didactic substance he had brought all Greek and Roman knowledge, and something even from Carthage, to contribute to its truth, precision and fullness; but it was rather by his cultural knowledge, which he used in heightening and expanding the theme to its true proportions, that he regenerated and transformed the matter of the verse and made the rural scene into the glory of Italy. The wealth of this preparation, and his seven years' toil, may seem disproportionate to the result in a poem so brief, but only to those who do not know that, the scale of the matter being allowed for, the power of a poem is in inverse proportion to its length. He used for his artistic method a selective, partial description, subordinating individuality and detail to social and general presentation, and he employed episode, suggestion and the emphasis that lies in enthusiasm to enlarge the theme and qualify it with greatness; in particular, he intended no exhaustion of the subject but only of the feeling of the subject, which is the method of great poetry, and hence come the rapidity, the variety, the completeness of impression which are the most obvious traits of the changeful lines. The "Georgics," most of all, reveals the master of the poetic art; and in a work somewhat limited by its choice of one though a great and enduring phase of human life and also by its national inspiration and its attachment to a particular social moment, the mind has leisure to notice the more its artistic modes, the choice and ordering of the material, the colors of rhetoric, the edge and immobility of style ever fresh and everlasting as sculpture, the wealth of mosaic, the pictorial, sententious and eclectic compositeness, the elaboration of the poem's beauty in the whole and in detail. It is full of a poet's choices; and, though popular with the cultivated class to which it was addressed, is essentially a poet's poem. True to himself, the stuff which Virgil worked in was his own nature; out of his heart brooding on the beauty of the visible world about him, on the picture of its human labors and the imperial care conserving all these things in happy and lasting peace, came the vision shaped and colored and idealized by his sympathies with man's life, his affections for the things of old time, his hopes in the present. The "Georgics" in a land of patriots and poets is still the unrivaled monument of the first poet-lover of Italy.

The "Aeneid," Virgil's last and greatest work, is a world-poem. It is one of that splendid cluster of world-poems, which by the fewness of their number, the singleness of their glory, and the great intervals of time that separate them, have, of all man's works most infinitude; though time attacks them, they survive like the pyramids; they are man's Bibles on the side that he turns to the human, like the Scriptures on the side that he turns to the divine. The distinctive feature of the "Aeneid" is the arc of time it covers, the burden of time it supports. After that song of Italy, of the land and the life, the genius of Virgil struck a deeper compass of reality and seized the theme at its heart. "Utter my toiling power," said Rome. The tale of the wanderings of Aeneas and how he brought the Trojan gods to Latium is only the fable; over and beyond all the character and event which it contains, and including these like an atmosphere, it is a symbol of the massive labor of the seven centuries that had for their crown and climax the pacified Augustan world.

*Tantae molis erat Romanam condere gentem.*

This massive labor, this toiling power, is the theme. It is not the Homeric world; no ten years' foray, brilliant with Greek personality, in the dawn of history; no passionate boy, though the most splendid of all Alexanders, great in his sulking wrath, his comrade-love and his battle-glory; no chieftains parleying in the council and warriors rushing in the field; not these. It is the Virgilian world — Rome at the summit of her Empire, rising from those seven centuries of interminable strain. Rome in the verse is its creative impulse, and governs the poem in its whole and in its parts. The sense of past time, too, always so strong in Virgil, is never relaxed. The "Aeneid" is the book of an old world.

Aeneas is, in his character, Rome concentrated — a man set against the world; and in him, too, is that perspective of the past. He has outlived his personal life; his city is in ashes, his wife is dead; there remains nothing for himself, only to live for others, to obey the will of the gods, devotion to a public end. He is characterized by patience which alike to the Pagan and the Christian world, to the Oriental and the Occidental mind, is the greatest virtue of man, and was the state virtue of Rome; to endure, however distant the goal, however frequent the defeat, however adverse men and fortune and the gods. The "Aeneid" is the book of victory deferred, as imperial Rome, to one looking backward on her past, was the last fruit of time, the late issue of long and perilous struggle through generations. Toil, which in the song of Italy was linked with the land, is here fused with the power of empire; but it is toil — the same Roman idea, though more informed with grandeur, and it draws with it the same rule of life, obedience, though more set forth with the stern absoluteness that belonged to Roman discipline. If Aeneas offends romantic sentiment by deserting Dido at Carthage, he conformed thereby to the Roman ideal of right in some of its deepest foundations; and even in the modern view, it may be suspected that if in place of the wing-heeled Mercury there had been some Hebrew prophet rebuking an erring David, the sympathy of the reader might run truer with the thoughts of Virgil. Rome would not tolerate the noblest of Antonys forgetting empire in passion for a woman; and Aeneas, in abandoning Dido, was the reverse of Antony, and measured to the Roman rule of life. Aeneas gains, and is truly seen, in proportion as the mind is free from the allurements of individuality, free from the worship of the ungovernable human power in life, and all that makes against the ideal of patience, obedience and rule; the grandeur of the individual is found in Mezentius and Turnus, creatures of self-will opposed to the will of heaven, and herein justly doomed to perish; if these latter seem the true heroes, it is as Satan is sometimes, and perhaps popularly, regarded as the hero of Milton, but to Milton Satan was infernal as to Virgil Turnus was impious. Aeneas stands at the opposite pole of conduct; and if he shares the defective attraction which the typical Roman character historically discloses, he the more illustrates that efficient power in life, of which the sense greatens as time clarifies the mind of the ardors of youth, whether in men or nations; for the ideal implanted in him, like every part of the poem, bears the mark of a world grown old.

The presence of Roman time in the verse, especially the sense of the sorrows that are the price of empire, is also profoundly felt in the diffusion of pathos through the poem, not the pathos of individual lives but of the general lot, which makes it the saddest book of the world.

It contains three great defeats: the destruction of Troy, the fall of Carthage, which is the atmosphere of fate in which the personal tragedy of Dido burns out on her funeral pyre, and the overthrow of Turnus; the true action is contained in these passages; and, in addition, though Aeneas is finally successful, his checks have been so many and his success is so long delayed and is so palely realized that his career, in the impression it makes, may almost count as a fourth defeat. Against this scene of disaster the majesty of Rome's final triumph in history, though it fills all the horizons of the poem, blazes in vain. Here are the tears of time. *Lacrimae rerum* seems almost the other name of the "Aeneid," as it is its best known and central phrase. The "chanter of the Pollio" had come to this. He who was the first to sound the strain of world-hope was also now the first to strike that parallel chord of world-woe which has reverberated down all after ages. The "Miserere" follows the "Gloria" as manhood follows youth. If the "Aeneid" were only a poem of heroic action, and not a symbol of life long lived, the suffering would be absorbed in the action; but the poem is heavy with thought and clouded with feeling like a sun struggling with eclipse. The intellectual force in it, the passion of thought, Virgil's overmastering sympathy with the victim — and Aeneas by his long sufferings is essentially a victim — shake its containing bounds, and again and again threaten its epical form. A thousand lines have the lyrical cry; they could, and do, stand alone, each one a poem. The dramatic power in the episode of Dido threatens to overbear the moral unity of the structure; the didactic depth of teaching in the descent to Hades threatens to intermit the sense of action and shift the scene to the academy; and at every turn, when the epic seems slipping from his hand, Virgil invokes Rome, returns to that ground-swell of his music, and fuses all disparate elements in its enveloping power. It is the thought of Ascanius and the Julian line that overrules the wrongs of Dido; and in the Elysian fields it is the encomium of Rome — the most majestic lines ever written by the hand of man — and the bead-roll of her heroes and the vision of her Augustan triumph that restore the epical interest and supremacy. It is in these ways most truly that, as Tennyson said, this "ocean-roll of rhythm sounds forever of imperial Rome."

Rome, too, sustains the verse in its weakest part, the mythology, and gives to that debilitated supernatural element the only reality which it contains. Virgil was born too late to be a true believer in Olympus; but in placing the prophecy of Rome on the lips of Jupiter and in identifying the fate of Rome with the divine purpose and will he made the mythological creed discharge a true and important function in the poem, and in fact its only function; except for this, Olympus is only a traditional adornment, a part of the mechanical scheme and surface pictorialness of the plot, and one element in that many-sided perspective of human history in which the poem is so remarkably beyond all others. If, however, Olympus is a shadow and Virgil recedes from it in his mind, on the other hand he is far advanced and moves forward in what was to Homer the shadow-world, the life beyond the grave; in his thought and sentiment there is not only the sense of profound reality, but he touches on the confines of revealed religion. Here most strikingly, in the sweep backward to the still visible but fading gods and in the sweep forward to the still unborn Christian ages, the "Aeneid" shows that characteristic of

# VIRGIL

greatness in literature which lies in its being a water-shed of time; it looks back to antiquity in all that clothes it with the past of imagination, character and event, and forward to Christian times in all that clothes it with emotion, sentiment and finality to the heart. If, as is sometimes said, Gibbon's history is the bridge between the ancient and the modern world, the "Aeneid" is the high central ridge where time itself joined both.

Virgil was so great a poet because he assimilated his vast mental experience, and turned it, in the true Roman way, to power over the future. His language itself — and he was the "lord of language" — bears the Roman stamp. Scarce any poet is so brief; like all the masters of poetic speech he seldom carries his sentence beyond three lines, and more often he clasps the sense in shorter limits, and notably in those "half-lines" which are so often spoken of as the special characteristic of his style, though they are also to be found in Shakespeare with like power. Oratory belongs to the epic as the lyric belongs to the drama, as its rhetorical means of intensity; and oratory was a Roman art. It belongs to Virgil equally with his winged music. It is the oratory of Brutus, not of Antony; and it is present in spirit and method, not only in the set speeches and narratives, but in the general flow of the verse; the weight of thought, the compactness of vision, the intensity of the lyrical cry of feeling itself, are indebted to it, for it is the native world of Roman speech, and Virgil in his song could only heighten, refine and amplify it, pour it in more lucid and tender voices of the spirit, which was none the less a Roman spirit. It is common to regard the earlier books of the "Aeneid" which are more inspired by the Greek element in Virgil's culture as the greater; but in the later books in which the inspiration of the home-land prevails more, and not less excellently in its own qualities, if the presence of Rome is less imperially impressive, it has more primitive charm. The early air of Rome is here, the youth of primeval Italy, when Empire was far away. In Mezentius and Turnus, and especially in Evander, there is an original impulse, a native stamp; and, most of all, in Camilla. Few poets cast a new type of womanhood. Camilla is the first of those ideal Italian women who have glorified the pages of Tasso and the canvasses, divine and human, of a hundred artists. If the later books of the "Aeneid" are less valued, it is partly because they are purer in originality, more Italian in their interest, and in limiting themselves to the evolution of a romantic past for the soil of Italy and the beginnings of Rome make a narrower appeal. To Virgil this task was, perhaps, dearer than the echoes of Troy and the sorrows of Carthage, but he worked with names that sounded less in the ears of the world. In one respect he succeeds marvelously; both on the voyage and in Italy he gives the sense of the early Mediterranean world as a place of wandering colonists and rising settlements in lonely places, a sense of the taking possession of the virgin land, with seas and coasts and spaces never to be crossed again; such a wonder-world did not come to man's view a second time, so effectually, till the days of Cortez and Magellan and De Soto, in the dawn of the Americas. The primitive time, such as it is shown in Evander, has the same reality, and his hospitality has retained in men's minds its place as the historic and ideal moment of the simplicities of the first life of men on still unviolated soil. If one's eye is on the Roman spirit of the poem, he will not find the Italian prepossession of its last books an obstacle to his interest; but rather the charm of a more home-bred inspiration will endear to him its humilities, its native character and the nobility of human feeling which is nowhere in the poem so constant, pervasive and pure. If Rome is less, in these passages, in her imperial form, Italy is more; and it is that Italy in which the true Rome resided and to which she returned, of which the Empire itself now seems a planet she cast from her larger and more immortal life.

The poem of Rome, however, even though such a nation as Italy fall heir to it, could not maintain its intimacy with the modern mind and continue to make a direct appeal to life, unless it were something more. There is a greatness in the "Aeneid" beyond the presence of Rome in the verse. It might seem that Virgil was by nature little fitted for the epic; his initiation into life had been through that "passive youth" which Shelley describes, the type of poetic boyhood, sensitive, impressible, inexhaustibly recipient; and all his days he was a scholar drawing into his brooding thoughts the spectacle of things till his knowledge was equal to the world-culture of his time; that such a man should give back to the world what he had received from it in the shape of a poem of action seems incongruous, and, doubtless, like Tasso and Milton and Spenser and Tennyson, in their several degrees, he experienced the natural difficulties of the task. Yet, to the brooding spirit, not thought, but action is the true sphinx of life; not what is dreamed or reasoned or desired, but what is done, what God permits, as the phrase goes, the power of unrighteousness that is nine-tenths of life; this fastens the eye, perplexes the mind, disturbs the heart. Virgil, born late and acquainted with the world long lived in, was of a contemplative mind; in the "Aeneid" thought shadows every word, a subtle judgment blends with every action clothing it, as music clothes the line, in an element of its own, pitying, appealing, affirming, according to the motions of the poet's soul; and hence the "Aeneid" has its grandest phase, by virtue of which it has entered into the hearts of so many later generations and still enters. It is a meditation upon life.

The modes in which the poem thus affects the reader are infinitely varied; sometimes so intimate as to seem the voice in one's own heart of one's own life, or so lofty and assured as to seem the voice of all men's hearts, or so world-sweeping in its pathos as to seem the voice divine. Unbroken is the sense of the difficulty of life, not merely under its old conception as a warfare, but as a thing of burden, of frequent mistake, of unforeseen and unmerited disaster, of repeated defeat, of uncertain issue; the toiling power of Rome is made up of the innumerable toils of miserable men, and about the main actors are the files of captive women, the sons burning on their funeral pyres before the faces of their parents, all the wretchedness of a military state for the private life. The element of difficulty felt in the reverses of the main fortune of the tale, in its birth in the terrors of the last night of Ilium, in the wrong landings, the insidious dangers of Carthage, the burning of the fleet, is, on the individual scale broken into a thousand cries of death and sorrow essentially personal and domestic. Life on land and sea is a field of battle, and everywhere are corpses rolled by Simois or the ocean-wave, and in every prospect the heart follows the remnant of men, in their beaten courage ever more courageous, but none the less victims of life. "Pain, pain, ever, forever," rings through the poem like a Promethean cry; the burden of Priam, the burden of Dido, the burden of Turnus, kingdom after kingdom, and by the way the strewn corpses of Palinurus, Euryalus, Pallas. In the Elysian fields Aeneas marvels why any soul should desire to see the light of life. Over all there hangs in heaven the doubtful interest of the gods in human fates. "If any gods be just" — "if there be any kindness in heaven" — these are the refrains of all the prayers. In the presence of the mystery of what is done on earth the reason, always unsatisfied, will not be silent and refuses to yield its just share in the conduct of life; if, in one age, the tale be of Eden and the Fall, this offends the mind's sense of justice; if, in another time, it be of the struggle for existence from the dawn of life, this offends the mind's sense of mercy; in knowledge of justice and mercy, the mind finds its own superiority to the environment in which it is imprisoned, and in its moods of sincerest reason still seeks refuge in the provisional prayer on Virgil's lips.

Lucretius had lived; and something of all this difficulty, pain and uncertainty had come to light in that great intellect. He was essentially one of the eternal Puritan brood, personal revolters against church and state, which in history have been the twin tyrants of mankind; he looked back on the past and saw there immense and long-continued error in important parts of life, the delusion and woe of whole peoples since time began; and he denounced superstition as the mother of human ills. He was an individualist, a man of conscious virtue, self-sufficing; he had an empire in his mind; he spoke out, a lonely intellect in a world stripped for his eyes to the bare principles of its being and in his words was the fiery seed of the new universe of scientific thought. Virgil was of a different strain, a natural worshiper, reverent of the rite, attached to the myth, clinging with his affections to the outward garniture of life and history; but his eyes were on the same things that Lucretius saw. He, too, was finding in philosophy the true goal. He felt from youth the compelling power of thought of Rome's greatest mind as he looked out on the long Pagan retrospect of life's beauty and sorrow. How did he save himself from the intellectual indignation, the despair of the divine, the earthly pessimism of Rome's great sceptic; for the face of Virgil, "majestic in his sadness at the doubtful doom of human kind," is the grave face of a believer. He saved himself by the power of love.

He was a lover of life; only an immense love of life could have so revealed to him the pity of it. At every touch he shows a spirit naturally dependent; teachable, yielding, hospitable, responsive, sympathetic, appealing, his heart flows out upon things, uniting with them at every contact, from his early loves of nature, romance and antiquity, his long passion of patriotism, on to his brooding over the fates of men; and yet with his self-surrender to the things of life there goes, equal with it, the true Roman self-control; it is a surrender that returns to him as strength. At every turn of the verse he evokes the moment of beauty from the natural world, and from life its moment of pain, with the clarity of the poet; charm, which is the one, and pathos, which is the other, are the words that leap from the heart in the memory of what he wrote, and after these the third is majesty, which is the principle of control in him, and completes and perfects his genius. These are wonderfully softened by his constant tenderness. The epics generally find no

place for children in them; but here there are three —
Astyanax, Ascanius and Marcellus — and two of these
are dead boys. Of all Virgil's loves, the greatest in power
is the love of human life; and it is this that makes the
poem so Christian-like, because it is embodied and con-
veyed in the forms of sorrow and especially of bereave-
ment. Yet the burden of that sorrow comes as the
burden of the Roman world running its long career of
battle-strife; here is the heart of Rome beating in the
only Roman breast in which it had become fully conscious
of itself. The world was ready to be re-born; there is no
break; the premonitions of Christian feeling are natural
to Virgil. It is this that makes him of all ancient writers
the nearest to modern times, of all epic poets the nearest
to all nations. The "Aeneid" is, I think, the greatest
single book written by man because of its inclusiveness
of human life, of life long lived, in the things of life. It is
the dirge of Rome; majestic in its theme, beautiful in its
emotions, sad in its philosophy, it is almost the dirge of
life; yet many a modern mind still turns from the contemplation of human life in history, like the thousands
of old days, to Virgil, and says with Dante, *Tu se' lo mio
maestro,* "Thou art my master."

# MONTAIGNE

Montaigne was one of the great confessors of life. The confession is a paradox; for he reveals himself, and it is the reader who stands revealed. A personal writer, whose whole story is about himself, as he says, matters of his own career, opinions, anecdotes, trivialities of the daily life, a diary of privacies; yet throughout it is not he who is interesting, but that human nature of which he is the showman. His work is not to represent life, as the novelist does in fiction, but to illustrate it by his own example. The fortune of those who have been drawn to him, now for three centuries, is identical; they all claim a share in his individuality. Emerson says of that copy he found in his father's library: "It seemed to me as if I had myself written the book, in some former life, so sincerely it spoke to my thought and experience." Byron heard the same personal tone in it. Not all of Emerson is there, not all of Byron; there are neither heights nor depths of the soul in the book; but human nature in the norm of its range, in its middle flight, in its average of the gentleman, a little knowledge, a little morals, a little religion, with much moderation and good sense — these are there, exemplifying the practical life of the great and small in the world in which Montaigne lived and in which his admirers have lived after him. In the practice of life that the world wills, Montaigne is a master; he is its moralist; the "Essays" contain its rule and counsels, and are vivaciously varied by the gossipy interwoven tale of his adventures, body and soul.

Montaigne, nevertheless, had in his own right the figure that arrests the eye and traits that jet from the memory in high relief. One thinks of him commonly in connection with his famous tower, the great Tour de Montaigne, that overhangs the entrance of the château, round, dungeon-like, massive, in the uppermost of whose three stories is the circular room, spacious, with its rafters on which were cut inscriptions, the author's mottoes of life, and its deep embrasured windows through which he looked out to three parts of heaven, on the garden, farm-yard and court, and over the sloping estates to the distant Perigord hills; here was his library, and Montaigne is thought of here, in retirement, like a solitary surveying the world. But this is a fantastic conception. He was in reality a man of affairs all his life; he had the mind of a man of affairs, with something superadded. The best inheritance he drew from his father, an active, capable, successful man, was the athletic vigor and business capacity that did him yeoman service in that age when both were needed to keep one's feet in the world about; but to his father he also owed that added something — he owed a careful education. The elder Montaigne, though not learned, was the friend of scholars, and experienced that new interest in the intellectual life which in his day was molding France as the Renaissance spread to the northwest out of Italy; it was a movement that dealt much with education and favored originality, experiment, eccentricity even; and it was, perhaps, by the touch of Italian conversation and ideas that the father determined that the son should be brought up with Latin for his mother tongue. He had already put the boy to nurse in the country with poor people, in order that he might have his mind and sympathy open to the life of the humble, and so contract a lively feeling of their condition; and now he secured proper instruction, a learned German who taught the child to speak in Latin from his earliest accents, while all who came in contact with him were compelled to conform to the rule, even the servants, so that this chatter, it is said, left traces in the country speech. The boy felt and talked in Latin till he was six years old, and later in life French was so much less natural to him that in moments of deep excitement the instinctive words in his brain were Latin. He was bred at college from six to thirteen, immediately put to the law, and made counsellor at twenty-one, in which capacity three years later he became one of the Parliament of Bordeaux, the city that throughout his life was the stage of his public actions and of which his father was mayor. The family by its integrity, kindness and energy, had long held a well-established place in the province. On his father's death, Montaigne who had married some five years before became its head. The inscription which records his accession may still be read at the château, as follows:

"In the year of our Lord 1571, aged thirty-eight, on the eve of the Kalends of March, the anniversary day of his birth, Michel de Montaigne, having long been weary of the slavery of courts and public employments, takes refuge in the bosom of the learned Virgins. He designs in quiet and indifference to all things, to conclude there the remainder of his life, already more than half-past, and he has dedicated to repose and liberty this agreeable and peaceful abode, which he has inherited from his ancestors."

When Montaigne thus sought the private life in the middle of his years, he had already lived a full and active career in a station of moderate distinction which had brought him in contact with various aspects of the human lot. He knew the life of the court and had led it at Paris and elsewhere with a young man's interest, with gallant adventures, with gaming and episodes and debauch, and on all sides he had formed ties with persons of power. He knew the life of the camp, and had followed it, as the custom was, at sieges and on marches to which a young man of his position would go at his will and come away at his choice. He knew the life of administrative affairs to which his post in the Parliament obliged him and by which he was brought into serious concerns affecting his locality and the interests of his faith and country. He had taken no leading part, but he had observed human life in many ways, and he had learned to keep his balance in a difficult age. He was a firm Catholic and loyalist, but he had the art of remaining on good terms with all parties, and in his own country which was in the disturbed region he suffered but little in the religious and civil dissensions that distracted and oppressed the times with the changing fortunes of Henry of Navarre. He was that marvel of the moral life, a man of integrity who is a master of compromise.

An entirely different phase is revealed in the only incident of distinction that marked his early years. This was his friendship with Estienne de la Boëtie, a fellow-counsellor in the Parliament of Bordeaux, famous as the youthful author of the most eloquent attack ever made upon the institution of Monarchy, which though then circulated was not published for many years, and known also as a poet. The two young men were of about the same age, and their friendship, which was meant by themselves to restore the classical example to the world, was terminated after six years by La Boëtie's early death. This attachment is one of the legends of literature, and in it Montaigne showed most heart beyond any other action of his life. He idolized it after the ancient model in his essay on "Friendship"; he wrote a minute account of the death-bed scenes, with the classical touch, but real; and his references to his loss are among the few passages of his writings that have poignancy. His first task when he became master of himself in the world was to edit such of his friend's papers as it seemed discreet to publish, but he reserved the immortal essay on "Monarchy" for less turbulent times and the next age. It was not in his character to find in his pious duties to the dead a legacy of unrest that might disturb the years which he had dedicated to "repose and liberty."

Montaigne's retirement was by no means absolute. Throughout the score of years that it lasted before death carried him off at the edge of sixty, he kept in touch with the business of this world; and his privacy was especially broken by two events, his travels into Italy and his incumbency of the mayoralty of Bordeaux. The Italian journey, which took place after eight years of labor on the "Essays" and when he was forty-seven years old, was primarily undertaken on the score of health since he had become subject to the stone, and he may also have desired to observe the effect of the first publication of his work, then just issued, on his reputation. He saw Paris, assisted at a siege, and made his way by Baden and the Tyrol to Venice, and thence to the chief cities of northern and central Italy, visiting the baths and taking the waters by the way. He was an excellent traveller. He rode on horseback, a habit which he greatly enjoyed, with a sufficient but not too expensive suite, in the style befitting a

French gentleman of his rank; and he took pains to live in the country according to its own customs, to mix with its people and lay aside his native prejudices, to get the full benefit of travel by means of a lively curiosity, an open mind and a hospitable manner. He was bound by no rule or plan, but zigzagged along according to his mood, doubling on his track or deviating from it as the fancy took him; and in all places he conformed and gave way and reaped his harvest of experience and observation. Social tact distinguished him. He got on with the papal critics of the "Index," who handled his "Essays" with some doubtfulness, just as he had done with Henry of Navarre, and they left him to make his own emendations. He gave a dance for the country girls at the Baths of Lucca. He made friends everywhere. In spite of acute attacks of illness, with discomfort and wearing pain, he maintained an even and settled demeanor, and thoroughly enjoyed the new scenes, the honorable entertainment and the variety of life and manners. The note-book which constitutes his Travels reveals the man as plainly and more simply than the "Essays." Posterity remembers out of it two things, the eloquent description of the ruins of Rome, and the offering which he was solicitous to hang up at Loretto — "a framed tablet with four silver figures attached, representing our Lady, myself, my wife and my daughter."

He spent a year and a half in this journey, and it was still unfinished when he received news of his election to the mayoralty of Bordeaux. He made his return without haste, and as soon as he had arrived told them, he says, "what they had to expect of me — no memory, no vigilance, no experience, no vigor; but also no hatred, no ambition, no avarice, and no violence." It was an excellent program that was thus promised in the distressed situation of affairs, and the character of Montaigne for justice, moderate temper and tact must have much commended him in that time and place; he pleased well enough to receive the unusual distinction of a re-election, and thus served for four years. It was characteristic of his career that he entertained Henry of Navarre at his château in the last year of his term, and that, a pestilence desolating the country at its conclusion, he declined to return to the stricken city to preside at his successor's election. He was an expert avoider of risks. He was careful to leave his château undefended in order not to invite attack, and this device succeeded; but he owed his extraordinary immunity from the ravage and insult of either party to his character and manners. Once when a hostile company had entered the château by a kind of stealth, Montaigne's hospitable good nature carried the matter so well that the leader took his party off without sign of the injury that had been intended; and once when Montaigne was stopped on the road and robbed, his bold spirit and fair temper so told in his favor that he was released and warned of other danger by the captain of the band. He was not deficient in courage, but what carried him through in so many difficult and delicate situations was his knowledge of men and his open appearance, his mastery of social intercourse. He had none of the traits of a recluse; he was more a soldier and a man of pleasure, used to the business of life, sincere, honest, moderate, and above all adroit. In his travels, his office, his adventures of whatever kind, he has the stamp of the man who lives, who knows how to take and give in a real world, and to whom living is more primary than thinking — in other words, the man of action.

Montaigne, the writer, none the less, was formed by his education. Education had an equal importance with life in stamping that image of personality. It was a classical education, but he did not get it at school. The college where he was bred in his boyhood years was one of the most distinguished in France, but it was one of those hells which civilization has imposed on the suffering youth of most generations. Montaigne tells us how he slipped away from his routine tasks and read by stealth his Ovid and Virgil and found his true world there. He gave his education to himself by reading in his manhood. The important books were of course the ancients. The Latin authors he read in their own tongue in which he was well grounded, and the Greek authors for the most part in the translations then made by the French humanists; and, generally speaking, he knew the Greek authors later than the Latin, and especially Plato came to him toward the close of his life. He was essentially a pupil of Plutarch, a sort of man who has become in our culture extinct but in the sixteenth century flourished in the new lands of the Renaissance; and especially he was an intellectual child of Plutarch, the moralist. When poetry began to grow shallow in interest to Montaigne, as it belonged to his nature that it should, history and biography became the food of his serious thought. They appealed to him because they illustrate life; and it was life that Montaigne held as the center of his meditation always — not life in its principles, but rather life as it is lived, the scene of life. For example, he says that he always had great curiosity to know how men died, and would eagerly inquire for all the details. Plutarch in his various writings gives immense illustration of life thus viewed in all its aspects, and with it a wealth of apposite reflection on human nature and the fortunes of men. The conduct of life broadly speaking is his theme, as it became Montaigne's. To all such knowledge out of antiquity Montaigne added the memoirs and narratives of the recent world. He applied this to his own ends. To him all these facts of life were not an affair of learning, not information, gossip, but means by which he came to a better understanding of human nature, or, as he said, of himself. His proper study, he affirmed, was only himself. The power of his education consisted in the vital connection he made through it between himself and the story of men's lives as he picked up its multitude of fragments in the biographical and historical records of past times. For principles of conduct, for maxim and apothegm, he fell back on Seneca, and with all the discursive philosophy of the later ancient world he was in touch; but he became a moralist because he was primarily an observer, and he was always more interested in the premises than in the conclusions of his thoughts, more absorbed in the curious spectacle of human phenomena than in the laws of human nature. He had an immense interest in things human, and this gave him the secret of originality. "I am human," he said. "I am immensely interesting to myself, I will write about myself." The "Essays" were thus engendered. This directness of Montaigne belongs to the man, to his vital energy. He had been formed by life, it is true; but in his mind, the mind of a man of affairs, there was, as I have said, something superadded; it was a meditative habit. There was, however, nothing of the closet in it, nothing of the abstract and logical, the speculative for its own sake; it was a thing of experience, empirical. The intellectual part of his book is a meditation upon life as something observed, recorded, practised;

the vivid reality of the book, which makes it seem often written by the reader, springs from this. A man of affairs, in his ripeness, meditating upon the business of living, with cogency, with brilliancy, with unexampled frankness — this was what life and education combined to make of Montaigne; and the "Essays" are the mind of such a man.

Montaigne was a born man of letters, but like many men so born he did not think of making the career. His father's house was a place of books, of scholars and the intellectual ferment of the age; he had been trained by men of learning and had mingled with the poets of the times; but he showed no early disposition to write a book. There was no adolescence in his genius. For learning he had the characteristic literary contempt. The first requisite for any career for him was that it should be a life. Montaigne had that secret, which has so often developed the highest literary faculty, the power to absorb life into himself directly, to let life have its way with him as an experience, and yet to maintain in the midst of it complete possession of himself, to lead his own life. He established terms with his environment. With that facility which seems rather a characteristic of southern than of northern peoples, he accepted the social fictions with all solemnity. He was a true Catholic in faith; and the truth revealed through the church, with the observance of its attendant and customary ritual, as things beyond the pale of what is merely human — this was accepted as being imposed by his baptism; he conformed, and did so with apparent sincerity. He was a true loyalist, and the system of state, with its ritual also, was accepted as being imposed by his birth in the country and under the crown; he conformed in secular as in religious matters to things established. But this being settled, he remained the master of himself in both thought and action, the man of his own choice. He was by temperament Epicurean, given to an indulgent habit of pleasure, with the wisdom of the moderates; yet his character was of a more vigorous stock than such words imply; he was hardy and sufficiently energetic. Indeed there was in his spirit a nobler capacity, a movement toward enthusiasm even, and a power of admiration that is most often found in alliance with more active and ardent ambition than belonged to his nature. The Stoical precepts awakened a glow in him, the personality of Socrates seized him with the fervor of hero-worship, Cicero disturbed him by his weaknesses. But this strength, this latent passion, this capacity to be morally great never reached the kindling point. One is aware of it by its heat, but never by its flame. He had dedicated himself to repose as well as to liberty; he would pass life agreeably — that was the main thing. He was active intellectually rather than morally; his curiosity was unlimited, and what it brought him was the food of untiring and discursive reflection; but, before all, he was a moralist in the scientific spirit of exploration, and not at all in the proselytizing spirit of the believer.

He discovered himself as a writer almost, it would seem, by one of those accidents of life which are also not uncommon in the history of literature. He was not an author, and apparently had no thought of being one, when his father put into his hands a book which he asked him to translate. It was a theological work of the times of the Reformation, a "Natural Theology" by Raymond de Sebonde, written in a curious sort of Spanish with Latin terminations and left at the château by one of the elder Montaigne's scholarly visitors, an attempt to show the truth of religion on grounds of human reason independent of revelation. Montaigne translated this work, and it was afterward published. Later he was led to compose an apology or defense of it, a paper included in his "Essays" and the longest of them. In the meditation of this important piece and in writing out his thoughts Montaigne seems to have found himself intellectually; and it may fairly be said that the various matter of the famous "Essays" flowed from the author of the "Apology" as truly as Scott's Novels proceeded in their long sequence from "the Author of Waverley." The conjunction of the two names is suggestive; for, at not far from the same mature period of manhood as Scott began his career in fiction, and from a similar foundation of life that had practically fed his genius unintermittently in the moral sphere by affairs and books, Montaigne like Scott at the moment of "Waverley" was at the moment of his apology for Raymond de Sebonde at the point of ignition; he had been prepared by temperament, experience and studies, in a purely practical way, without literary premeditation, to become the great moralist of life that the "Essays" revealed. Montaigne, like Scott and Cervantes, was the product of life, in which studies, it is true, were a large element, but of which reality was the substance and vigor; his book is consequently one of those greatest books in which life is supreme. The center of it is Montaigne himself, because that was the point where for him life converged all its forces; and hence, too, it is often and habitually a book of apparent egotisms, of trivialities, of confidences, as of a man talking with a friend and of a friend, with the frankness of privacy; but this personality which is the center of Montaigne' world is also the center of all of us, it is human nature, it is ourselves. In this book life is so supreme that the reader himself lives in it.

Montaigne's subject which he unfolds in the "Essays" is the scene of life, that existence of which "all the world's a stage." He does not do this by the methods of the imagination, as the poet and novelist do. He brings to the task observation, history, biography, all that experience has given him from his personal career or that he had drawn from recent times, and in addition the great bulk of recorded life that the philosophers and essayists and historians of antiquity had gathered, a mass of detail that was as modern to him as the facts of journalism. This great body of real experience and moral reflection upon it which man had accumulated at the end of the classical civilization had been displaced by the Christian ages, but in Montaigne's day it flowed back upon men's minds through the channels of the Renaissance; and it has now again been displaced by the insurgence of the modern ages of colonization, industrialism, mechanical science, and in its stead we have a different history and other biographies and travels which have not yet developed that finality as an accumulated result of long living which belongs to antiquity. Montaigne thus stands, as it were, in the Renaissance gap between the Christian and modern ages, and surveys life "looking before and after," by the undying lamp that he had found in the Roman tomb. He has placed Christianity on one side, and, having made his peace with it, it troubles him no more; he has hung up the votive images in the shrine of Loretto, and will die when the time comes in the proper odors and acts; but merely as the reasoning animal that is earthly man he will examine human nature without regard to its spiritual part which is a thing whose habitat is the church. Human nature, so considered, is the same that it was in classical times and is perhaps there more simply observed because of the absence of any entanglement with revealed truth. Montaigne thus, though he did not live in the past, lived, in a sense, in the thoughts of the past, and hence one feels in the "Essays" a certain breath of remoteness at times, a certain mustiness of thought. The idea of death, for example, was a fixed idea of ancient moralists; and Montaigne is much concerned with it, as if it were as important for him as for Cato and Seneca, as if he were under the same need of Stoical rather than Christian preparation for it, more as a mortal end than an immortal beginning. This idea is, no doubt, part of his literary legacy; he could not avoid prepossession with it, his authors being what they were; but its importance in his reflection indicates a pre-Christian mood in his mind, marks the infection of his paganism, discloses the intellectual and moral atavism which was imbedded in the Renaissance. The Stoical insistence on the idea of death is the trait of a dying culture; it could not fill the mind of a Christian in that antique way unless he were already detached in soul from the lessons of his own faith to some degree. In Montaigne this interest, except in so far as it was purely literary, marks a reversion to a past type of intellect, a dislocation from his age which assimilates him with the great world-minds independent of their origin from any particular age; in fact, while seeming a mere reversion mentally, it signifies really his modern enfranchisement. Such an escape into the past was the way to a cosmopolitan point of view.

This cosmopolitan habit was, in fact, Montaigne's distinction. What an excellent traveler he was is seen in his account of the Italian journey; but he was a better traveler in his mind. (An enlightened spirit, a mind hospitable to new things, a marvelous power of detaching himself from his own heredity and civilization belonged to him; his mind was not repelled, but freshened by novelty and strangeness.) In the reports of travelers from the Perus and the Indias he sought out manners and customs, the differences from what was established in European habits and ideas; he was interested in what these savages and pagans had made of themselves in their own worlds apart. The page of antiquity, too, in which his curiosity was so much absorbed, held a broad and various world, the old Mediterranean civilization of many races, institutions, religions, thoughts, careers. This past in all its diversity was, too, it must be remembered, far better known to him than the middle ages or even his own times of which the human story had not yet been spread in books in anything like the same degree. His world of intelligence was substantially the classical world; there were the things he knew, his intellectual interests, his dominant mental memories. When he was made, during his Italian residence, a citizen of Rome, an honor that gave him so much delight, no one living better deserved the title; for he was truly a citizen of that eternal Rome which endures in the mind of man. Indeed, he had something of what may be called a colonial dependence on the life of antiquity, and his outlook and feeling toward Rome and Athens were not unlike the attitude of the scholars of New England toward London and Paris in the last century. He was more at home there than in his own age; his outward life and action were in his own neighborhood, in the religious and civil strife of a province with which he made terms for the day and the hour, but the

life of his mind was in the company of the antique world
and its affairs. He naturally fell into the philosophic
attitude which prevailed in that exhausted paganism; and
from the survey of the scene of life familiar to him out
of that Greco-Roman past and under the guidance of
Roman thought that gave his mind direction, he gathered
that general impression of the feebleness of man's nature
which kept on deepening with years until it became the
master theme of his matter, and made the famous "What
do I know" the legend of his shield in literature.

This impeachment of man's faculty for knowledge
was nothing new. It was made up of a résumé of the rags
and scraps of those old sceptics in whom the intellect,
which had awakened in Greece and had a long career,
found its first disillusionment in the pursuit of truth. It
had a curious place in Montaigne's day as being the
complement of the idea of the necessity of revealed truth
miraculously made known to the race; but it was not in
that aspect that Montaigne cared for it. The feebleness
of man's natural faculty for truth fell in with Montaigne's
general convictions with regard to human nature; it harmonized
with the Epicurean ease of his temperament.
The idea of sex, to approach his philosophy in another
way, was a cardinal interest in his mind. He makes his
confessions with equal frankness and discretion, but with
unconcealed thought. He brings no imagination, no romance
to bear upon the matter; he is scientific, naturalistic,
and unashamed. As the higher spirituality, which
he leaves to the Church, is absent from his philosophy, the
higher ethics is absent from his morality. To live with
ease in this world involves concessions to established
conditions; and as Montaigne conceded to the Church and
the State, he conceded also to nature, and was seemingly

no more aware of any conflict in one case than in another; this, it seemed to him, was good sense, the quality in which, in the judgment of his readers, Montaigne is more eminent than any other writer. And, in truth, viewing the scene of human life in its action and its thinking, apart from any divine element, as the stage of the world where man is only man, and seeking its examples in the confusions of his own age and in the retrospect of decadent and expiring Rome, Montaigne has within these limits a singular gift for reasonableness, for setting forth the life that the world wills, for good sense. The weakness of human nature, whether knowing or acting, being accepted as primary there remains for Montaigne only the question of an easy adjustment thereto, of a search for "repose and liberty"; and such good sense is the key.

In the discursive setting forth of human life and nature under these lights Montaigne developed one great virtue, toleration. It isolates him in that age, and does him honor forever. A conviction of the futility of human faculties in the pursuit of truth carries with it the sense of uncertainty in doctrines and induces a mood of indifferency toward all tenets, whereby the habit of toleration becomes natural; and, in addition, familiarity with the diversity of human opinion and of moral practice, that has filled the world both in antiquity and among the newly-found regions of the earth gave him the poise and freedom of the traveled mind, of the man acquainted with men and cities, of the man detached from the slavery of one environment. A classical education had exercised on Montaigne one of its great freeing powers; it had made him familiar with a civilization, not specifically and theologically Christian, but of an overawing type; it had redressed the balance of ecclesiastical prejudice, and restored the secular life to its due proportions as a thing of this world, of reason and of nature, apart from revelation. In Montaigne's case, indeed, life had become essentially a purely secular affair, and he considered it as a moralist quite as if he had been born in the fourth century and remained unconverted. Toleration was the natural habit of a mind so bred, and so capable of entering into another age. It may have been grounded, if one examines the matter curiously, rather on a kindly philosophical contempt of human nature than on the doctrine that the way to truth lies through the conflicts of an untrammeled liberty of thought and speech; it may not have been the toleration of a free government, such as is now conceived; but in the days of the religious wars and at the end of the sixteenth century in France, it was the mark of a singularly enlightened spirit. The spectacle of France at that time, and the personal experience of Montaigne who had friends on both sides of the struggling factions, no doubt aided him, by virtue of his repugnance to the folly and turmoil of the scene, to establish the principle in himself; but it also belonged to his conciliating and compromising temperament, to his power of facilitating life, to his classically bred intelligence, and to his native kindliness. Toleration was in him a human instinct, strongly supported by his knowledge and experience and approved by his judgment, and not merely a conclusion of philosophy or principle of government. He was as singular, too, for his hatred of cruelty. What he has to say of torture in legal processes, of the imposition of cruel punishments, of public executions and the like matters, also marks him out in the age. He was one of those who had become humane as well as reasonable in his converse with that antiquity which was then infusing secular vigor into the blood of the world as an antidote to the ecclesiastical poisons that had long corrupted free human nature. Yet in his "Essays" there is one singular silence. He does not mention nor even allude to the massacre of St. Bartholomew, which was one of the great events of his lifetime, and by which he must have been deeply moved. It is an indication of his good sense. His retirement, after all, was indeed profound intellectually, in the great round Tour de Montaigne, by the Perigord hills; there he freely speculated and gossiped in his learned way in the still air of delightful studies; but practically when in the midst of state-affairs, and there was question of publishing his friend La Boëtie's attack on "Monarchy" or of a St. Bartholomew's Day, he kept a close mouth. This sense of contradiction between the intellectual and the practical life is necessarily felt in Montaigne; it affects the sincerity of the man, for many readers; but it belongs to the psychology of the conformist in every age. Montaigne has lived by his thought rather than by his life, and by his privacy rather than by his publicity; yet thought and life with him moved with singular intimacy and equality; and as his career, despite its prudencies, will be held manly, energetic, honorable and above all wise, so his thought, despite its reticencies — and they are many and serious — will be held bold, free, advancing and again above all wise. Repose and liberty, could he compass and reconcile them, were a possession worth many practical compromises.

Montaigne's name, for mankind, is that of the great doubter. The modern spirit, in this one great phase of its manifestation, may be said to begin with him, in literature. He was not aware of the career that this scepticism was to run, of the deep reach and radiations of its undermining power in later days, agnostic and pessimistic, as far as to the base of life itself. He did not question the worth of life; he had found life a pleasant thing; but he certainly doubted the worth of the higher life. He repeatedly expresses the doubt that the exercise of the higher faculties interferes with the pleasurable good of life and introduces a disturbing element injurious to human happiness. He makes that interrogation of civilization, in developing which Rousseau found him so fruitful a master. Montaigne, merely as a conformist, has eliminated much from life; and his temperament led him along that path to a general elimination of the nobler faculties, the superior aims, the dangerous toils of the ideal, which he knew rather by observation, seeing what trouble these things brought upon the private life and public tranquillity; and in his view of the world, the life of nature, whether individually seen in the poor and humble or collectively in the newly-found savages, seemed possibly preferable to the type of civilization. Perfectibility was an idea that he did not know. Repose and liberty were the ends of life for him and weakness its condition; not to impose too great a burden, not to accept too heavy a yoke, not to open too distant a scope, not to propose too far a goal, rather to avoid the heights, this was wisdom. It is the philosophy of one who places happiness in recognition of the limitations rather than in cultivation of the energies of life; to enjoy life it is most needful not to overestimate its worth. Such a scheme, so little exacting of force, is naturally crowned by the virtues of ease, by moderation, reasonableness, good-sense, the virtues of Montaigne.

He was at one with his theory; he is its illustration,

and after all it is himself and not his theory that is interesting. The page grows antiquated and dull with outworn knowledge in proportion as the theory occupies it, tatters of the past in science, thought and scandal; but it grows vivid and contemporary as soon as he puts himself into the sentences. For him he is himself the model of life; the human nature that he exhibits with such vivacity is that with which he has grown acquainted in his own bosom. He tells piecemeal in the rambling method of the "Essays" all the story of himself, his birth, education and career, what has happened to him, what he has done, his tastes and habits, the secrets of his meals and his toilet, the course of his disease, the most trivial, the most dubious, the most private matters; he makes the world the familiar of his person, of his mortal being, of his quality of man. This intimacy which he ingenuously allows, as a thing the most natural to him in the world, wins credence for his sincerity in his intellectual confessions, in his examination of his thoughts and impressions, in his remarks on the ways of the world that he lived in; and this sincerity has the appearance of being absolute. It gives to his thought that quality of echo, which makes it seem the whisper of one's own experience, the utterance of one's own unframed words. Montaigne ingratiates himself in the bosom of the reader by a thousand ways, but by none more than by this of being his spokesman; it is pleasant to confess by proxy, to let another tell those truths of which human nature, in its tacitness, is half-ashamed, expose those half-lies which it is reluctant to acknowledge but of which it is aware; and it is pleasant to find the philosophy of the pleasurable, the unexigent, the not too serious, stated with so much unconcern, and to feel the compromises of life take on an aspect of such reasonableness. It is in these things that the personality of Montaigne is so attractive; in the Epicurean, the Sadducean moments of life, in its average actuality of living among people of the world, he is good company; the doubt in his mind has great pardoning power, and may contain indeed a general amnesty for life.

In a temperament such as Montaigne shows in his career, his thought and his personality there is defined a universal type of man, a constant mood of the human mind, a spirit of life speaking intelligible words to men in every reflective age. It is of the fourth century or the sixteenth or the twentieth indifferently. Its reality was never more vital than in Montaigne, its words never more vivid than here; he is by far its best incarnation. The time was ripe for a lukewarm gospel; the long triumph of fanaticism was waning in its last fierce excesses; the hour of the moderates had come. After ages of dogmatism, his unconcerned "What do I know," is the voice of a new world; after centuries of spiritual strain, in in every form of fervor and travesty, his radical acceptance of this world as man's proper sphere to which he should adapt himself is a welcome relaxation; after the torture, assassination and massacre, the turmoil of sect and feud, the misery of warring faiths, his sceptical toleration is a truce of reason that men might be glad to have on any terms. In his works it may seem hard to discern the morning lights; but, as happens in great books, the past and future blend there with long rays. The conjunction of his acutely alive mind with the matter of antiquity often strikes the reader as a union of the quick with the dead; but that is an illusion due to our own relaxed hold on the classical authors. He found the lettered ages of Rome and Athens more modern than any intervening century, nearer to him than his own times, superior to them; and so it came about that his book involves a great span of time, and remembers Socrates as it foreshadows Rousseau. In the midst of all this precept out of Seneca and anecdotes of the philosophers' lives, there is a constant cropping out of the great modern traits — the free exercise of reason, the appeal to nature, the restless curiosity, the plea for toleration and humaneness, the interest in education, the disposition to examine all things anew and bring them to the test of practical reality, to think out the world afresh. Montaigne's modernity is clouded, too, no doubt, not only by his antiquarianism, but by his attitude of ease toward life. It seems incongruous that one who was so little a reformer as he should be counted among the leaders of a new age; but if he did not proselytize for a cause, he exemplified what is the best and profoundest of all reforms, a reform in the habit of thinking; he thought for himself. He was great in independence of mind; whatever he thought, it was his own. He was great, too, in force of character; whatever he did was his own. He was, as has been said, the man of his own choice. Individuality such as this is an undying ideal; it is superlatively modern; and Montaigne is thus a great type of the modern man, primarily in the conduct of his mind, and perhaps also more truly than would readily be confessed, in the conduct of his life. He was not a weakling, though his philosophy may easily be mistaken for that of a weakling. Justly interpreted, do not his concessions, compromises, reticences show strength of judgment, strength of good sense, prudence, which in practical life often avail quite as much as strength of mere opinion? Nor was truth, of itself, a large part of life for Montaigne; it was at best an uncertainty. He was not a martyr of ideas, but he was a man of ideas. He spent several years in collecting, digesting, and illustrating these ideas in the book, continually adding something to the earlier forms, and left there this portrait of himself, body and spirit. The terms on which he stands with his reader are those of friendship, and for friendship a man must be born; and it must be acknowledged that not all men are born for friendship with such a one as he describes himself. There are many who echo Clough's words — "I do not greatly think about Montaigne;" and Clough was classical, sceptical, modern, but he was serious-minded. Montaigne is not an author for serious-minded people, in that sense. He has too great detachment of mind, too great insouciance of conduct; he is in all senses too free a man.

It might seem that a book which is described as a confession of life, and one in which human nature finds itself absolved in the very bosom of the reader, is just such a one as should appeal to grave persons. But Montaigne has not the proper manner of the confessional; he is garrulous, not truly penitent, but rather scandalously interested in his own story; the confession of man's nature has quite as much the character of an exposure of life. Certainly it is a book of the disillusionment. It implies immense experience of living, of life long lived by many generations in many conditions and long meditated upon by many diverse minds. It is a book of the mature life, and century-ripened. The sublimities, the enthusiasms, the heroics of life are not here; the fiery hopes, the stimulations, the divine despairs — there is nothing of that, neither gospel, nor rallying-cry nor death-challenge. These things have long been. But the man who is acquainted with human nature in his own breast and in living men, who commands the vistas of history, of literature, of various philosophies, who knows the past issues of human hopes and toils, the man of experience, finds a certain justness in the thought of Montaigne that harmonizes with the latter-day moods of life and is the more acceptable because it is graced with that (lightness of spirit, that not too serious view, that tone which might so easily become mocking and yet never mocks) Though the herald of the modern age, Montaigne was deeply implicated in the past, in what man has been. In the "Essays" one finds the lees of antiquity, and somewhat the lees of life; it is the book of an old mind, of an old man, of a retirement from the world; to read it justly, the reader must have lived. Montaigne requires an afternoon light, and a mind content with the private life, with reason and nature and good sense.

# SHAKESPEARE

THE primary thing in Shakespeare was his sense of action. He seized all life as action in his thoughts; he led his own life as action in himself, as a career. That is his Englishry. He was a practical man; as a boy he was enterprising, in his maturity he was discreet. The traditions of his early days at Stratford show a lively, capable, eager youth, active, adventurous, expedient, quick to get into trouble, quick in marriage; and the flight from Stratford was a departure into the large scene of life, a going to London, to the field of ambition. The family had seen better days, and was in difficulties; he meant to bear up the name; he succeeded, in the end, in re-establishing the family estate in his native place. The traditions of his early days in London show the same fundamental temperament; he had no scorn of beginnings, whether he held horses at the theater, or by whatever door of trifling service he entered on the great scene that was to be his kingdom, he would get in where he could; he accepted the terms on which life was to be led in his time and place. He learned easily because he was facile to receive; he learned much because he put what he knew to use as soon as he knew it; he was quick to experiment with his faculties and what they found to work with. The stage was developing comedy and tragedy and a verbal style proper to display them; there was a stock of plays rapidly outgrown, a public demand to be met, money to be made. He made himself apprentice to the best masters of comedy and tragedy, he tried his hand at re-making the old plays, he used what he found on the stage, adding what he could of prettiness and quibble, of grace and softness in the phrase, of heat and vivacity in the dialogue, of golden cadence, comic play, tragic thrust; and gradually he moved forward, emerged, became playwright and poet, the mark of passing and impotent malice, popular with the many, well-beloved by his comrades, successful. If the history of these days were known in detail, it would not differ from the great type shown in Scott, Cervantes; infinite interest in life, unceasing industry in work, the power to live which makes men great, and with it the apparent unconsciousness of genius, the reality of the individual life, the near regard to the private good. Whatever else there may have been, the theater was to Shakespeare a profession, a career; he made himself master and head of it by the toilsome process of daily life; and he measured his success in it, in one way at least, by the substance of what it brought him, wealth, position, a county name.

At London, where he led this career for twenty-five years, he had complete worldly success. His life there leaves two impressions on the mind. The first is that of immense labor, not only in the composition of the plays, but in the other necessary business of the stage and management, the acting, the preparation, the provincial tours, the court performances, the life of the theater and its finances, the practical realities; it must have been a very busy life, and its wearing effects are plain in the rapid and deep maturing of his manhood, and in his comparatively early death. The second impression is of the ease, quiet and friendliness of his temperament, his companionableness and his reserve, a human and noble nature; the characteristic epithets given him that have survived from his friends' lips are the two words "gentle" and "sweet"; though a few ill-natured phrases were flung at him, he escaped with the highest good-fortune the venom that the literary life vents even on its favorites. He was helpful; in his youth he befriended Jonson, and in later years he collaborated with younger men. His comrades of the theater show him that wholesome loyalty which mixes respect and affection so that they are indistinguishable. He seems to have had by nature those unconscious, intimate, incommunicable traits that oftenest come only from breeding and make men free of the society where they are. Young Southampton was not only his patron, but his friend; and in that difficult role of poet and patron Shakespeare was proud and happy in his noble friend, and gave the tribute of affectionate compliment in verse and that glory of style that lies in courtly hyperbole, and all that was due from the greatest of poets, but he gave his heart also. Shakespeare accepted the conditions of the literary life with respect to rank and fortune in his day as simply as he met the state of the theater. It is likely there was no better courtier when he went to court, as it is likely that there was no better buyer when he went to view lands and houses, no better judge of the public taste in plays. He was equal to the business of life on all sides that required worldly ability, and temperamentally as equal to it in the things of affection and comradery, of the heart, of humanity in social intercourse. The patron, the mortgage belong in his life, together with the scores of friends and the innumerable affairs to do; they are naturally there, for he was a man like others who lived the common life of man, earned and ate his bread in it, and to whom this action of life in and about and for himself was a very palpable thing. It is not a life that has left much record of itself, not diversified by adventure, not the scene of known passions; but the golden silences that lie like autumn mold upon his memory are in harmony with that thought which discovers there a life, dedicated indeed to the creative dream, but yet within the limitations of its own world distinguished by daily labor and daily kindliness, not too self-conscious, storing up provision for the future, respect from the world, the affection of friends, the things that should accompany old age — a life well-lived, well-acted, in its earthly lines. Such a life is consistent with the highest genius even in men in whom the sense of life as action is not so supreme as it was in Shakespeare; in him it was born of that genius where everything set with a great tide toward reality.

Action is the core of the drama; it is what gives attractive and arresting power to the word "dramatic," focuses the attention, makes the eye look and the spirit expect at the fall of those syllables. To Shakespeare, in his youth, immersed and absorbed in the dramatic movement that made a captive servant of him, mind, moods, energy, ambition, hope — that overmastered him with what was to be his fate therein, life was the object of his thoughts, but life primarily as a story. The story of life was there before him in the old plays on the stage, in the books he read, in the tales he thumbed over; at first a story of English kings and Italian lovers, of the convulsions of state, heart-break and the words of clowns, comic confusions, tragic discords, enchanted woodlands. He found the chronicle plays in vogue, fragments of history; and here and there, beginning his art, he re-established a scene, heightened a dialogue, concentrated a passion of anger or pity; it was piecemeal work by which he came to the power at last of defining a plot, a play of his own, an interpretation and representation of the story in a way of his own. The material he used was external, given to him, persons and incidents; he did not invent them, he found them; and his manipulation of them at first was, naturally, mainly in the language, the verbal investiture of person, act, scene, that part of the work which was most flexible, most plastic, readiest for a youthful hand and most tempting for lips that had suddenly unlocked a flood of such poesy, eloquence and passion in speech, colors of nature and the heart, as had never before poured from an English fount. It is this flow of language, vehement or smooth or impassioned, reflecting natural beauty or personal graces, prone to pathos and sentiment, rhetorical, dragging along with it all the affectations of the hour, experimenting with its own powers, intoxicated with its own poetry, exuberant with its own life — it is this marvelously musical, facile, intellectual power of language, this mastery that is not merely verbal, but is of the essence of expression, poetic not purely dramatic — it is this that in the earlier works plays over the story, atmospheres it, inhabits it, and in its surplus of light, feeling and imagery, in its lyrical effusion, overflows without submerging the dramatic interest, threatens the eminence of the action. From "Love's Labor's Lost" to "A Midsummer Night's Dream," this lyrical obsession mounts prevailing; thereafter it recedes — the tints of the morning, the bloom of spring, the hour of the bloom of life had passed. Shakespeare, loosing the passion of language to the full as never English poet did, had not lost his foothold on the reality of life, on the story, the drama, the action; and, deepening in his dramatic faculty he came, in the end, to that subtile mastery of language which belongs only to the greatest genius, lords of the brief and broken phrase. Four words created light; and something of that same miracle lingers in the power of the poet who is truly divine. The gradual victory of dramatic over purely poetic diction in Shakespeare reflects the victory of life itself, of the action over the illusion of life, in him.

There was a second rivalry with the dramatic instinct in Shakespeare besides this of the lyrical impulse. It lay in the intellectual temptation, the power of the naked thought. What is technically called the sentiment, that is, the wise saying, the axiomatic verse in which the reflecting mind is condensed with a purely intellectual value, was an inheritance of the drama from old time; and Shakespeare, particularly in his middle life, was apt at linking such counsels together or in developing them from the dialogue. It is an analogous faculty that he employs in those wit-combats of the characters that are preeminently intellectual in tone. The wit of Rosalind and Beatrice is more closely united to the dialogue; but in the passages of advice, from Biron's gentle sermon on love to the sage wisdom of Polonius and Ulysses, and even on to Prospero's great farewell there is a recurring interruption of the action in play after play, due to the emergence of thought in control of the scene; and as Shakespeare's lyricism gives to the plays that atmosphere which isolates them among the works of dramatic genius and sets them apart in an unapproached realm of creative art, so his wisdom gives to them that intellectual dilation by which they excel all others in majesty of mind. Other dramatists have represented life with equal impressiveness in its being, but none have represented life so conscious of its own significance. Here again, as in his lyrical moment, Shakespeare in his intellectual moment seems to depart from the story, the drama, the action, but he does not really depart, or if he does so it is only to bring back to the drama the offerings of all the Muses. And in a third tributary element of the drama, in the spectacle, while he uses the embellishment of the scene to the full measure of what his times allowed, he introduces the masque as an adjunct, like a song or a dance, harmonious with the scene but not an essential of the action. These three things, then, diction, sentiment and spectacle, which were the open temptation to woo him from the essential dramatic point of view, the action, he either overcame or successfully subdued them to the enrichment and enlargement of the action; the main drift of his art, the main purpose of his mind were the same, with whatever slackening or bending of the current, toward the story of life pre-eminently, toward character and event, toward reality in its most human form. Beginning with the more intractable material of history, he came to use preferably romantic story in which his imagination was more free in creative power; and in the end, to such a height did this power reach that he seemed to create not only character and event, but also the world in which they had their being; to such a complete victory did his dramatic instinct, prevailing over all other impulses, carry him who always remained at heart a dramatist.

Shakespeare was so completely a dramatist, interested in the action of life, that when he took the autobiographical mask in the "Sonnets" he seems transformed into his opposite, into the lyrical poet unlocking his own heart; here, it has been believed, he told his dearest secrets, his intimacies, the most sweet and bitter disgraces of his days and nights, his springs and autumns; and so inspired is the dramatic action of his mind in this play in the forms of the sonnet, if it be such, that it is only by an effort of detachment, by reflection and judgment, that one sees there only the working of that supreme faculty under the appearances of personality. The secret of the "Sonnets" has been so many times discovered, and escaped in the discovery, that this view, now best supported, may justly have its lease of life in turn, and the physical basis of fact on which the poet's imagination worked — such strands and suggestions of actuality as he used in the romances — may be found in Southampton's personality; but the black lady, the dear, disloyal friend, the rival poet will still wear in their faces, have in their form and moving, an insoluble mystery, because, whatever the drama, they move in a cloud of lyricism, so intense with tenderness, sorrow, unavailing cries, that here all seems the form and substance of the soul itself. A dramatist who makes his own soul the scene of the drama, using the forms of personality, must necessarily leave a mysterious work; but in the "Sonnets" what is plain is the drama, what is obscure is only the basis of the drama, whether it be fact or convention, or mingled of both; whatever be the personal element, it is conceived, handled, developed dramatically, its truth is at bottom dramatic truth.

And if it be difficult to trace Shakespeare's personality with any assured steps in the "Sonnets," how much less is it to be probed in the plays proper! Those attempts that have been made to correlate the bare facts of his history with the sequence of his works, to synchronize his

## SHAKESPEARE

life-moods with the comedies and the tragedies, to make the plays render up the spiritual states of the man in his personal being, are ingenious; but the conditions of production, when Elizabeth might ask any day for a "Merry Wives of Windsor," or some noble family desire a hymeneal spectacle like "A Midsummer Night's Dream," or James be pleased with a Scotch theme, or the public itself, little indulgent to the moods of those who provide entertainment, might have to be recaptured to the play — such conditions are little favorable to "periods" of the private soul. The chronology of the works, too, is not convincing. Did Shakespeare, in whose mind the perspective of life varied no more than the perspective of the heavens in the celestial telescope, think to have all that world of his courtesy to his private fortunes in a son's death, a friend's fall, a mistress's fickle change? Shakespeare was of the objective type of genius, a trite but useful phrase for a very palpable fact. He never mistook his soul for the soul of the universe. He passed, as other men, from youth to manhood, and the deepening of his nature in the process, as it was worked out under the control of absorption in creative dramatic art is plainly discerned; he seized life in its action more logically, more ideally, more profoundly; he compassed and penetrated and filled it with omnipresent thought; height and depth, passion and fate and gloom, he laid it bare; he saw it. He passed through the disillusionment; but it was a disillusionment not of the suffering heart, but of the seeing eye; and after the disillusionment came, what comes to all, the lassitude, the indifference, the repose, the relaxed sense of fate, the concession to optimism, the fantastic world; the calm of Shakespeare was the subsidence of life in him, the smoothing of the great wave of passion, the stilling of the tumultuous voices of thought.

Such a history he had, in whatever special forms of personal feeling; it is the normal life of great genius, absorbing imaginatively the passion and thought of life in the world; and from time to time, out of this continuing personal reaction on life in normal growth there would proceed modifying influences, lines of choice in subject, of intellectual direction, of creative mood, passional harmonies blending with the given theme — to such a point temperament would have its will, more or less, with the work according to time and circumstances; but such a continuing and aging mood attendant on the plays is a far different thing from "periods" determinative of the type of the plays in a sequence which makes them proceed from Shakespeare's personal fortunes as a mortal spirit with changes from cheerfulness to gloom and again to equanimity. Shakespeare was a dramatist by nature as well as by profession, or he became subdued to what he worked in; he was the servant of the public; and, much more, he was fascinated by life in its externality, life as it was in other men, other times, other places; he was insatiate in informing himself of its story in history, in novels and romances, in ancient and modern authors, wherever it was to be found. He was not that egotist who writes himself large and calls that the world; art in him was not self-revealing, it was the revelation of a world that had been from the foundation of being and would continue when his works were buried deeper than any plummet could sound. This objectivity, this self-effacement in art, this interest in the story of life, his absorption in life's movement, in action, is Shakespeare's gift of greatness. It explains his limitations. Spirituality, properly speaking, the celestial immortality of man's nature, is not found in Shakespeare either in character, thought or aspiration. The religious life sleeps in his works; and many a generation will marvel at it. He was interested in life, the action of life; and that is a thing confined to this world. He is mundane, secular, in a way scientific; he saw the spectacle as it is in time.

The second main consideration bearing on Shakespeare's genius is the fact that the world he saw, dealt with and knew was an aristocratic world. It was given to him first historically, in those chronicles in which his hand learned to mold the human stuff, a kingly world of the Henrys, the Richards and John, with feudal challenge, battle incidents, the life of the council, murders in prisons or on the block, treasons, dethronements, the sorrows of queens, Norfolk, Hotspur and Falconbridge; a life focussed on aristocratic fortunes and pivoted on aristocratic power. To Shakespeare the people was always the mob, and negligible. The sphere of humor, too, in which the vulgar enters, is dependent on the aristocratic sphere from the comedy of the camp-fire and the tavern to Bottom's craftsmen and the court clowns, up to Lear's Fool. Later, the Roman plays gave him the same aristocratic state in an antique form, dictatorial, imperial, with the mob of citizens, though more in evidence, more contemptible. The ordered world for him was the world of courtly life; all else, though contiguous or entering in for entertainment or service or in the mass of battle, was essentially subordinated, exteriorized, as environment. The romances, which, after the chronicles, had given him the raw material, reinforced his conception of life as an aristocratic structure by expanding it socially into a community of gentle-folk, Venetian, Veronan, Paduan, in

Arden, Attica, Illyria, or on French or English meadows; a life where everything breathed civility, the sentiment of high breeding in chivalry and courtesy, the cult of phrase, the dress and behavior, the interests, ambitions, intrigues, recreations, language, manners and customs of an aristocratic ideal. Even in those regions of the imagination, where he reared his own state in its lordliest form, with the effect of an incantation of genius, in the English realm of Lear, the Scotch court of Macbeth, the throne of Denmark, the Venetian principality of Cyprus, the Egypt of Antony, or in the woods of Cymbeline, the country-side of Perdita, the island-kingdom of Prospero, he impressed upon it aristocracy in its most majestic, noble and gentle forms as the seal of its being. Shakespeare's genius is, in fact, the finest flower of the aristocratic ideal of life.

Aristocracy is, in a sense, the state of nature historically developed in society as the survival of the fittest in the selfish struggle for existence. Shakespeare received it as the past of the world, contained in the forms of history and romance, the life that had always been, in which the masses, held in economic slavery under whatever name, furnished that wealth monopolized by the nobles which gave these latter liberty of the higher sphere of life, the sphere of intelligence, ambition, art, where they were enfranchised and armed for the possession of the chief goods of life. Aristocracy, so based on the enforced tribute of mankind, naturally develops individuality, the open career for those who are in command of wealth, opportunity, leisure; it spreads the scene for strong natures, highly endowed, superfluous in vital force and selfish desire; it is the breeding place of human greatness of the positive, self-assertive, world-conquering kind. Shakespeare received this aristocratic ideal from the times in which life had been great, from the Greek, Roman, English periods; but he received it also at a peculiarly fortunate moment in the special movement of its historical development; he received it when the coarser, denser forms of military and tyrannic power, of feudalism, monarchy and dogma, were dissolving in the finer, milder, freer modes of rationalism, individuality, culture; he received it at a culminating moment of its excellence — from the Italian Renaissance.

Personality, the essential fruit of aristocracy, the crowning victory of nature in working out her will, came forth from the Italian Renaissance in one of its highest forms, the form of superb personal power. The idea is so native to Italy and has played so great a part in her history that it seems racial — a race-element in her greatness. It was then concentrated in the ideal of the Renaissance prince, whether as a pattern in Machiavelli, or as an illustration from history in the nobles and leaders of the Italian cities; but stripped to its essentials it is no more than the individual will to live, the dominance of that will, the ideal of conquering the world to oneself, of subduing life, of having one's way, one's will, one's desire, of the assertion of the power to live that is the thirst of great souls. The aristocratic ideal of life in the Italian Renaissance developed in the central line of its advance in history this idea of the dominance of the personal will in life, the prepotency of individuality; and in so doing it freed human faculty, energy and desire in a way to a degree which gave to Italy its brilliant period of many-sided genius and impelled the human spirit in every civilized country and recaptured the lost provinces of Rome to the dominion of a spiritual civilization the seat of whose power is in the ideals of men. The Renaissance was so great a movement. Though not a material conquest, it was vaster in control than that of Alexander or of the elder antique Rome. Shakespeare took its full impact, lived in it, fed on it, absorbed its passions, its principles, its being, became its spirit in the North, was its transcendent and overwhelming genius in literature, its greatest monument in time. This is Shakespeare's position; he was the flower of the aristocratic ideal of life; he was the crest of the Renaissance; he was the incarnate spirit of that mighty power of life to live mightily which belongs to the aristocratic ideal as a right of nature and was the passion of the Renaissance in history.

The drama, it must be borne in mind, was always a European art. Shakespeare's universality, which is often made the occasion of so much marvel, is in its origins closely connected with this fact. The early English drama, with its miracle-plays, moralities, school-comedies, Senecan imitations, displayed cosmopolitan traits and originals belonging to a common mental culture and a general artistic condition; and the Elizabethan drama, in its Shakespearian culmination, though locally English, proceeded out of the European mind, its general past, its ideas, principles, moods, its order of life, its accumulation of sentiment and romance, its forms of imagination; and in this Shakespeare from an early point in his career was more deeply imbued than any of his contemporaries. What, then, constituted the European mind, its intellectual memory and moral passion, its conception and ideal of life, its poetic culture and means of art, was more variously, richly and profoundly present and active in him than in any other writer. He may never have been out of England; but he was the most European author then living. It is not an accident that on his stage locality ceases to exist. Italy has her immortality in the drama more in Shakespeare than in her own literature. "Hamlet" is the chief literary monument of Denmark. This does not happen by the caprice of an individual, but marks that quality in Shakespeare by virtue of which he is the genius of Europe. The human spirit, from time to time, detaches from the world of known geography a country of its own lying apart, a land for itself; such was Arcadia, in which Sidney and others wandered; such was the region of chivalry where Spenser and others traversed the romantic scene; and such was the realm of Shakespeare's stage, the magic circle where none dared tread but he. It was a world abstracted from the great scene of life in Europe as it then lay before the thoughts of men, in its breadth out of the historic past, in its variety of living energy, its medieval and classic garniture, its Renaissance luminousness, space, vivacity; it was this scene of the European consciousness of what life had been and was, idealized and generalized, and made to issue in poetry with the power and brilliancy of a new creation, the realm of Shakespeare's art. The aristocratic ideal of life is its organic principle and determines the quality of the scene, the nature of the event, the impulse of the characters; all the flowering of phrase and fancy, of sentiment and passion, all the adornment of taste in whatever form, all that constitutes mood, temperament and atmosphere, is representative of the European fashion of courtliness, scholarship, art, the reverie and dream that belong to the Renaissance characteristically, its pastoral, dramatic, rhetorical modes, its vari-colored romanticism; but, most cardinal of all, what is the mainspring of its life, is the human force loosed in it, that prepotency of the individual, that dominance of the personal will, which was the master-spirit of the Renaissance everywhere and finds in Shakespeare's world the place of its great career. This is not a local, a national, an English thing; it is a world-idea, and the imagination of Shakespeare, mastered by its inspiration found any country a fit stage for it in that environment of an ideal courtly life which was also not local or provincial, but a great world-scene. Shakespeare's universality in matter goes back to the fact that he was never anything else but cosmopolitan, in the nature of his knowledge, the ideality of his art, the sources, compass and illustrative power of his dramatic work. What is most contemporary, realistic and locally English in this work is on its fringes; in its beginnings and interludes, subordinate; in proportion as the work becomes great, profound, comprehensive, it possesses more purely the European character, it develops ideal freedom, it belongs not to Italy or Denmark or England, but to the genius of Europe.

The dawn of the Renaissance spirit, incarnating itself in English dramatic poetry, was in Marlowe, who was perhaps in his own passion of life more at one with the heart of the Renaissance than was Shakespeare, but he was less nobly, less perfectly, less splendidly, at one with it in its manifold fullness of expression. Marlowe first put on the stage the career of great passions, characters of immeasurable ambition and unquenchable thirst; but in "Tamerlane," "The Jew of Malta" and "Faustus," the theme is not sufficiently correlated with the real play of fact and force in human affairs, it is seized with too much intellectual abstraction and presented too spectacularly and fragmentarily in the scenes; some experimenting with the modifying power of history over imagination and invention was needed before it could find its dramatic limits and free itself from fantasy, enthusiasm and exaggeration in artistic expression. Shakespeare followed Marlowe in turning to English history for the material of his art. The idea of tragedy was, indeed, already defined for him in the European tradition as a thing of the fall of princes, of royal misfortune and the vicissitude of splendid fates; and in this way Shakespeare's tragic course was charted out for him beforehand; but in working out dramatically the lots of the English kings he also kept a close hold on the idea of a life-force in personality determining temperament, character and the issues of the action. What in Marlowe was extravagantly set forth as the fixed idea in his characters, bearing almost the impress of madness, remains in Shakespeare, but subdued to the requirements of the environment and of human nature, to probability. "Richard II" is a pathetic instance of the fall of a prince, but the story is linked with that infatuation of the idea of divine right which is the dominant idea of Richard, absorbs the eloquence, grace and chivalry of his nature and contains his fate. In "Richard III," the prepotency of the selfish force develops its bloody way with a power to take possession of the king's soul that recalls the self-maddening tyranny of the Roman emperors, till he becomes the fiend, the enemy of society and of the state itself, whose fall clears the air like a departing thunderstorm. Romeo exhibits the mastering of passion in the youthful soul; love in him is ecstasy. The dominance of the personal will, possessed by an idea inciting it, asserting itself with unbridled desire, naturally leads to madness, and in Shakespeare's great characters of this sort mania is never far off; in Macbeth there is the capital instance of the blending of the borders between reason and unreason, and, as is Shakespeare's way, this elemental trait in the play permeates it, objectified in the witches, reduplicated in Lady Macbeth, but concentrated in the vivid mental action, the bodily starts and stares, the repeated challenge of fate, in Macbeth's shaking but never quite dethroned "state of man." "Timon" is a lesser illustration. "Hamlet" and "Lear" thrust this part of life into the foreground; and in "Othello," the near neighborhood of the excess of life to madness, of the noble nature to ruin through its own power to live, to be possessed by a passion, an idea, a sorrow, is the ground of its tragic scene. The personal will is necessarily anti-social, and hence opens in its career the whole field of tragic conflict in endless ways; the drama is its natural scope in art, and there it is the most potent power to conjure with; it is, by far, the most interesting thing in the whole of that action of life which Shakespeare contemplated so absorbingly. The Renaissance spirit concentrated and intensified the sense of it, carried it to the extreme, made an ideal of it, in history; Shakespeare took it over into the sphere of imagination and then gave such examples of it in the transcendent forms of art that his characters became, each in its kind, the supreme models of what is possible to human nature and faculty in personal force, the types of man.

The fullness of life in all its forms, which makes the plays great, has as its underlying basis this life-force, the affirmation of life, in its energies, its desires, its revelations, in the conscious spectacle of being, and with the more brilliancy because of the transcendent idealization to which the scene of life here has been subjected. All Shakespeare's male characters are self-seekers, in a true sense; the exceptions, Kent, a feudal type, and Horatio, a modern form of the Kent temperament, are also men of strength. Though with the visitation of thought, melancholy, peculiar misfortune on the scene, there is occasionally the sense of a withdrawal from life, in Hamlet, Antonio, Hermione, it is rather a forced and regretful retirement than a true withdrawal; the denial of life is truly present in Shakespeare only as an unshaped suggestion. The age was one of action, of faith in life, and the ideals it projected were those of the positive, achieving, realizing kind; and in Shakespeare the life-force moved in his world of art with the fruitfulness, the teeming variety, the creative overflow into being that it has in nature. Men recognize and remember this life-force in him by the immortal figures of the plays, Romeo, Hamlet, Lear, the score or more that have entered into the world's memory enduringly, eternal realities, with ideal fascination, either for their beauty or their intimacy with men's bosoms or their awe in fate or some other mode of consanguinity with man that is Shakespeare's seal upon them; these figures best illustrate that power of life and will to live, in high personal forms, showing the far reach, the majesty, the pity and terror of the forces of life in the soul in their energy accomplishing the utmost possible to man unfolding his nature in the vicissitudes of fortune; but the whole Shakespearian world, no less than these, in its various planes of character, incident and plot, is the outcome and realization in art of this same life-force more widely diffused in humanity of every kind and sort. That infinite variety that so distinguishes the plays, such that each seems a fresh revelation of a new world, so embracing that they seem in their wholeness to leave no lot in life unexpressed, no mortal joy or sorrow unrecorded in its own cry, no thought almost untold, — that scene of life from the tavern-companions of Falstaff and the craftsmen of Athens up to the solitude of Cæsar in power, the solitude of Lear in grief, the solitude of Prospero in wisdom, — all this proceeds from the life-force manifesting itself with the multiplicity and abundance of humanity. Shakespeare engaged his mind with the movement of life in its wholeness; he let the life-force pour through him, from clown and fool and trull up to the highest incarnations of the will in passion, wisdom, sorrow, the types of man; and this seen in imagination is the Shakespearian world. He was not an observer, bringing back word from this or that tract of life or group of mortals or peculiarity of fortune; he was a creator — his world is always whole, as entire and perfect in the Indian boy of Titania as in the Rome of Cæsar. The spirit of the Renaissance, insatiable for life, whispered to him this secret; but in the act and passion of creation he exceeded the Renaissance and took his station with those mightiest few who are not for an age, but for all time.

The courtly sphere, the aristocratic ideal, the culmination of life in the career of great passions led up to that triumph of life which is the spectacle the Shakespearian world presents with inexhaustible profusion, splendor and vitality; but this world, though an emanation of the spirit of the Renaissance and its climax in literature, was itself sphered in a larger conception universal in the tragic art; it lies, like the antique drama, in fatality, in the mystery and under the sway of an infinity that envelops the life-force round about more profoundly and densely than the dark ether envelops the forces and imagery of nature. The prepotency of individuality, the dominance of the personal will are the great forms of life; but the power to live, however supreme in its manifestation, is a wrestling with the unseen angel of life; and to Shakespeare in the long and brooding absorption of his contemplation of the action of life in mortality, what finally emerges from the strife as the master-spirit there is the dominance of fate against which the life-force is shattered. It is commonly said that fate in the antique drama is external and operates from without as destiny, and that in the modern drama it is internal and operates from within as character; the distinction brings out the larger scope of personality and its greater importance in the romantic drama of Shakespeare; but in either case the fatality resides in the action, in the play of the forces determining the tragic catastrophe, in that which is essentially beyond and outside of the sphere of the personal will and operates free from its control, against its desire and to effect its ruin. The error, the weakness, the cause that initiates the play of fate may be of different degrees of ignorance or consciousness, of generosity or criminality, of responsibility or irresponsibility; but, once loosed in whatever way, fate in the end rules the issue. In what is known as Shakespeare's period of tragic gloom, that is, in the plays of his manhood's maturity, in which his creative genius works with its most profound power in realizing the states of the soul, the characteristic trait is the gradual emergence in his art of the sense of fate in the world, its accumulation in his mind, its possession of his genius which then gave forth those dramas on which his fame as a master of the knowledge of life most rests and in which fate controls the scene of life in the wreck of fortune, the riving of the soul within, the catastrophe where tragic death loading the stage impresses the mind less as the penalty than as a release of the sufferer from the power of life to torture and betray, a dismissal of the soul to the peace where life is not. To Macbeth, Othello, Lear and also to Hamlet, death is welcome; and to the spectator also their death brings relief, calm, peace. Shakespeare, in these days pre-eminently saw fate as that against which personality is shattered, not merely dramatically by a star-crossed fortune as in Romeo, with the pathos of the death of youth, beauty and passion, but more essentially as by a law inherent in the greatness of the life-force itself to destroy it; for these are not special but typical instances of the action of life — slight changes of circumstances might have altered the fortunes of Romeo, but no change could ever have altered the fate of Macbeth, Othello, Lear, Hamlet. In these four Shakespeare sets personality against fate, front to front, and the story is felt to be a universal chapter of life, of the implication of the human spirit in that vicissitude of nature and fortune which has in every tongue borne the same name and that is stronger than life.

The realization that such is the nature of human life was attended in Shakespeare's mind by a storm and stress that is read not only in the great dramas, but also in the cynical acquaintance with humanity shown in "All's Well that Ends Well," and in the savage temper toward its baseness displayed in "Troilus and Cressida." The concentrated, intense, ideal realization of the tragedy of existence, of humanity victimized in its forms of noblest nature or of most superb power, though most brilliant in the four great tragedies, is not confined to them; it extends and spreads into many others in different planes of character, mood and thought. The action of life takes on that quality of impenetrable mystery which the face of life has always worn, in every literature, in the highest works of imagination. Mystery is an increasing element in Shakespeare's dramas from the first, continuing, growing in depth, growing also in intangibility; poetically, it is etherealized in "A Midsummer Night's Dream" full of the idea of illusion in art as the wood is of moonlight; reflectively, it is precipitated in Hamlet's thought; and, at the end, as the illusion of life it fills "The Tempest;" but the finer and most secret form of mystery in Shakespeare is not poetical or intellectual or metaphysical, but springs from the action itself and is dramatic. It is in Macbeth's superstitious interrogation of the witches, in Hamlet's questioning of the soul in his soliloquy, in those half-lines of tragic climax where life grows silent before the presence of fate; it is in Othello's mind-dazed question:

"Will you, I pray, demand that demi-devil
Why he hath thus ensnared my soul and body," —

the mystery of the fates of man; it is in Lear's invocation of the elements:

"I never gave you kingdom, called you children," —

dismissing them from the moral world as if they alone were free where all was guiltiness in the worse storm of life beating on his white, old head. It is in such passages as these, where Shakespeare's dramatic faculty is at its lightning-stroke that the inner secrecy of the mystery is lighted up, shown but not revealed, in the depth of consciousness. Reason has no solvent for it, justice does not measure with it, mercy is unknown to it. The attempt to make fate ethical in Shakespeare, to identify it with moral law in the universe, however it be made, fails; it was not as righteousness that he saw life; he saw it with the simpleness of his genius, as a dramatic struggle, and, emerging thence, the dominance of fate shattering life mysteriously, beyond the intelligible grasp of man's reason or the moral sense. He saw, in other words, above all else, the dramatic mystery of life.

Shakespeare was thus, through and through, a dramatist; and he was the dramatist in whom the old tradition of the art, even from Æschylus, as a representative of the courtly life and a tale of the fall of princes, culminated. The idea of humanity, in the modern democratic sense, was never in his brain; the types of man that he created were, in their greatness, those of the aristocratic life; and the tragedy he set forth was not that of the spirit of life, the modern world-pain, but of the careers of individuals highly endowed by nature or fortune in a world which seemed to exist to be the theater of their will, ambition, passion; he was the dramatist of a class-society. The aristocratic ideal of society and of action in it, however, is the will of nature, and still prevails in every state; and it makes a universal appeal to men. The ground of this appeal is little affected by the absence in Shakespeare of democratic sympathy; for the scene of life which he does present includes all classes; human nature is common and constant, and the career of life in fortune, ambition, passion is now the same that he depicted; the Shakespearian world, however modern conditions may be changed, is still life as it is known to the thoughts of men. The dramatic mystery is that which is closest to mankind in daily experience, the mystery of what is done, of what happens; the poetic, intellectual, metaphysical modes of mystery exist for the few, but the mystery of the event itself is for all, and it is seized by them in Shakespeare's way as not a thing of reason or ethics, but as a fact impenetrable, leaving the soul according to its degree affected by the scene. This is the normal human attitude toward calamity, toward tragedy, of any kind; its force expends itself not in explanation, but in experience. The sense of life as action, too, and the ideal of it as lying in the prepotency of individuality, and the dominance of the personal will is natural to all men, and the thing dearest to their bosoms as their thought and desire of life; the power to live, — to loose the energies of the soul in achievement, enjoyment, experience, to affirm life in its fullness, variety, richness, intensely, extremely, insatiably, to the utmost of the force that is in one — this is the impulse to self-expression, to self-realization, that drives men in their ambitions and passions of whatever nature, the action and movement of life in the world; and in this world as it lies outspread in the knowledge and thoughts of men brilliant personal force most attracts admiration, confers fame and secures imitation, oftenest without regard to moral quality. Force is the idol of life that is hardest to combat in civilizing man. In the Shakespearian world the affirmation of life in general is as broadly various as in the world of nature, and in individual types it reaches a height of beauty, power and majesty that is unrivaled in nature because seen through the ideality of art, and these types have a history and a revelation of their being such as is only possible in imagination; men, consequently, passing into this world as they read or behold the plays find there that enlargement of life and its career, that intensification and revelation of it, which, though denied to their experience, truly endows them with the greatness of life, gives them understanding of the soul and the faculties lodged in it, the heights and depths of its passion, the reaches of its thoughts, the shadows of fatality amid which it moves under the stars. The universal appeal of Shakespeare lies in the power with which he has seized life in its intense forms, its richest efflorescence, its magical fantasy, its fascination and horror, its vulgar generality, its high types, its manias and humors, the whole of life, and given it back to men as an increase of their own power to live, a world in which they come to true consciousness of themselves. Life is what men desire; Shakespeare gives them life, according to their own ideal, the triumph of life, yet life which at its height is tragic and shocks them with that mystery of the actual which is the profoundest reality.

The secret of life solves the riddle of Shakespeare, whose greatness has no other mystery than the mystery of the greatness of life. He is the spirit of life made manifest in its own dramatic motion, imprisoned, embodied and unveiled in art. Here are the fates of men, grotesque, heroic, terrible, or stately in prosperity with the olive crown and the sheaf of Ceres, almost as many in number as the lots set forth to be chosen by the souls at birth. It is an earthly life limited to the mortal scene; no illumination falls on it from heaven, no divinity inhabits its sphere. It is essentially Pagan in its ideal, its art and its philosophy. It is the supreme work of man's hand so rendering life in its aspects of mortality. If one were to mold in sculpture the face of life, it would be, one thinks, that over which every joy and sorrow, every thought seems to have moved — the infinite of human expression — leaving its trace in the living flesh, — the face of Shakespeare. That would be, could it be won back from time, the ideal face of life, the Sphinx of our existence.

# SWINBURNE

ALGERNON CHARLES SWINBURNE, sprung of the strength of English blood, was born in London, April 5, 1837, the eldest son of Admiral Charles Henry Swinburne, and Lady Jane Henrietta, daughter of the third earl of Ashburnham. His childhood was summered in Northumberland and wintered in the Isle of Wight, so that the ancestry of his senses as well as of his blood was of the sea. He was bred at Eton and Oxford, where though not undistinguished in scholarship he took no degree. He became acquainted with Italy and France by travel. From his boyhood and in college days he was devoted to the literary life, and thereafter literature was his sole career. A life secluded in friendships and studies has been his portion, as a man; and the fruits of it, by which he lives to the public, are an abundance of prose and verse which has come forth unintermittently for nearly forty years; he stands now alone, the last of the great English poets of the nineteenth century, with a fame never to be forgotten in the annals of that time thronged though it be with poetic names and voices of matchless splendor and music.

The gift of Swinburne is to be capable of passion. Enthusiasm is inseparable from him. Perhaps the simplest aspect of his genius lies in his revolutionary songs. The old French fire burns its last in his torch. It is the flame that descended for an hour upon Coleridge, that wrapped Shelley life-long and in death, that by tradition now belongs to the English race of poets from Milton to Landor with every well-loved name to aid; and in his generation Swinburne will ever be remembered as its herald, a figure sole and supereminent, the poet-republican —

> "I am the trumpet at thy lips, thy clarion
> Full of thy cry, sonorous with thy breath," —

that is his attitude, in the modern battle for liberty, like Taillefer at Hastings. It began with his songs for Italy, in the great days of her patriots, the first-fruits of his sympathies with the land and of his personal admiration for Mazzini. He does not state the grounds of his faith, for it is not an intellectual passion that seizes on him; it is a fervor that burns, an exaltation that lifts and heightens, a flood of feeling that pours forth and inundates with light and music and with the confluence of many strengths in one superb moral force — the revolutionary cause. Its monotone, though in part due to the quality of the resonance and to the sameness of the imagery, is essentially emotional, the monotone of profound and unchangeable depth in the feeling itself which is a constituent of the eternal nature of man. The passion is a capacity to hate as well as to love. There is no such master of the curse, in modern days. He strikes home and to the pit with it, and with a mien and phrase and a volleying after of fire and wrath fit to hurl Satan down to the abyss. These are curses to rejoice the heart. They mark their victims indelibly for hell. *Vice versa* his hymns to Landor, Victor Hugo and Mazzini are adorations. These three were the living hands that had fed him in youth with their touch, their words, their presence on earth. The fire they nursed though they did not kindle, had long life in it, a deep core of heat; and whether the year was '66 or yesterday, whether the scene was Rome or Paris, Crete or Muscovy, the poet still brooded there the passion-bolts of his invective or peans for victor and martyr. In his own land Swinburne's revolutionary ardor changed and took a new form in an illimitable patriotism, a pride in England, an Elizabethan might of land-love that carried the fate of the Armada in its bosom as its dearest memory and expressed itself in an exuberance of panegyric and delight that makes his verse seem contemporaneous with English liberty and the ocean-rhythm of England's empire. This love of liberty and dedication to mankind had, too, its far fount, under dark centuries, in Athens,

"Dear city of men without master or Lord;"

thence the poet had drunk, most truly, the draught of his inspiration, the intoxication of his faith in man. The stream of his revolutionary song is unmatched in volume, splendor and force; it has flowed life-long, and still wells; it is blended of many loves of persons and histories and memories, of time and of eternity; it is a great passion, great in personal intensity, great in its human outreaching and uplifting aspiration, great in sincerity. Here is immense manhood-strength, seeking, by the poet's right, to pour itself through the impoverished veins of "miserable men."

Even in so brief an opening glance at Swinburne's work the fact of his scholarship, his provenience from literature, stands prominently forth. I suppose that no English poet has ever had so wide and familiar acquaintance with the poetry of foreign climes. He began with a felicitous command of the classical and romance languages. He took the Taylorian prize, in his college days, for French and Italian, and won other similar distinction in the ancient tongues. He has written, as a poet, in Greek, Latin and French with literary mastery. In English his studies have been prolonged and comprehensive, and not restricted to poetry. Out of this varied scholarship sprang his prose works, a long series beginning with his elaborate exposition of Blake's genius and including for its bulk an examination of the Elizabethan drama, together with the study of Victor Hugo. To be grouped here, also, as dependent on the critical activity of his mind are the poems so many in number which, whether in the form of ode, elegy or sonnet, are dedicated to the literary fame of those writers whom he had deeply studied. In this large body of verse his criticism is condensed and, so far as the matter permits, is put into the form of poetry with a full heart of praise. He indulges himself in this luxury of praise, in a minute and lavish tribute to the writers of many books and plays, to the nameless as well as the famous dead. Swinburne truly is nowhere more the poet than in this inexhaustible capacity to be moved to hero-worship and the affectionate eulogy of those who from Sappho and Catullus down the long line seem to be in the intimacy of genius his own. His criticism is woven of such noble recognitions.

This literary element, explicitly exposed in his prose criticism and in the critical as distinguished from the imaginative portions of his verse, is implicitly active in the whole mass of his poetry. Its influence is observed most plainly in the structural form of his dramas. He had achieved such familiarity with past literature that his mind became capable of an attitude of contemporaneity toward it; he was thus led, in opposition to the usual attempt of a literary poet to modernize what he derives from the past and naturalize it in his own age, rather to archaize his own forms. Swinburne's detachment from his own time was gradual, but he moved toward a reproduction of both the Greek and the English antique. "Atalanta in Calydon" was his first experiment in this way, but "Erechtheus," his second Greek play, was more perfect in the success that it aimed at. Similarly his earliest dramatic work "The Queen Mother" and "Rosamond," though Shakespearian in diction and reminiscence, was yet not a conscious reversion in art; but the play of "Locrine," and the trilogy of "Chastelard," "Bothwell" and "Mary Stuart," a chronicle history as he himself describes it, were attempts to write anew in the Elizabethan manner of the drama. The same may be said of "Marino Faliero," while "The Sisters" and "Rosamund, Queen of the Lombards," the other two dramas, stand somewhat apart.

In the trilogy of which Queen Mary is the theme, the effort for contemporaneity with the past is also to be observed, other than artistically, in the historical veracity of the characters in themselves and of the scene of events. Attentive and exhaustive study of the facts of the record is noticeable, the historian's fidelity; and it is rather in obedience to the necessities of history than of art that the poet has swelled and lengthened the drama to such a remarkable compass, and owns that the work has such proportions and has been so treated as to deserve the name of an epic drama. He seems desirous that it should be judged of as a history as well as in its aspect as a work of imagination. This indicates the depth in him of that feeling for past fact, which has controlled the artistic form of the drama in his general use, both Greek and English. He disengages himself from contemporary realities — standards, ideas, convictions — but subjects himself to the realities of another place and time so far as he can re-embody them; he thus by native aptitude and with the aid of scholarship, does become in a singular degree a citizen and freeman of many literatures and at their different periods, a poet in whom what would be imitation and reminiscence in others becomes genuine because he plays the part he assumes after due study and with deep feeling; he thus succeeds beyond all others in writing literary drama that accords with past principles of composition.

Such a power to free oneself from one's own age and move in the guise and fashion of other times and places, illustrated here by the use Swinburne makes of the drama, involves aloofness from the world. He is, in fact, in his greater work of the imagination, remote from current life. He lives, withdrawn in his own thoughts, in that sphere of the poetic imagination where there is a true timelessness, — the solitude thronged with figures that appear at any moment from any age and drift across the vision or play their mimic parts before the mind's eye and disappear. It is the world of the great artists. Locrine, Erechtheus, Meleager are natural there; so are the stormy passion of the Scotch peers, the craft of English statesmen, the spectacle of Venetian pride; or Sappho or Faustine. The world of Swinburne is well symbolized by that Zodiac of the burning signs of love that he named in the prelude to "Tristram of Lyonesse," — the signs of Helen, Hero, Alcyone, Iseult, Rosamond, Dido, Juliet, Cleopatra, Francesca, Thisbe, Angelica, Guenevere; under the heavens of these starry names the poet moves in his place apart and sees his visions of woe and wrath and weaves his dream of the loves and the fates of men. He is a myth-lover, a dreamer, a companion of the myths and the dreams of the past, an artist of the imagination. The aloofness that belongs to Swinburne's verse is not due only to his effort to archaize the forms of his art, but much more to the fact that he reverts to great imaginative themes which, in themselves, are remote from the modern world, and conceives them in a spirit of poetry that now seems to have its death-limit of a great age in his sole surviving genius.

The artistic conservatism of Swinburne, which disposed him in the rigidity of his mind to the preservation and choice of anterior poetic forms, and to the treatment of antique and legendary themes or subjects of historic grandeur, is also felt in his desire that these themes should be kept in their primitive state. He revolted against modernization of the old in all its forms. The dramatic bent of his own genius may have predisposed him against idyllic treatment by any transforming method; but, apart from that, there was, deep in his nature, a rooted abhorrence of any change in the essentials of the antique or medieval matter, a feeling reflected in his care for the accuracy of history in his trilogy. He was a purist, in opposition to his contemporaries. This was exemplified, for the Arthur Myth, in "The Tale of Balen," and again in "Tristram of Lyonesse"; he stood for the medieval, romantic narrative in the one case, and for the naked majesty of primitive love and fate in the other. There is a truthfulness, an austerity of truth, in all this which is temperamental in the poet and marks the strength of his individuality. In a certain way there is the spirit of Pre-Raphaelitism in it, a formal reversion to severer artistic methods, to a primitive poetry, to a more stern and bare figure of life, a reversion to art as opposed to mere manipulation of material, a recognition of the truth that the great themes of imagination are given to man, not created by him in any passing generation, that they are of man but not of men. This reverence of Swinburne for the past, in form and matter, in the things of art, is a part of that ritual of hero-worship to which he gives such fervid and personal expression and which is summed generally throughout his verse in his ever recurring hymn to Apollo, to the Sun-god, the inspiration of all poetry. The poet's faith is in this past of art, both form and matter and personality, instrument and theme and singer, and he sustains it against the temporal hour by virtue of his own enfranchisement in the mind from time, of his own liberty in the mastery of many literatures and epochs, of his own contemporaneity with poetry in a multitude of its forms and moods. Swinburne's conservatism is one with his hero-worship, one with his scholarship, one with his life-long passion for literature, a poet's passion for life in the imaginative world. The love of literature, a scholar's love, is the most fundamental thing in him; it is a jealous and deep-hearted love and controls him in his theories as well as in his practice, in his mental outlook as well as in his secret inspiration; it may make him aloof in person, remote in theme, reversionary in art, but it gives him a wide domain. The revolutionary cause even was for him a literary heirloom from the poets. Swinburne is a poet of culture through whom flows the broad stream of the many thoughts of men.

Swinburne first took the world with melody. The opening chorus of "Atalanta in Calydon" was, in the ears of men, a new singing voice on earth. Its music stamps the memory of whoever hears it beyond any possible oblivion. The cadence and the phrase are both characteristic of the poet's original genius, and so is their inseparability; they are one in the manifold of their syllables and they flash out in their fall what can only be called a color of sound. This is the peculiar and arresting poetic gift of Swinburne, the lyrical iridescence of the verse like a mother-of-pearl sea, like a green wave breaking in tempest, like a rainbow-spray before the beak of his driving song; it is a marvel that changes but fails not, a witchery of language, a vocal incantation in the rhymes, an enchantment in the mere pour of sound and pause and elision,— a purely metrical gift. The chorus of the "Atalanta" serves melodically as a prelude to all this lyrical change, just as it arises most spontaneously in the memory, in the recall of his music.


"When the hounds of spring are on winter's traces,
  The mother of months in meadow or plain
Fills the shadows and windy places
  With lisp of leaves and ripple of rain;
And the brown bright nightingale amorous
Is half assuaged for Itylus,
For the Thracian ships and the foreign faces,
  The tongueless vigil, and all the pain.


Come with bows bent and with emptying of quivers,
  Maiden most perfect, lady of light,
With a noise of winds and many rivers,
  With a clamor of waters, and with might;
Bind on thy sandals, O thou most fleet,
Over the splendor and speed of thy feet;
For the faint east quickens, the wan west shivers,
  Round the feet of the day and the feet of the night.

Where shall we find her, how shall we sing to her,
　　Fold our hands round her knees, and cling?
O that man's heart were as fire and could spring to her,
　　Fire, or the strength of the streams that spring!
For the stars and the winds are unto her
As raiment, as songs of the harp-player;
For the risen stars and the fallen cling to her,
　　And the southwest-wind and the west-wind sing.

For winter's rains and ruins are over,
　　And all the season of snows and sins;
The days dividing lover and lover,
　　The light that loses, the night that wins;
And time remembered is grief forgotten,
And frosts are slain and flowers begotten,
And in green underwood and cover
　　Blossom by blossom the spring begins.

The full streams feed on flower of rushes,
　　Ripe grasses trammel a traveling foot,
The faint fresh flame of the young year flushes
　　From leaf to flower and flower to fruit;
And fruit and leaf are as gold and fire,
And the oat is heard above the lyre,
And the hoofèd heel of a satyr crushes
　　The chestnut-husk at the chestnut-root.

And Pan by noon and Bacchus by night,
　　Fleeter of foot than the fleet-foot kid,
Follows with dancing and fills with delight
　　The Mœnad and the Bassarid;
And soft as lips that laugh and hide
The laughing leaves of the tree divide,
And screen from seeing and leave in sight
　　The god pursuing, the maiden hid.

The ivy falls with the Bacchanal's hair
　　Over her eyebrows hiding her eyes;
The wild vine slipping down leaves bare
　　Her bright breast shortening into sighs;

The wild vine slips with the weight of its leaves,
But the berried ivy catches and cleaves
To the limbs that glitter, the feet that scare
  The wolf that follows, the fawn that flies."

The lyrical vein here opened disclosed richer ores in the succeeding choruses and antiphonal arrangements of the plays. A new master of song-craft was plain to see. But there was that in the Hellenism of this play which gave the quality of an exotic to the verse, which shadowed and veiled the permanence of the gift and made it appear more magical than real. Its reality and permanence as the natural gift of an English poet was first and surprisingly established in men's minds by the publication of the first series of "Poems and Ballads" from which Swinburne's fame properly began. Here the lyrical quality was pre-eminent, greater in range and variety and in effect than in any later volume; here, there, were not only the cadence and the phrase, the flow, the color of sound, the intermingling of musical senses with the whole range of emotion and thought, but such delicacy and litheness and volume in the verses as made them a new revelation of language as a medium of expression. It was as if a new magical art had arisen, and Swinburne was its master. The verse was like sword-play, for brilliancy and precision, for short and long, for speed and glitter and nerve. Familiarity with it has now lessened the pleasures of surprise and wonder; but as the poet has gone on through later years, and from time to time has put forth his strength in novel ways, he has maintained and increased his early fame as a metrical master perfecting a native gift with all the resources of an exact and subtle scholarship in the resources of his art, its aim and limits, as a form of music in words. In all these things he is accomplished.

Perfect, however, in meters, he is less sensitive to purity in structural form. His lyrics are apt to be shortened dramas, his dramas to be fragmentary epics, his narrative to be a blend of lyric passion and dramatic episode. "Tristram of Lyonesse" is his most characteristic poem in this respect as in all others; it is the poem most representative of his qualities, each at its best. The poet's command of intellectual form, of the proportion of matter to expression, of the economic rendering of character, event and thought, of that logical condensation which is effected by art, is less manifest. Form in all its modes, and they are numerous, is essential to the greatest poetry. Swinburne is eminent for metrical form, in the highest degree; and in this he is lyrically unrivalled, so far as the form only is concerned. Of form in its structural and intellectual modes he has less, but prefers complexity to singleness and an ample fullness to economy. Blank verse also does not take his imprint so sympathetically as the lyrical measures, though as studiously labored as his rhymed and lyric lines; it is rather by the melody with which he first captured men, and by no other equal bond, that he holds the world under the fascination of liquid cadences and light lilts and choral harmonies that first fell on human speech from his lips.

The second salient trait of Swinburne's work, and one not less impressive and individualistic than his lyricism, is its rendering of the experience of passion. The theme is most pervasive in his earlier verse, and is there so frequent and takes on so many forms of imagination that a misleading idea was fixed in the public mind of the narrowness of his range in poetry. The poetic fiction under which he develops the theme is multifold, and exhibits the various sources of his culture; it has three main phases, classical, medieval and Pre-Raphaelite. The guise of Pre-Raphaelitism is the earliest and most palpable in the verse, and the fact is connected with the poet's association in life with the group of artists, Rossetti, Morris, Burne-Jones and others, with whom he had come in contact in college days and later, and to whose art in painting and cast of imagination generally Swinburne's was most cognate. His mind formed the habit of allegorizing in human figures abstractions, such as Love, Fear, Grief, and presenting these pictorially and symbolically. They are figures essentially without the motion of life, designated by attributes of color and wreath and wand, canvases or cameos in words; the poems in which they are the human element of interest are also highly conventionalized in their literary art, generally under French or Italian influences. Such are the opening poems of his work, set first in the collected edition, "A Ballad of Life" and "A Ballad of Death." The initial note thus struck often recurs, but as an artistic method it is diminishingly employed by the poet in the progress of his works. The classical source of his song is a much deeper spring, and from the moment when it blends with the verse lifts it far away from estheticism, conventionalized art and any limitation of narrow modes, peculiar fashion and formalism. The theme at once takes its great form as that of the everlasting opposition in human nature which is historically summed up as the antithesis of classical paganism to monkish Christianity, or more broadly as the contrast of the bodily with the spiritual element in life. Swinburne still further defines the discord as the opposition of the worship of Venus to that of the Virgin Mary; and thus begins for him that denial of Christian symbolism which he carried to the extreme of expression in the poem "Before a Crucifix."

The reversionary instinct, so noticeable in all his art, is here at work unchecked. He seems, like another Julian, to bring back the worship of the Greek divinities, affirming their permanence essentially in human nature, and he takes the traditionary dying words of Julian as the motto, one may add the motif, of the poem in which he most eloquently set forth his new paganism, the "Hymn to Proserpine":

"O Gods dethroned and deceased, cast forth, wiped out in a day!
From your wrath is the world released, redeemed from your chains, men say.
New Gods are crowned in the city; their flowers have broken your rods;
They are merciful, clothed with pity, the young compassionate Gods.
But for me their new device is barren, the days are bare;
Things long past over suffice, and men forgotten that were.
Time and the Gods are at strife; ye dwell in the midst thereof,
Draining a little life from the barren breasts of love.
I say to you, cease, take rest; yea, I say to you all, be at peace,
Till the bitter milk of her breast and the barren bosom shall cease.
Wilt thou yet take all, Galilean? but these thou shalt not take,
The laurel, the palms and the pean, the breasts of the nymphs in the brake;
Breasts more soft than a dove's, that tremble with tenderer breath;
And all the wings of the Loves, and all the joy before death;
All the feet of the hours that sound as a single lyre,
Dropped and deep in the flowers, with strings that flicker like fire.
More than these wilt thou give, things fairer than all these things?
Nay, for a little we live, and life hath mutable wings.

A little while and we die; shall life not thrive as it may?
For no man under the sky lives twice, outliving his day.
And grief is a grievous thing, and a man hath enough of his tears:
Why should he labor, and bring fresh grief to blacken his years?
Thou hast conquered, O pale Galilean; the world has grown grey from thy breath;
We have drunken of things Lethean, and fed on the fullness of death.
Laurel is green for a season, and love is sweet for a day;
But love grows bitter with treason, and laurel outlives not May.
Sleep, shall we sleep after all? for the world is not sweet in the end;
For the old faiths loosen and fall, the new years ruin and rend.
Fate is a sea without shore, and the soul is a rock that abides;
But her ears are vexed with the roar and her face with the foam of the tides.
O lips that the live blood faints in, the leavings of racks and rods!
O ghastly glories of saints, dead limbs of gibbeted gods
Though all men abase them before you in spirit, and all knees bend,
I kneel not neither adore you, but standing, look to the end.

. . . . . . . . . . . . .

Though the feet of thine high priests tread where thy lords and our forefathers trod,
Though these that were Gods are dead, and thou being dead art a God,
Though before thee the throned Cytherean be fallen, and hidden her head,
Yet thy kingdom shall pass, Galilean, thy dead shall go down to thee dead.
Of the maiden thy mother men sing as a goddess with grace clad around;
Thou art throned where another was king; where another was queen she is crowned.

Yea, once we had sight of another: but now she is queen, say these.
Not as thine, not as thine was our mother, a blossom of flowering seas,
Clothed round with the world's desire as with raiment as fair as the foam,
And fleeter than kindled fire, and a goddess and mother of Rome.
For thine came pale and a maiden, and sister to sorrow; but ours,
Her deep hair heavily laden with odor and color of flowers,
White rose of the rose-white water, a silver splendor, a flame,
Bent down unto us that besought her, and earth grew sweet with her name.
For thine came weeping, a slave among slaves, and rejected; but she
Came flushed from the full-flushed wave, and imperial, her foot on the sea.
And the wonderful waters knew her, the winds and the viewless ways,
And the roses grew rosier, and bluer the sea-blue stream of the bays."

The essential elements of Swinburne's imagination and method are all here present in this delineation of opposed divinities each powerful over human life. The identical theme is set forth again under the guise of medieval fiction in the poem "Laus Veneris," where the knight of the Venusberg legend sets in antithesis the pagan and the Christian scheme of life, and embodies in himself the apostacy from Christian ideals —

"For I was of Christ's choosing, I God's knight, —"

and his adhesion to the lady of the myth;

"For till the thunder in the trumpet be,
Soul may divide from body, but not we
    One from another; I hold thee with my hand,
I let mine eyes have all their will of thee."

Apart from the theory and the imagery, these poems are also identical in the tone of sad, dark farewell which converts each of them into a lament for love, for life itself. The protagonist of either poem has finished with life. Both poems have the motion of life, a vital breath in their lyrical expression of emotion profoundly modified by thought; but about the imagery, the figures of Aphrodite, the Virgin, the Lady of the Venusberg, and also the Crucifix that defines the conception of Christ in "Laus Veneris," — about all these there lingers the Pre-Raphaelite habit of imagination; the imagery has more affinity with modes of sacerdotal art, with symbolism and the attributive in imaginative power than it has with the free vitality that is more properly the sphere of poetry.

The new paganism, of which these two poems are elemental expressions receives a widely varied illustration in the body of poetry that is grouped about them. Several of these are dramatic lyrics containing a situation or a slight story; others are hardly more than exercises in verse, often in French forms; still others are deeply meditated or elaborately studied after the sentiment, the phrasing and the thought-movement of the Greek antique. The whole spirit, however, is romantic in mood and conduct and more nigh to the essentially medieval than to the modern or to the ancient. The dominant memories of Swinburne, however, whether intellectual or imaginative, lie in classical antiquity; and, so far as he has need of any divine principle in his verse, in concrete forms, he has found approach to the Greek gods most facile. He achieves the most genuine appearance of belief in the gods that has fallen to the fortune of any English poet, perhaps of any poet in any modern literature. The recurring hymn to the Sun, under its many forms, which has already been alluded to, is a deep note of his temperament. The classical immersion of his mind had made clean work of all Christian symbolism; it had swept it away; and in its place came, for imaginative purposes, the Greek forms of old divinity and myth, but less as idols of hope than idols of memory. The close of the "Hymn to Proserpine" gives his point of faith with most precision; death is the end of all, but he chooses for his companions in death the dead gods,—he will descend to Proserpine where all have gone. His faith is a farewell; a *Vale* not an *Ave*.

The new paganism in which imaginative reminiscence plays so great a part, effecting this renascence of antique symbolism in the poet's mind, also finds expression in a more direct and concrete presentation of the experience as well as of the theory of passion, both in the form of dramatic incident or situation and in the form of allegorized figuration in art. Whether set forth under a classical or later name, Sappho or Faustine or Félise, or in the namelessness of a dream of passion, Swinburne delineates the moment with vividness of sensation, with languid hazes, with lights and shadows as of some Venetian picture; or in his symbolical poems he builds up a figure, a background, a landscape as of some mythic painting, though using mainly cadence as his means of evoking it. "Dolores" is a poem of this last type, and characteristic of his genius, in subject, handling and tone. In all these poems which, in various ways, by dramatic, lyric and meditative modes, set forth the theme of the mortal ways of desire, the accompaniment of the verse is a lament, seldom light, usually profound and often touched with bitterness. Pain is the master-emotion in the verse, unconcealed, rebellious, self-pitying. The knight of the "Laus Veneris" is filled full of it; so are the cadences of "Doleres"; so are some of the lightest and most delicate of the lyrics.

The poem which sets forth this aspect of the paganism of a modern spirit with nobleness of feeling is "Hesperia," which after its fine nature-opening, goes on with its human burden in these lines:

"From the bountiful infinite west, from the happy memorial places
  Full of the stately repose and the lordly delight of the dead,
Where the fortunate islands are lit with the light of ineffable faces,
  And the sound of a sea without wind is about them, and sunset is red,
Come back to redeem and release me from love that recalls and represses,
  That cleaves to my flesh as a flame, till the serpent has eaten his fill;
From the bitter delights of the dark, and the feverish, the furtive caresses
  That murder the youth in a man or ever his heart have its will.
Thy lips cannot laugh and thine eyes cannot weep; thou art pale as a rose is,
  Paler and sweeter than leaves that cover the blush of the bud;
And the heart of the flower is compassion, and pity the core it encloses,
  Pity, not love, that is born of the breath and decays with the blood.
As the cross that a wild nun clasps till the edge of it bruises her bosom,
  So love wounds as we grasp it, and blackens and burns as a flame;
I have loved overmuch in my life; when the live bud bursts with the blossom,
  Bitter as ashes or tears is the fruit, and the wine thereof shame.

As a heart that its anguish divides is the green bud cloven asunder;
  As the blood of a man self-slain is the flush of the leaves that allure;
And the perfume as poison and wine to the brain, a delight and a wonder;
  And the thorns are too sharp for a boy, too slight for a man to endure,
Too soon did I love it, and lost love's rose; and I cared not for glory's;
  Only the blossoms of sleep and of pleasure were mixed in my hair.
Was it myrtle or poppy thy garland was woven with, O my Dolores?
  Was it pallor of slumber, or blush as of blood, that I found in thee fair?
For desire is a respite from love, and the flesh not the heart is her fuel;
  She was sweet to me once, who am fled and escaped from the range of her reign;
Who behold as of old time at hand as I turn, with her mouth growing cruel,
  And flushed as with wine with the blood of her lovers, Our Lady of Pain.
Low down where the thicket is thicker with thorns than with leaves in the summer,
  In the brake is a gleaming of eyes and a hissing of tongues that I knew;
And the lithe long throats of her snakes reach round her, their mouths overcome her,
  And her lips grow cool with their foam, made moist as a desert with dew.
With the thirst and the hunger of lust though her beautiful lips be so bitter,
  With the cold foul foam of the snakes they soften and redden and smile;
And her fierce mouth sweetens, her eyes wax wide and her eyelashes glitter,
  And she laughs with a savor of blood in her face, and a savor of guile.

She laughs, and her hands reach hither, her hair blows hither and hisses,
    As a lowlit flame in a wind, back-blown till it shudder and leap;
Let her lips not again lay hold on my soul, nor her poisonous kisses,
    To consume it alive and divide from thy bosom, Our Lady of Sleep.
Ah daughter of sunset and slumber, if now it return into prison,
    Who shall redeem it anew?  But we, if thou wilt, let us fly;
Let us take to us, now that the white skies thrill with a moon unarisen,
    Swift horses of fear or of love, take flight and depart and not die.
They are swifter than dreams, they are stronger than death; there is none that hath ridden,
    None that shall ride in the dim strange ways of his life as we ride;
By the meadows of memory, the highlands of hope, and the shore that is hidden,
    Where life breaks loud and unseen, a sonorous invisible tide;
By the sands where sorrow has trodden, the salt pools bitter and sterile,
    By the thundering reef and the low sea-wall and the channel of years,
Our wild steeds press on the night, strain hard through pleasure and peril,
    Labor and listen and pant not or pause for the peril that nears;
And the sound of them trampling the way cleaves night as an arrow asunder,
    And slow by the sand-hill and swift by the down with its glimpses of grass,
Sudden and steady the music, as eight hoofs trample and thunder,
    Rings in the ear of the low blind wind of the night as we pass;
Shrill shrieks in our faces the blind bland air that was mute as a maiden,

Stung into storm by the speed of our passage, and deaf where we past;
And our spirits too burn as we bound, thine holy but mine heavy-laden,
As we burn with the fire of our flight; ah love, shall we win at the last?"

The procession of Swinburne's studies of passion, highly composite in artistic material and method as they are and diversified by their kinship with many moods and periods of the spirit of poetry, have, together with their vividness of sensation and their sad meditative burden of the emptiness of mortal things, a monotone that is unmistakable, as omnipresent and profound as the monotone in his revolutionary verses. It is the monotone of fundamental emotion in the one as in the other, and springs from a depth of habitual feeling that is a part of the poet's temperament. The experience of passion is not seized dramatically in the true sense, it is seized lyrically, and the ultimate mood is that of the weariness of life which in place of a dramatic exhaustion of the action in tragic catastrophe, issues only in an exhausted emotion; it belongs to the type that it should end in weakness. The end of the feeling is a transformation into thought; into meditation; in this intellectual climax the mood takes on the appearance of philosophy, of a surrender of life to death, of the prayer to Proserpine before the descent of the poet to the shades of the underworld. This philosophy in which the lyrical mood of Swinburne under these impulses evaporates is most beautifully and winningly given in the verses so well known by their melody alone, "The Garden of Proserpine." They contain the summary of his verse of life-experience for the individual, of emotional experience properly, and are the death-song of the pagan ideal, not in its historic but its esthetic sense, as it was conceived and presented by him:

"Here, where the world is quiet,
  Here, where all trouble seems
Dead winds' and spent waves' riot
  In doubtful dreams of dreams;
I watch the green field growing
For reaping folk and sowing,
For harvest-time and mowing,
  A sleepy world of streams.

I am tired of tears and laughter,
  And men that laugh and weep,
Of what may come hereafter
  For men that sow to reap:
I am weary of days and hours,
Blown buds of barren flowers,
Desires and dreams and powers
  And everything but sleep.

Here life has death for neighbor,
  And far from eye or ear
Wan waves and wet winds labor,
  Weak ships and spirits steer;
They drive adrift, and whither
They wot not who make thither;
But no such winds blow hither;
  And no such things grow here.

No growth of moor or coppice,
  No heather-flower or vine,
But bloomless buds of poppies,
  Green grapes of Proserpine,
Pale beds of blowing rushes
Where no leaf blooms or blushes
Save this whereout she crushes
  For dead men deadly wine.

Pale, without name or number,
  In fruitless fields of corn,
They bow themselves and slumber
  All night till light is born;
And like a soul belated,
In hell and heaven unmated,
By cloud and mist abated
  Comes out of darkness morn.

Though one were strong as seven,
  He too with death shall dwell,
Nor wake with wings in heaven,
  Nor weep for pains in hell;
Though one were fair as roses,
His beauty clouds and closes;
And well though love reposes,
  In the end it is not well.

Pale, beyond porch and portal,
  Crowned with calm leaves, she stands
Who gathers all things mortal
  With cold immortal hands;
Her languid lips are sweeter
Than love's who fears to greet her
To men that mix and meet her
  From many times and lands.

She waits for each and other,
  She waits for all men born;
Forgets the earth her mother,
  The life of fruits and corn;
And spring and seed and swallow
Take wing for her and follow
Where summer song rings hollow
  And flowers are put to scorn.

There go the loves that wither,
  The old loves with wearier wings;
And all dead years draw thither,
  And all disastrous things;

Dead dreams of days forsaken,
Blind buds that snows have shaken,
Wild leaves that winds have taken,
 Red strays of ruined springs.

We are not sure of sorrow,
 And joy was never sure;
To-day will die to-morrow;
 Time stoops to no man's lure;
And love, grown faint and fretful
With lips but half regretful
Sighs, and with eyes forgetful
 Weeps that no loves endure.

From too much love of living,
 From hope and fear set free,
We thank with brief thanksgiving
 Whatever gods may be
That no life lives for ever;
That dead men rise up never;
That even the weariest river
 Winds somewhere safe to sea.

Then star nor sun shall waken,
 Nor any change of light:
Nor sound of waters shaken,
 Nor any sound or sight:
Nor wintry leaves nor vernal
Nor days nor things diurnal,
Only the sleep eternal
 In an eternal night."

In his later work the theme of passion was less brilliantly treated than in these first poems, and few of the passages in which he reverts to the subject are so significant, characteristic or successful. Passion as an element in human life attracted him rather in more dramatic ways, as it exists in the great trilogy of Queen

Mary felt in diverse modes by those about the Queen from the tender and noble figure of Chastelard to the weakness of Darnley and the strength of Bothwell; or it attracted him as the life-element of the myth of Tristram and Iseult, that in which they had the perfection of their being and the completion of their fate. In both cases this is the drama of passion, not its lyricism; and in both cases, too, it is divorced from the after-sickliness of thought that attends it in the youthful poems, and is free from the envelopment of the pagan world, from dead gods and past time; it stands by itself, in its own right, a part of nature and life universal, a reality. No English poem surpasses "Tristram of Lyonesse" in the quality of passion; it is great as a representation of passion, primarily, and equal to the fame of its theme. Yet it is rather upon the younger verse, in the early passionate efflorescence of his poetic nature, that the fame of Swinburne as an original, unique and powerful exponent of the passion of life in the ways of desire, brilliantly illustrating the multiform romantic spirit, must rest.

The meditative power of Swinburne's mind gradually displaced the passionate impulse of the senses, in his verse. He is a very thoughtful poet. The intellectual burden of his poetry first appeared in the vigor with which he seized and held to the idea of fate; fate is as elemental in his work as passion and is its true complement. The conception at the beginning may have been only a part of his Greek legacy, made familiar to him in his study of Greek drama and adopted from it into his own literary scheme of art and philosophy of life. In "Atalanta of Calydon," fate is set forth in the choruses; it is associated there with the feeling of bitter hostility to the gods. There is a Lucretian sternness and fierceness in all of Swinburne's invective against those aspects of religion which were to him what superstition was to the old Roman; and he uses violence of phrase in the expression of his mood. It is thus that he comes to a climax of thought in the attack on the supernal powers which ends in the words, "the supreme evil, God." The thought is arrived at through the spectacle of the suffering of the human race, and applies, as it were, to the Zeus of Prometheus.

"Thou hast fed one rose with dust of many men;
  Thou hast marred one face with fire of many tears;
Thou hast taken love, and given us sorrow again;
  With pain thou hast filled us full to the eyes and ears.
Therefore because thou art strong, our father, and we
  Feeble; and thou art against us, and thine hand
Constrains us in the shallows of the sea
  And breaks us at the limits of the land;
Because thou hast bent thy lightnings as a bow,
  And loosed the hours like arrows; and let fall
Sins and wild words and many a wingèd woe
  And wars among us, and one end of all;
Because thou hast made the thunder, and thy feet
  Are as a rushing water when the skies
Break, and thy face as an exceeding heat
  And flames of fire the eyelids of thine eyes;
Because thou art over all who are over us;
  Because thy name is life and our name death;
Because thou art cruel and men are piteous,
  And our hands labor and thine hand scattereth;
Lo, with hearts rent and knees made tremulous,
  Lo, with ephemeral lips and casual breath,
  At least we witness of thee ere we die
That these things are not otherwise, but thus;
  That each man in his heart sigheth, and saith,
    That all men even as I,
All we are against thee, against thee, O God most high."

In such passages, of which this was the earliest, the life-weariness that belongs to exhausted passion is extended over the whole of life, and the philosophy set forth is frankly atheistic. The passing away of the successive hierarchies of gods that have been exalted in the heavens, including the entire symbolism of Christianity, is as constant a theme of Swinburne's imagination and meditation as is the transitoriness of the generations of men and their works; nor is there only this denial of the gods, but with it goes that implacable hostility to them and their ways, which has been alluded to, giving often to the verse an edge of scorn and hate. Swinburne derived from Greek literature the point of view, so far as the history of man under the Olympian dispensation was concerned; he derived from the revolutionary poets an attitude toward historical Christianity in its medieval forms and in its institutional power, which was a practical repetition of the same point of view; however he approached supernatural religion he collided with the eternal mystery of God's dealing with mankind, and also with the temporal dispensation of the professional ministers of God, the priesthood wherever found. The anti-Christian verse is, of course, incidental to and a part of the great mass of revolutionary verse, and belongs to the poet's crusade against the social powers that be, to his ranking himself with the spirit of Burns and the later upholders of the powers of light, that is of human intellect, liberty and love. But, besides this aspect of it, there is a philosophical side to his thought, apart from its revolutionary intention, by virtue of which it must be regarded abstractly as his own poetic attitude to the mystery of life itself. Fate is the simplest word to describe the power in whose dark and infinite grasp Swinburne habitually sees the universe of man.

Deeply impressed as the poet is by the conception of fate in life and in the universe, he does not embody it in either his dramas or his dramatic narrative with great power; he rather describes it than presents its operation; it is a presence rather than a force in his verse. The story of Atalanta, and also that of Erechtheus contain fate, in piteous and cruel forms, but the will of the gods in either case seems arbitrary rather than fatal. In the Trilogy of Queen Mary the element of fate is discernible in the constant reminiscence, through the play, of Chastelard's execution and in Mary Beaton who is the embodiment of that memory and shall remain with the Queen until the latter's death at the block expiates the original wrong, or at least crowns it as a consummation; but the linking of fate which should connect one with the other directly and impressively, and as a law of necessity is not shown. In the other dramas there is a similar laxity in the causal operation of fate, — the fatal necessity of the action is not felt as power, but is described as story. In "Tristram of Lyonesse," it is the passion, not the fate of the lovers' love that is in the foreground of interest. In the shorter poems the method of presenting the general subject-matter is more abstract and by means of passages of invective. "Anactoria" is the best example, where the outcry against the divine power is repeatedly raised, with a fierce vindictiveness:

> "Is not his incense bitterness, his meat
> Murder? his hidden face and iron feet
> Hath not man known, and felt them on their way
> Threaten and trample all things and every day?
> Hath he not sent us hunger? who hath cursed
> Spirit and flesh with longing? filled with thirst
> Their lips who cried unto him? who bade exceed
> The fervid will, fall short the feeble deed,

> Bade sink the spirit and the flesh aspire,
> Pain animate the dust of dead desire,
> And life yield up her flower to violent fate?
> Him would I reach, him smite, him desecrate,
> Pierce the cold lips of God with human breath,
> And mix his immortality with death."

At the conclusion of this poem is the first expression of any possible human victory in the strife with the gods. It takes form in the thought that, whatever misfortune may be visited upon Sappho in life, yet after death she will have an immortality in her words still breathing on the lips of men:

> "Albeit I die indeed
> And hide myself and sleep and no man heed,
> Of me the high God hath not all his will.
> Blossom of branches, and on each high hill
> Clear air and wind, and under in clamorous vales
> Fierce noises of the fiery nightingales,
> Buds burning in the sudden spring like fire,
> The wan washed sand and the waves' vain desire,
>
> Sails seen like blown white flowers at sea, and words
> That bring tears swiftest, and long notes of birds
> Violently singing till the whole world sings —
> I Sappho, shall be one with all these things,
> With all high things for ever; and my face
> Seen once, my songs once heard in a strange place,
> Cleave to men's lives, and waste the days thereof
> With gladness and much sadness and long love."

This hope of immortality in the mind and for the service of man is the prelude to Swinburne's later exposition of man's faith in himself.

The earlier attitude of hostility to the gods yields in the poet's maturer years to a prevailing mood of high-

# SWINBURNE

spirited indifference, which is felt rather toward fate under the forms of the imagery of nature than under those of divine beings. The passage which best concentrates it is the speech of Tristram, concerning fate which is described only by negatives as the unknown infinite in the universe:

> "How should it turn from its great way to give
> Man that must die a clearer space to live?
> Why should the waters of the sea be cleft,
> The hills be molten to his right and left,
> That he from deep to deep might pass dry-shod
> Or look between the viewless heights on God?
> Hath he such eyes as, when the shadows flee,
> The sun looks out with to salute the sea?
> Is his hand bounteous as the morning's hand?
> Or where the night stands hath he feet to stand?
> Will the storm cry not when he bids it cease?
> Is it his voice that saith to the east wind, Peace?
> Is his breath mightier than the west wind's breath?
> Doth his heart know the things of life and death?
> Can his face bring forth sunshine and give rain,
> Or his weak will that dies and lives again
> Make one thing certain or bind one thing fast,
> That as he willed it shall be at the last?
> How should the storms of heaven and kindled lights
> And all the depths of things and topless heights
> And air and earth and fire and water change
> Their likeness, and the natural world grow strange,
> And all the limits of their life undone
> Lose count of time and conscience of the sun,
> And that fall under which was fixed above,
> That man might have a larger hour for love?"

It is in this identification of fate with the universe of greater being, in a form of apprehension which hovers between pantheism in its aspect of nature-force and in its aspect of humanity, that Swinburne's mind rests in its final meditation. The hymn entitled "Hertha" sets forth the matter in full and at great length, with a principal dependence in the imagery on Igdrasil, the tree of life. In its main philosophic intention the poem is hardly to be distinguished from Emerson's "Brahma," which is the type of such poetic thought; but Swinburne gives it a new turn and transforms its meaning by grafting into it the idea that mankind is the highest personification of the divine known to man and hence that true worship and religion is in the energy of man's self-expression, in the apotheosis of himself that is self-achieved. The key stanza is this:

"A creed is a rod,
    And a crown is of night;
But this thing is God,
    To be man with thy might,
To grow straight in the strength of thy spirit, and live out thy life as the light."

The poem in its last line makes the identification of man with the infinite spirit plain:

"Man, equal and one with me, man that is made of me, man that is I."

The same doctrine is more elaborately stated and with a more comprehensive inclusion of many past elements of Swinburne's thought, especially with relation to the passing away of the gods and to the history of superstition, in the "Hymn of Man," which Swinburne himself describes as "the birth-song of spiritual renascence" and which concludes its Miriam-like outburst of triumph over the fall of old religion with the exultant cry:

"Glory to man in the highest! for Man is the master of things."

This is the French apotheosis of Reason in its most modern form, and may be regarded, perhaps, as essentially a hymn of positivism.

It thus appears that Swinburne's mind, guided by the preconceptions of his Greek studies and the revolutionary impetus of his native genius, has been deeply concerned with reaching an intellectual faith with regard to the scheme of man's life as it has been seen by him in history. In this attempt he has clung most tenaciously to the idea of fate, a vague conception diversely seized by his mind and set forth in a variety of ways. The denial of the gods was inherent in his intellectual position; and the gods having passed away, there remained only such an adjustment of mind to the world emptied of old divinity as is possible to many a modern brooder over thought besides the poet himself who may be, somewhat at least, a type of such sceptical men. In the one hand there was the resource of the conception of the unknown infinite which is approached by human thought most commonly through the majestic phenomena of nature, and of which the nature-poetry of the book of Job, whence come the imaginative method and scriptural cadences of that speech of Tristram that has been quoted, is the ritual of expression. On the other hand there was the resource of positivistic and humanitarian insistence on the religion of Humanity, the creed of doing as the other is the creed of knowing. The apotheosis of human energy is natural in any greatly progressive or violently active age of the world; and in the nineteenth century, with its unmeasured pride in itself and its incontestable greatness of achievement in both the realms of knowledge and action, faith in man sprang up and has flourished as if it were the ancient Igdrasil itself; it has seemed as if man were a god of nature and a providence for the future, — at least that has been the tendency of man's late ideals in science and philanthropy. Man at least thinks himself — what Swinburne says the gods were not — piteous. Swinburne has caught the infection of both of these intellectual moods; he has on one hand accepted imaginatively the theory of the unknown natural infinite and on the other the doctrine of the greatness — as he frankly says, the godhead — of man; not, it should be observed, of men in their parcelled and particular individuality, but of the race, — the apotheosis is a thing of collectivity, and without such collectivity would not exist. Perhaps his own words should be given:

"We men, the multiform features of man, whatsoever we be
Recreate him of whom we are creatures, and all we only are he.
For each man of all men is God, but God is the fruit of the whole;
Invisible spirit and blood, indiscernible body from soul.
Not men's but man's is the glory of godhead, —"

In working out this side of the theory, it follows of necessity that the poet should find himself in a midmost ethical stream, that he should end less as a philosopher than as a moralist; he would finally be absorbed in the vindication of that law of life which is humanly discerned and applied as the will of "righteousness" from age to age. The gods pass like leaves of the forest, in their generations, even as men do; but righteousness is an abiding thing. It is this that is stated, very nobly and magnificently indeed, in the chief poem of Swinburne's later years, "The Altar of Righteousness." This poem is the climax of his intellectual attempt in solving the universe, or in reaching at least a working relation with respect to it; it is the ultimate conviction, the last word, — this of the majestic permanence of righteousness.

Does it seem singular to any that the poet of passion should be one with the poet of righteousness? There is really no discord in the case; the two elements, at least, never cross in the verse. A poet gives a representation of life, and the variety of his representation depends on the richness and complexity of his nature. Swinburne was endowed with power to render with unrivalled vividness, with brilliance of word and melody of cadence the experience of man's life in passion; he was also endowed with intellectual curiosity and restlessness, with mental vigor, with irrepressible and inexhaustible sympathies with the public causes of mankind in political and religious social life, and he had thence his power to interest himself in the ideas that lie back of all life, in the philosophy of the divine element appearing in the history of the race and in its changes under the shaping of time from Greek to Christian, and so on to the last results of modern speculation. He expressed himself from year to year, according to the faith that was in him, and he reached in his maturity the clear position which needs no plainer definition than his own lines contain. The original idea of adverse fate has faded in his mind, it would appear, to that of the immanence of the unknown in nature, indifferent and kindless to man, but not consciously cruel and deliberately scornful like the old gods; and this in turn yields to the prominence in his later thought of the essential necessity that mankind is under to know no god except his own spirit, to advance that spirit as the life of the race itself, and to find the conscious law of righteousness in its bosom age after age its only oracle and guide to destiny.

The third great monochord of Swinburne's verse, after passion and fate, is nature. The poet's genius is one of singular directness, though the fact is masked and obscured by the conventionalized, curious and classically reminiscent character that so much of his work superficially bears. The same directness that appears in his dealing with the experience of passion, and with the theory of the divine element in the universe, marks also his treatment of nature. He is a nature-poet, but rather in the energetic than the esthetic sense. The reminiscence of his boyhood upbringing by the seas of the Northumberland coast and of the Isle of Wight is always present in his verse of every kind. His description is not deficient in either abundance or beauty of detail; but he seizes the landscape mainly as a whole, he feels the forces abiding in it as power, he is exalted by its effluence in him as an emotion; in a word, his treatment is ample. Here, too, that extraordinary trait of primitiveness, that love of the primordial things in thought and life, of which illustration has already been afforded in the preceding pages, breaks out with great force. It seems often that his mind is absorbed, not so much in natural objects in their individuality as in natural elements, in their larger life of the constitution, the whirl, the vast spectacle of nature. Fire, air, earth and water are the four elements from which his very vocabulary seems made up; flame, wind and foam, and all the forms of light are so much a part of his color-rhythm that they become an opaline of verse peculiarly his own; his mannerism in diction and style is chiefly a thing of his fascination with these elemental phases of matter and sensation which are more abstractions of motion, hue and luminousness than simple objects of sight and hearing. The blurring effect of this mass of indefinable sensation, especially when metaphorically employed, even more than the overcharge of vocal sound in the verse, accounts for that impression of vacuity of meaning that Swinburne's poetry in general makes on readers not habituated to his manner. The main fact is that in the sphere of natural imagery his mind tends constantly to escape from the limited and particular object into the more abstract primary elements of nature, and to use these metaphorically without definition to color his verse with sensation that is rather emotional than perceptive; it is thus that he produces these effects by virtue of which his poetry is generally thought to have more affinity with the art of music than has been achieved by other poets. Color-tones of nature have as much to do with this as simple sound-tones of rhyme, alliteration and cadence; all the senses, and not the ear alone, are occupied with this music which lulls and dazzles the mind with a magical and exquisite pleasure.

The nature poems of Swinburne in the precise sense, however, are many and various and among them some rise higher than others. He has himself, in his own review of his poetic work, named those which to himself seem most significant, and his own choice coincides with that of his readers. He dwells there upon his closeness to the scene and repeats the same traits of the general landscape that he has described in verse. No summary can equal this in justice, brevity and breadth. The poems he selects are the four poems of the West Undercliff, "In the Bay," "On the Cliffs," "A Forsaken Garden," the dedication to "The Sisters," "Off Shore," "An Autumn Vision," "A Swimmer's Dream," "On the South Coast," "Neap-Tide." It will be found on examination that primitive nature is at the heart of all of these poems as plainly as it is in the last class he names — "such as try to render the effect of inland or woodland solitude — the splendid oppression of nature at noon which found utterance of old in words of such singular and everlasting significance as panic and nympholepsy." The terror of noon is precisely one of those primordial things the fascination of which — not to speak of the wonder of his merely knowing it — stamps Swinburne's genius, in its approach to nature, with the aboriginal mark of the race. With this capacity to feel the old mood belongs the general largeness of his outlook and horizon, and through both these traits he comes into sympathy with polytheistic habitudes; at that moment of noon his genius hovers between the Sun-god in heaven and Pan on earth with an equal possession of mythologizing mind; and, in general, it is the grand features and glomeration of things that holds him — heaven with all its stars, its winds and clouds; earth in great tracts of barren places or of "cliff and crag, lawn and woodland, garden and lea;" and most of all the sea.

Swinburne's ocean-poetry is the crown of his nature verse; in it he is not only most exalted and fluent and vivid, but he winds the sea-voices truly into his song. He was the child of a sailor-race, and in his boyhood the sea was his open highway of dream, imagination and sentiment, of the vision that comes to great poets in their youth. It was the thing of nature most clung about by his spirit; the sun — so he represents it — had his adoration, but the sea his love. The sea, too, had other imaginative values to him. It was his nature-symbol of England. The thought of England as the oceanic power was natural ever after the Armada and the Elizabethan poets, and in later days is supported by the imperial dominion spread and based in all directions upon the waters; to Swinburne, the singer of the Armada and the patriot for whom the greatness of England lay in that quality of race of which her sea greatness is the memorial in time, England is, as it were, the emanation of the sea in humanity, one thing with it and, one may say, the spiritual form of it; so it seems to his eyes. The sea, too, is his nature-symbol of liberty, of that in the spirit of all mankind which is the greatest object of human effort, the condition and the consummation of greatness in nations or men, the state of being in which alone they truly are at all. The historic association of liberty with the sea-races, from Athens down, helps in this idealization, which, in itself is natural to the thoughts of all men and universal in poetry. And again, through the operation of his own poetizing revery and fancy and the familiar growth of his spirit in conjunction with and through an environment of sea-experience, the sea became in Swinburne's secret thoughts the nature-symbol of his own genius, a thing of untameable and primitive nature blending with the cause of liberty and the glory of England and the universal hope and life of mankind; he thought of himself, mythically, as the child of the sea, and he repeatedly praises a sea-death as the appropriate end of such a child.

This fancy, which is more genuine in feeling than might seem possible, is expressed in many passages of his poems, but it is the formative idea in one distinctive poem, which may fairly be regarded as an autobiographical myth of the idealizing sort, such as Shelley's "Epipsychidion," that entitled "Thalassius." It is a delicate and highly-finished work, and is also perhaps the most broadly instructive, the most comprehensive of his experience and theory, of any of his poems. Thalassius is the child of the Sea and of the Sun, and the verse relates his history from birth to the moment of his perfecting in life, under the symbolism of classical mythic imagery. He is educated by a foster-father, and fed

"For bread with wisdom and with song for wine,"

after the antique manner familiar to us in Shelley's verse of Laon and Prince Athanase; the identification with the poet is made plain in the details of this instruction:

"High things the high song taught him;

. . . . . . . . . . . .

How he that loves life overmuch shall die
The dog's death, utterly:
And he that much less loves it than he hates
All wrongdoing that is done
Anywhere always underneath the sun
Shall live a mightier life than time's or fate's.
One fairer thing he shewed him, and in might
More strong than day and night
Whose strengths build up time's towering period:
Yea, one thing stronger and more high than God,
Which if man had not, then should God not be:
And that was Liberty.
And gladly should man die to gain, he said,
Freedom; and gladlier, having lost, lie dead.

. . . . . . . . . . . .

And hate the song too taught him: hate of all
That brings or holds in thrall
Of spirit or flesh, free-born ere God began,
The holy body and sacred soul of man.
And wheresoever a curse was or a chain,
A throne for torment or a crown for bane
Rose, molded out of poor men's molten pain,
There, said he, should man's heaviest hate be set
Inexorably, to faint not or forget

Till the last warmth bled forth of the last vein
In flesh that none should call a king's again,
Seeing wolves and dogs and birds that plague-strike air
Leave the last bone of all the carrion bare.

And hope the high song taught him: hope whose eyes
Can sound the seas unsoundable, the skies
Inaccessible of eyesight; that can see
What earth beholds not, hear what wind and sea
Hear not, and speak what all these crying in one
Can speak not to the sun.
For in her sovereign eyelight all things are
Clear as the closest seen and kindlier star
That marries morn and even and winter and spring
With one love's golden ring.
For she can see the days of man, the birth
Of good and death of evil things on earth
Inevitable and infinite, and sure
As present pain is, or herself is pure.
Yea, she can hear and see, beyond all things
That lighten from before Time's thunderous wings
Through the awful circle of wheel-winged periods,
The tempest of the twilight of all Gods:
And higher than all the circling course they ran
The sundawn of the spirit that was man."

The body of the poem continues with the life experience of the hero, and at the end, at the moment of his perfecting, the Sun-god blesses him with words that may be taken as the ideal of the poet's life:

"Child of my sunlight and the sea, from birth
A fosterling and fugitive on earth;
Sleepless of soul as wind or wave or fire,
A manchild with an ungrown God's desire;
Because thou hast loved nought mortal more than me,
Thy father, and thy mother-hearted sea;
Because thou hast set thine heart to sing, and sold
Life and life's love for song, God's living gold;

> Because thou hast given thy flower and fire of youth
> To feed men's hearts with visions, truer than truth;
> Because thou hast kept in those world-wandering eyes
> The light that makes me music of the skies;
> Because thou hast heard with world-unwearied ears
> The music that puts light into the spheres;
> Have therefore in thine heart and in thy mouth
> The sound of song that mingles north and south,
> The song of all the winds that sing of me,
> And in thy soul the sense of all the sea."

In this poem the nature-poetry of Swinburne finds its highest and most beautiful idealization in human life; it is, in fact, the crowning work of his hand, in so far as he drew his inspiration from the life of his spirit with nature.

Admirable in portraiture as the pure nature-poems of Swinburne are, in their mere rendering of scene, atmosphere and landscape mood, they gain in poetic power in proportion as the element of human life is brought into them in any form, whether as a personal tone of the poet or as incident, memory or vision, or as a main action. In "Thalassius," the idealization of nature is superfine and places the poem in the highest rank of those few imaginative and spiritualized allegories of life which can appeal deeply only to a narrow circle of readers in any generation, men who are numbered by two's and three's rather than by scores. In numerous poems, however, Swinburne has blended description with autobiography in the most charming way, especially in those coast poems which he has associated with the name of his friend, Theodore Watts-Dunton, himself a nature-lover with the primitive bases of feeling in him belonging to earlier ages and a more earthly generation of men; and also, and peculiarly, in the poems of swimming the blend of nature with life is accomplished with a fine effect. The great instance of such a description in which nature is not only the scene but the giver of the action is the swim of Tristram in the dawn of the Sun just before the battle in which he receives his death-wounds. The passage is long, and fuller of pure natural beauty than any other scene in the poet's verse, and it is besides unique in literature, sole by itself in its saturation with the sea and the dawn and the joy of the swimmer, made one joy of all; but no presentation of Swinburne's nature-verse can spare the concluding lines, with the glory of their physical delight:

> "Till the sweet change that bids the sense grow sure
> Of deeper depth and purity more pure
> Wrapped him and lapped him round with clearer cold,
> And all the rippling green grew royal gold
> Between him and the far sun's rising rim.
> And like the sun his heart rejoiced in him,
> And brightened with a broadening flame of mirth;
> And hardly seemed its life a part of earth,
> But the life kindled of a fiery birth
> And passion of a new-begotten son
> Between the live sea and the living sun.
> And mightier grew the joy to meet full-faced
> Each wave, and mount with upward plunge, and taste
> The rapture of its rolling strength, and cross
> Its flickering crown of snows that flash and toss
> Like plumes in battle's blithest charge, and thence
> To watch the next with yet more strenuous sense;
> Till on his eyes the light beat hard and bade
> His face turn west and shoreward through the glad
> Swift revel of the waters golden-clad,
> And back with light reluctant heart he bore
> Across the broad-backed rollers in to shore."

Such poetry brings back that early world in which old Triton blew his wreathed horn, and not in a vision only, but as the everlasting life of nature and man.

Swinburne is at heart a nature-worshipper, and it is through the symbolism of nature that his religious instincts find their fullest and unimpeded flow. His classically reminiscent and anti-Christian poems alike contain a literary alloy and belong in substance to scholarship, to progress, to things of civilization, to society; in proportion as he lays these things aside and reverts in primitive freedom to the world of nature, to awe of the sun and delight in the waves and indefinable moods of the moors, the barrens and the glens, he recaptures the original soul, becomes himself purely, pours out his spirit directly, intensely, overflowingly, — he lives the poetic life. The deepest sympathies of his genius are with force, with things of power everywhere, with the energies of life. The truth about him is the exact opposite of what has been widely and popularly thought; weakness, affectation, exotic foreignness, the traits of estheticism in the debased sense of that word, are far from him; he is strong, he is genuine, he is English, bred with an European mind it is true like Shelley, like Gray and Milton, but in his own genius, temperament and the paths of his flight charged with the strength of England. In his nature-verse there is sympathy with power, grandeur, energy, marking the verse unmistakably as that of a strong soul; in his social verse of all kinds, political and religious, there is the same sympathy marking it, making it clarion-like, to use his own metaphor, for liberty, progress, man, for the truth and love of the Revolution, for the ideal of the Republic as the great and single aim of the race. In his passion-verse there is the same breath of the power of life; and that farewell to life in which the pagan mood ends, by its insistency, its poignancy, its plangency, the sweetness of its regret, the bitterness of its despair, is the death-recoil of a great power of life, of joy and dream and aspiration in youth, of a power to seize the things of nature and of the spirit, to live over again the experience, to think over again the thoughts of man, to have man's life. It belonged to so strong a nature and genius that the larger note should be ever increasing in the song, blending in widening harmonies, to rest in the unities of nature, of man, and of man's hope in society.

Swinburne's nature poetry has the added charm of affording some access to his personality, since it is closely connected with his habits of life, his friendships and the loved and familiar places where he has passed his years. Memory and companionship have a large share in their inspiration, and the trace of French and Italian travel and of holidays along English shores is a trodden trail in the verse. He will remain a figure of the Northumbrian headlands and the South Coast forever in the imaginative memory of literature; there he is seen in the verse, alone or with a friend, on horseback or a-foot or a-swim, in his habit as he lived in his own country and with a love for the soil and the breaking sea, his English birth. Such a back-ground of personality, of the human life of a man, is deeply desired by a poet's lovers who thus reach an unnoticed share in his privacy; it is the craving and the due of their gratitude and answers to his unknown intimacy with their own spirits. A finer approach, however, is given by Swinburne in the numerous poems which he has dedicated to childhood, all of an intimate personal tone, and revealing his heart and mood and speech in the gentlest part of household privacy, in his love of children. The verse, as is usual with him, has a monotone, the permanence and depth of an unchangeable emotion that wells always from the same spring; it is made up of pure affection, repeated over and over, of kin to a child's kisses, for which it calls, to which it answers and through which it exists, a delicate, intimate, worshiping poesy, of which the like in English is not to be found. There is here the Delphic christening of the babe, one after another, the birthday ode to the boy faithful with each revolving year, the death-rite of the little life in sad cadences of brief refrains; and unique among even these records of life is that rosary of daily song which counts the month of absence and gives the weariness of the child-emptied house through the lengthening hours of summer bereft of its soul. To be capable of such a series shows the man's heart better than all else in his verse; and happy was the boy's head that drew this light to shine upon it and flash out the gold of the poet's affection like sunshine falling there in far absence, in memory, in presence as the two heads bent together over the legend and the picture by the fire. The sense of the household is as intimate and private here as in Cowper's verse; the house and the garden and the hours are pure English; all is native to the soil, the flowerage, the home of England. In this verse the solitary and secluded figure of the scholarly poet is familiarly seen in the gentlest associations and the happiest acts of life.

The nature of Swinburne's personal life is also, though less plainly and unreservedly, shown in the large number of poems addressed to his companions, on one or another occasion, but naturally most of these are memorial verses. He has been "fortunate in friendships," and the hold of love in them was strong. The most of the friends to whom he dedicates verse are naturally in the group of artists and men of letters with which his own fame is associated, Rossetti, Burne-Jones, William Bell Scott, Morris, Watts, Maddox-Brown, Watts-Dunton, and others, with whom he found his principal companionship in literary and artistic sympathy; but the list includes many besides these, distinguished or eminent or memorable for old association with Landor or Shelley or some other. A life which leaves so rich a personal memorial of its human loves, however secluded, has won for itself or received by its own grace one of the true felicities and happiest rewards found by man. Hardly less near than these attachments, the verse discloses the ties, as of student and master, with Landor, Hugo and Mazzini, which Swinburne regarded as the highest honor and greatest blessing upon his younger head; and in a degree yet further removed the verse continues to show, with an ever greater volume and widening range, his tribute to the dead masters of literature, not conventionally or perfunctorily or affectedly, but in a genuine and deeply-felt outpouring of admiration and gratitude and that strange, mighty love that only the dead can arouse, a thing of the pure and untrammeled soul. He was ever a lover of heroes, of great deeds and famous works; for him the heavens of fame were constellated more with poetic and spiritual names than is the case with other men; he was faithful to the pure fires there and saw the eternity of poetry as a flame outburning all others in beauty and everlastingness; he worshipped in his verse poetry, freedom, truth, and the fames that are indestructible names of these in human memory. "On the Cliffs" is a poem in which there is both the vision and the rhapsody of this, in very noble and unusual imaginative forms, and stands as the type of his mood toward fame, which for him more truly than for men at large was what Shelley called it, "love disguised." In all this volume of human appreciation, for the great fames of the past, for the elder masters who touched him with their hands, for the company of familiar friends in private life, there is to be observed the same strength of soul, the same affluence of response to life, the same capacity for the passion of life in its largeness which has already been spoken of as the fundamental thing in the poet's nature, but here seen in its noblest phase as a power to love.

Liberty, melody, passion, fate, nature, love and fame are the seven chords which the poet's hand, from its first almost boyhood touch upon the lyre, has swept now for two score years with music that has been blown through the world. He sang in the lines of his earliest dedication, in the opening lines of it, —

> "The sea gives her shells to the shingle,
>   The earth gives her streams to the sea;
>  They are many, but my gift is single,
>   My verses, the first fruits of me."

and a certain singleness has abided in the gift to the end. He has been faithful to his early lights, his first loves, and has served the ideal of his life with an unswerving rectitude, a tireless industry and an unflinching courage. He has been the laureate of the Republic in Europe as the continental cause of liberty in every tyrannic or partially enfranchised land; he has been a national poet of England, and has besides enriched English literature with a music never heard before, with the most stately tragedies of his time, and with its most imaginative romantic poem of passion and with a multitude of noble single poems of great variety of theme, mood and art. He has supplemented this poetic gift with a large body of prose which contains the wealth of a poet's appreciation of a main portion of the most famous English literature as well as of the greatest modern poetic mind of France, — a treasure of intuitive criticism such as no other English poet has left. This is the fruit of a long labor of life. Strength is dominant in his genius; the things of strength are in his verse; it is English genius and English strength, racial in lyric power, in free intellect, in bold speech, — none more so — and English also in its poetic scholarly tradition. The reversionary tendency of his art, the imaginative remoteness of his themes, the primitive predilection of his temperament have been pointed out, with the resulting detachment of his genius in important ways from his own age and generation; but if a certain aloofness has come into his work from these causes, he has been thereby withdrawn into what is most primary in art and most elemental in nature and life. He has been genuine, as only high genius can be, in all that he has done. In private life he has lived in seclusion; but he has been one of a company of sympathetic friends, and has besides numbered among his companions many others of the men of distinction of his times. He has never failed in public sympathy with great occasions and events. As a poet, notwithstanding his genius and labor, it must be said he found the world inhospitable. The measure of praise that he won has gone no further than the acknowledgment of the victory of a poetic power that could not be denied; it has not much increased with years; it has never been adequate, just or intelligent. There is, perhaps, the consciousness of this in the concluding words of his remarks on his collected verse, which he addresses to his friend and house-mate through these latter years: "It is nothing to me that what I write should find immediate or general acceptance; it is much to know that, on the whole, it has won for me the right to address this dedication and inscribe this edition to you." The poet, like all men of simple greatness, is free, it would seem, from the desire for applause, but not from the human want of some loving comradeship in his art. There are, in the wide world, here and there a few — a number that will increase ever with passing generations and is even now perhaps manyfold greater than the poet knows — in whose hearts his poetry is lodged with power.

O'Toole Library
Withdrawn